CW00411276

NEW ZEALAND'S FAVOURITE BRANDS

AN INSIGHT INTO SOME OF NEW ZEALAND'S MOST ICONIC BRANDS

VOLUME 1

Publishers
Neil C. Tanner
Phone 61 2 9953 0099
Email tannercp@bigpond.com

David A. Higgins
Phone 61 2 9981 1868
Email dhiggins@idx.com.au

Editorial Director
Monica Higgins
Email monica@greenfairy.com.au

Design and Production
Peter Remfry

Sales
Colin Gestro
Emma Gestro
Affinity Ads
09 449 2500
Email emmagestro@affinityads.com

Published by New Zealand's Favourite Brands Ltd
ABN 80 003 203 183
TCP Publishing
67 Wyong Road, Mosman NSW 2088, Australia

Special thanks to Ewa Jaremkiewicz, Mike Hutcheson, Roger MacDonnell,
Kelly Farrimond, Barry Armstrong, Ian Williams

Printed in Singapore

Print Logistics

Tony Tanner
All Print Matters
www.allprintmatters.com.au

ISBN 0-9756087-0-3

ISBN 0-9756087-0-3

This book is dedicated to all the people who have built and protected New Zealand's home grown brands.

Contents

Contents by Category

Roger MacDonnell

Roger MacDonnell has devoted the majority of his career to the growth and development of Colenso Communications and the Clemenger Group in New Zealand. He spent the first 12 years as Colenso's creative director, and developed benchmark campaigns for Cadbury Crunchie and Toyota, which helped establish Colenso as New Zealand's number one agency.

Colenso also describes itself as the agency for brand leadership. Roger's passion is to build brands through targeted creative communication. He has been CEO of Colenso since 1989 and chairman of the Clemenger Group in New Zealand.

More recently the group has acquired additional communication companies including Aim Proximity (New Zealand's largest direct marketing agency), Porter Novelli Public Relations, Dashwood Design and Total Media.

This group now dominates the New Zealand market and Roger sees the current opportunity as the integration of these specialist services.

During this period, Roger has provided marketing advice and high quality creative work to many of New Zealand's companies and brands and established a number of enduring relationships including Toyota (22years), BNZ (23 years) and Air NZ (8 years).

His creative contribution to brand growth has seen Roger receive the Advertising Professional of the Year Award and election to the exclusive New York Copy Writer's Hall of Fame.

This unparalleled knowledge of New Zealand, its people and its brands, uniquely qualifies Roger to be part of the *New Zealand's Favourite Brands* selection panel.

"If we put on a blindfold, most of us can't actually tell the difference between most products and services.

Rampant technology and extreme competitiveness have made 'product parity' one of the biggest problems faced by marketers.

Yet in this competitive world, some products stand head and shoulders above the rest. The reason for this is the power of the brand – the emotional high ground that is part of a consumers relationship with that brand.

In this country, the very New Zealandness of some products and services has made a number of kiwi brands a unique part of who we are."

Roger MacDonnell
CEO – Colenso BBDO

Barry Armstrong

To me brands are like people. Some you like – instinctively. Some you love – passionately. Some you trust – implicitly. And there are those you avoid like the proverbial plague.

As a former creative director for thirty-something years with multi-national advertising agencies McCann-Erickson, Needham Harper & Steers and DDB, I have had the opportunity to handle the advertising for a number of multi-national companies and the responsibility of nurturing many world famous brands such as Coca-Cola, McDonalds, VW, Guinness, Eveready, Castrol, Ford, L'Oreal, Nestle, Gillette, Goodyear, Barcardi and Pepsi.

I've also experienced the fulfillment of being one of the midwives at the birth of some indigenous brands, for example Fresh-Up and Air New Zealand. As well as having a hand in their upbringing I have also worked on the development of other local brands such as Fisher & Paykel, Watties, ALAC, Canterbury, Bendon and Griffins.

Sadly, some of our favourite New Zealand Brands which many of us grew up with are no longer with us today. Some have fallen victim to off-shore takeovers. Others have suffered a major identity crisis at the hands of ego driven executives who set out to put his or her own mark on the brand, with the consequence that consumers have been given cause to question their relationship with the product or service. Isn't this exactly how we react when a close friend has a personality change?

The Kiwi brands that have survived and flourished in the combative and competitive New Zealand market truly deserve our accolades and their inclusion in this publication.

Barry Armstrong
CEO Quattro Communications

Mike Hutcheson

Mike has played a high profile role in the New Zealand business scene for over 30 years.

In 1969 he was a co-founder of Colenso Communications, which over the years has proved to be a flagship of the New Zealand advertising industry.

During the 1970s and 80s, Mike founded Replica Homes Ltd, and Low Energy Homes Ltd. In 1985 he founded Hutcheson Kowles Marinkovich Advertising, and in 1991 Marcoa Direct Advertising, which sold to Colenso in 1994.

In 1997, Mike was appointed executive director, then managing director of the global advertising agency Saatchi & Saatchi.

Mike's success in the advertising industry was recognised early. In 1967 he was awarded the Trenchard-Smith Trophy for highest marks in Australia and New Zealand Advertising Institute exams. In 1968 he was awarded the Reader's Digest Scholarship for New Zealand's Most Outstanding Young Advertising Man.

A published author, Mike also writes a regular humour column for *The Independent*. He sits on the boards of English To Go Ltd, Project K, Auckland Festival 2003 Committee and Spirit of Adventure Trust, among numerous others.

With a successful advertising career spanning over three decades, Mike is exceptionally well qualified to know instinctively when he sees a favourite New Zealand brand.

Brands are an endangered species. Their habitat is a fragile one, occupying an ethereal place called the collective mind. Like Shangri-La, this place can only be discovered by those who believe in ideas. It can't be found using technology or modern machines. Unfortunately such machines drive modern business. Machines that are in turn driven by accounting cycles whose rhythms are quarterly or, at best, annual. These business cycles, far shorter than the gestation period of brands, mean that brands are easy prey to predatory accounting practices.

Short-term fiscal demands often mean that brands are sacrificed at the altar of retail selling, which seems to devour their blood. Hence we see brands which were once part of the vibrant colour of our lives disappear like shimmering soap bubbles when financial parameters are used to measure in one dimension that which exists in four. Maybe accountants will eventually learn that feelings can't be measured with a ruler.

This book is a salute to some Kiwi brands that have, do and will continue to exist – with careful nurturing.

Mike Hutcheson

Kelly W. Farrimond

Born and bred in New Zealand, Kelly has in excess of 30 years' experience with major international advertising agencies in Canada, Australia, key Asian countries, South Africa and New Zealand. In the last 10 years, Kelly's responsibilities have included running the Asia-Pacific operations of Foote Cone and Belding and Mojo and, more recently, George Paterson Bates' Melbourne operations. In addition, Kelly has also served on several boards, including the Starlight Foundation, the Alfred Hospital in Melbourne and the Australia-India Council Board.

During his career, Kelly has worked on and been responsible for creating campaigns for many major brands which are, in some cases, world brands and in other cases household names. In Australia, these brands included Qantas, Fosters, VB, Meadow Lea, National Australia Bank, K-Mart, Kodak, Vegemite, Pepsi, Mercedes-Benz and Nestlé.

Kelly returned to New Zealand in 2000 and is now a principal of Farrimond Limited, a communications agency in Auckland that works with client partners including Jim Beam, Burger King, Nestle, Electrolux, DB Breweries, Kimberly-Clark, Bell Tea and General Motors. Having worked with major brands in many countries, Kelly is well qualified as an expert, instinctively knowing and understanding what makes a brand the people's favourite.

"I'm delighted to be involved with this, the first book covering New Zealand's most important brands, a book that will record for history the story and success of brands born in New Zealand."

Kelly W. Farrimond
Managing Partner
Farrimond Limited

About the Publishers

Neil C. Tanner

Born and educated in England, Neil started his working life with Nestlé in their London head office.

Brand management came early in Neil's career when he became brand manager for Twinlock, an international office equipment supplier in the early 1970s. One of the brands Neil launched during his tenure at Twinlock was the Sasco range of management wallcharts.

It wasn't long before the advertising industry beckoned. Neil joined Young & Rubicam in London during a vibrant period of the company's history. Working in the newly developed role of an account planner on Cadbury Foods & Confectionery and Johnson & Johnson, Neil gained a first-hand insight into the communication that builds and develops brands that last. At that time, only two other London agencies employed account planners to ensure the overall brand direction was correctly maintained for a healthy, long-term future.

Having spent a number of years in advertising communication with Young & Rubicam, Neil moved back to brand management at a senior level with Brooke Bond Oxo, later renamed Unilever Foods. While at Unilever, Neil became one of their youngest marketing managers. The portfolio of brands included Britain's number one tea, Brooke Bond PG Tips, as well as the famous Oxo, Haywards and Fray Bentos names.

The desire to travel brought Neil to Sydney in 1983 and very soon after he started his own below-the-line marketing group, Creative Sales. It was here that Neil's pioneering approach to integrated communications ensured the group grew to employ over 100 people to become Australia's largest – with most of the country's blue-chip brand management walking through its doors during the 1980s and 90s.

Over this period, Neil established and chaired a stand alone advertising agency within the group.

Creating and building brands has always been at the forefront of Neil's career, and entering the publishing field to create a volume that celebrates brands and their success stories was the most natural progression.

David A. Higgins

Iconic Kiwi brands are part of what define the nation David Higgins still calls home, even after 17 years living in Australia. It is his passion for New Zealand's most favourite brands that inspired David to publish this book.

With a degree in Commerce from Victoria University, Wellington, David went on to establish a career in both brand and sales management. He worked in Wellington and Auckland for major international companies including ICI and Cyclax Cosmetics.

After a period in sales at ICI, David returned to brand management to establish the ICI Swimming Pool Chemical Division. During his employment at ICI, David spent some time in the UK working for the export division of the parent company where he gained true insight into global brand management.

After a move to Sydney in 1987, David took up the position of marketing world leading alcohol brands such as Tia Maria, Jim Beam, Carlsberg Beer and Ballantine's Scotch Whisky.

These experiences lead to a role in direct response marketing for an Australasian company. His love for those Kiwi Brands he worked on during this time sparked the initial seeds of an idea for a book about New Zealand's favourite brands.

Wanting to extend and broaden his own career beyond pure brand management, David established an import and marketing business that covers both Australia and New Zealand markets. David is still the director of this company today.

While this is David's first foray into publishing, he is pleased to have his vision turned into a reality that New Zealand families can celebrate and revel in for many years to come.

David sees this publication as a true legacy of New Zealand, its people and its brands.

Monica Higgins
Editorial Director

With a degree in media from Sydney's Macquarie University, Monica is an established freelance journalist and contract editor. Her freelance roles range from film and theatre reviews, feature articles and humour columns in major Australian publications to copywriting and editing duties for several Australian brands. *New Zealand's Favourite Brands* marks Monica's first journey into editing a New Zealand publication.

Born in Wellington in 1978, Monica moved to Sydney Australia with her family in 1987. And although her adult life has been spent in the latter country, she still identifies strongly with New Zealand and those brands that helped to shape her formative years.

She remembers Marmite on toasted Vogel's bread for breakfast (she's yet to find an Aussie bread quite as tasty), and afternoon teas of icy cold Raro with mum's fluffy cakes made with Edmonds Baking Powder (mum still has Edmonds shipped to her for that "Sure to Rise" effect).

She can recall car trips through the Rimutakas where dad would pass her a Nestlé Barley Sugar so her ears popped, and camping holidays in the Wairarapa, enveloped in a Swanndri to keep her warm and dry ("Daddy, your jacket smells OLD!").

And, most of all, she remembers rainy Sunday afternoons where the sounds of excited voices shouting "Go, you bloody All Blacks!" would fill the lounge room.

Monica is immensely proud to have been part of this publication as it has taken her on an often times, teary trip down memory lane.

Foreword

Neil C. Tanner & David A. Higgins
Publishers
New Zealand's Favourite Brands

When we decided to publish *New Zealand's Favourite Brands*, we had no idea how much interest there would be, simply as it only contained New Zealand-born brands. As the publication comes to fruition, it is apparent just how many companies see this as a great opportunity to celebrate and showcase their great home-grown success tales.

The ways in which iconic New Zealand brands began, how they grew and why they developed into trusted household names is not only a successful story but a fascinating one too. Lying within the pages of this book are stories of businesses humbly beginning in home kitchens, in the back rooms of shops and in residential garages – all established by people who demonstrate that Kiwi ingenuity.

Many of the brands that existed when we were growing up in New Zealand are no longer with us. Others, however, have gone from strength to strength and can now be described as iconic New Zealand brands.

Some of the great brands that have survived the test of time are featured in the pages of this publication. We have also recognised emerging brands that have begun to capture the imagination of consumers and are rapidly gaining the all-important element of trust and performance.

It is interesting to speculate as to why some brands have fallen away. At times, a brand's disappearance is through international acquisition, often leading to the introduction of a similar global brand to replace the local name. In other cases it is through poor management and simply not keeping abreast of the forever evolving consumer market.

So then, why are brands successful? The key reason for a brand's success and longevity is that it strikes a chord with consumers. Clearly, successful brands have strong values, values that are only matched by their distinct images and superb product performance – all of which appeal to the various sectors of the New Zealand population who place their trust in such favourite brands.

Finally, we thank our Brand Selection Committee for their patience and diligence in the very difficult process of selecting some of New Zealand's most iconic brands. Drawn from New Zealand's most eminent communications specialists, our committee has a deep appreciation of what constitutes the success of the brands displayed in this publication.

Nostalgia is...
PEN PORTRAITS OF BRANDS GONE EAST, WEST, OR LAID TO REST

by Ian Williams

To tell the truth, Rinso hasn't been top of mind for some years. Yet it used to be the washing powder of choice for millions worldwide, including my mum back in Harrow, Middlesex. Indeed, I hadn't even noticed it was missing from local supermarket shelves until this assignment came along. So much for my brand awareness.

What makes one brand last lifetimes, while others sink without trace? In Rinso's case, a detergent named Tide gobbled up most of its market share. Strangely, the only country where it is now marketed is Turkey.

However, contrary to the Rinso experience, the demise of most brands is due to decisions made by the brand owner. Takeovers and mergers result in the disappearance of many brands, or they get renamed and reformulated to give them a new lease of life. A few brands fail because claims made for them don't stand up to scientific scrutiny.

Although market researchers spend millions positioning a brand, or repackaging or reformulating it to meet changing consumer needs, it only takes one tiny negative mention in a consumer magazine or TV program to send sales plummeting – cigarettes and cancer being a case in point.

Remember Senior Service, Player's, Craven A, Capstan? Probably only if you're in a rest home. Or did you, like me, switch to "milder, safer," filter cigarettes – the Rothmans and Benson & Hedges? The latter's brilliant advertising – just the pack and the health warning – was enough to make even the staunchest anti-smoker eat their words.

Or, what about your teeth? Did you brush them with Pepsodent and "wonder where the yellow went"? Mine seemed to stay on my teeth, so it was no surprise to discover that in 2003, Unilever sold its once dazzling market-leader to a Canadian company. Pepsodent's then share of the North American market – under 1 per cent.

In 1965, one of my first assignments at my first advertising agency was writing a commercial for Griffin's wine biscuits. Forty years on, the same biscuits are still selling like, well, hot biscuits. Not so Auslebrook's, Hudson's or Bycroft wine biscuits. I could claim that my commercial ensured the survival of the Griffin's brand. I could, but I won't. In fact, Griffin's biscuits could all be called Nabisco biscuits if truth be told, since Nabisco owns the company.

I also worked on the Coca-Cola account, being involved in the 1966 launch of that company's new lemonade, unaccountably named "Leed." Leed Lemonade's bubbles, "tingled right down to your toes," but its market share never got much above toenail height. Even so, once the Schweppes and the Coca-Colas of the soft drink world trained their big guns on the local lemonade makers, Ballins, Thompson and Western lost their fizz too.

Number 2

In comparison, when rebranding is performed by the company that owns the brand, no-one gets hurt. TEAL (Tasman Empire Airways Limited), New Zealand's first international airline, and a first to use flying boats, managed 25 years of life on the waves before being renamed Air New Zealand in 1965. By that time its routes extended far beyond the Tasman Sea, and its fleet had been replaced by aircraft that landed on land and not water, so rebranding was warranted.

However, the rebranding exercise was as fraught as the current debate about changing New Zealand's flag. I well remember the furore as possible name changes were bandied about, Kiwi Air and NZ Air being popular choices. Naturally, diehard advocates of the status quo were also to the fore.

No such problems for NAC (National Airways Corporation). It simply disappeared from the face of planet Earth. Formed in 1947, and operating within New Zealand, initially with DC3's, and later with Vickers Viscounts on the main trunk routes, NAC's virtual monopoly position ensured it enjoyed year-in-year-out high profits. In spite of takeover and merger rumours that kept the airlines' respective ad agencies on tenterhooks, the domestic carrier survived to

TIMETABLE DEC.—JAN. 1956

TIMETABLE DEC.—JAN. 1956

Retailing has always had a high risk element. Apart from the obvious High Street casualties such as Mackenzies, F.W. Woolworth, the DIC and John Courts, long-established specialty retailers such as Hope Brothers (menswear) and the Maple and Smith and Brown (furniture) have fallen by the wayside.

Beauty products, lingerie and bras, jeans brands, entertainment... Remember Saturday nights at the pictures? Dressing up. (Or down.) The interval when everyone popped out for ice-cream. Not like now when the orally-fixated sitting immediately behind you munch popcorn non-stop throughout a movie.

Beer, too, has its ups and downs. I can't remember when I last had a Lion Red, although once I drank nothing but. The history of New Zealand brewing is littered with once famous local brands which have succumbed to outside pressure from nationally marketed ones. Thankfully, specialised brewers are now resurgent.

Of the brand categories that don't seem to have changed all the much, mention must be made of petrol. Perhaps that's because taking over an oil company isn't one of those off-the-cuff decisions taken around a boardroom table or even at the golf clubhouse. Nevertheless, once upon a time in Kiwi land, there lived a totally home-grown brand of petrol called Europa. And if you can get your head around a Kiwi company calling its petrol "Europa", you'll probably understand why it eventually sold out to BP. Musically-inclined nostalgia buffs may remember Europa's swan song: "People on the go go Europa."

Finally, mention must be made of the companies responsible for creating the advertising that made the brands above memorable or unmemorable, as the case may be. My first employer, Dormer Beck, became Dormer Beck Stuart Wearn, then Dormer Beck Campaign, then Campaign, and finally (after merging with Mackay-King – also a former employer) Saatchi & Saatchi.

Such is the life of a brand, from the ridiculous to the sublime, and then of course, as the wise of the world know only too well, even the sublimes can sometimes become somehow ridiculous.

Ian Williams is an advertising consultant and journalist based in Dunedin.

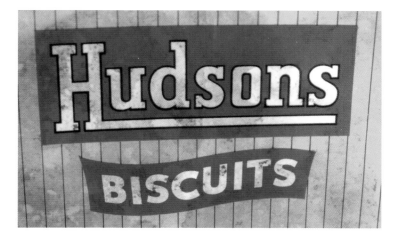

enter the jet age before finally being amalgamated with its international cousin in April 1978.

Still, what's the disappearance of a name compared to the disappearance of an auto brand? Austin, Morris, Triumph, Sunbeam-Talbot, Wolsey, Packard, Studebaker, Trekka...are tears welling from your eyes, too? As for Pan-Am, Trans World Airlines, BOAC, Air Congo...I could go on and on – and I will.

Supermarket shelves are all the poorer for the demise of Irvine & Stevenson's range of products, featuring brilliant examples of the designer's art. I bet Peacocks and St. George jams tasted brilliant, too!

Banking is almost as volatile as the airline business. Hands up those who remember the Commercial Bank of Australia, the Bank of New South Wales, the Post Office Savings Bank, or even Trustbank?

Emerging Favourite Brands

While researching for iconic Kiwi brands, we came across some exciting newer brands that we believe will become New Zealand's Favourite Brands of the future.

THE TWO PAGE EPIC ON HOW 42 BELOW CAME ABOUT

Here's the thing about writing a history of something. You have to have a reason for doing it and you have to not get caught up with wandering off track. Which is exactly where I went wrong with my Introduction to New Zealand History course at Waikato University. History lecturers often tell you that history is "written by the victors in any given conflict" however if you try and actually make up history yourself in an examination room you get the wrath of the four horsemen thrown at you. In fact, I was the only person that the late great Dr Michael King ever gave an F-. He seemed to think it was a monumental achievement. To this day I'm convinced he saw me as a true follower of the historic tradition of telling a convincing lie, and respected me immensely because of it.

All histories also have to have a beginning, a place where everything starts. I was going to say how the idea for 42 BELOW first came to Geoff Ross as he was travelling in a plane from America, but then I thought I should go back further and talk a little about Geoff's dad the boat builder/farmer whose influences led to Geoff coming up with an idea about vodka in the first place. Now, I've never met Geoff's dad but Geoff sat me down once and told me all about him, I just don't remember what he said. I think it was important. Just as an aside, I should tell you that a good deal of my University essays were built around what I called "thinking beyond the set topic". This was actually a way for me to intellectualise writing 3000 words about something I didn't know much about. It worked a treat in European Art where I completely made up a history of my family and how it related to the European art tradition. It was complete fiction but it got me my only A+.

Anyway Geoff Ross, the son of a boat builder/farmer, was on a plane from America reading a shite in-flight magazine which had an ad in it for some unknown brand vodka made in the States. "What a bunch of arse" thought Geoff. "America is the home of John Lee Pettimore, same as his daddy and his daddy before. It's all about bourbon not vodka. Vodka has to come from a country where the weather is a bit more crap". This naturally got Geoff thinking about the unique climate we have back here in New Zealand. "Hell, if any country should be where vodka comes from, it should be New Zealand". And that's when the idea for 42 BELOW vodka was officially born.

I, on the other hand, was officially born in Christchurch's Burwood Hospital during the worst snow storm they had had in 10 years. This in itself isn't that interesting; the real story is in how I was conceived. I don't know what this story is because whenever I try and bring the conversation up with mum she goes all quiet. All I know is that it had something to do with a protest against the Vietnam War and too much undrinkable home made alcohol. Which is exactly what Geoff started manufacturing as soon as he got off the plane.

In fact Geoff's first efforts at making vodka were so shite that it all went straight out to the farm to be used as a general purpose solvent in the boatshed. It's one thing to have an idea about something in your head. It's quite another to make that thing actually happen. It's like the first time you kiss a girl. You think it's going to be as easy as it looks on telly. But in reality you stick your nose in her eye, and no one says anything, and you go home already knowing that you are no longer going out. In fact she ended up going out with her best friends older brother pretty much the next week. Now she has three kids to him and lives up north somewhere. But I guess it's still better to take the opportunities when they come along rather than wondering about what might have been. Like when I was hanging out with this girl Rebecca for a while, and damn she was so hot for me but I was too blind to see it at the time and then she went overseas and ended up marrying this underground actor guy. And now I see her with him in all the American celebrity magazines and she looks soooo sooo hot and I could have totally had her.

Geoff kind of figured the same thing with the vodka. He saw the potential in the product. So rather than pack it all in when he discovered vodka production was actually a bit tricky he set about learning everything he could to make it work. He tried different stil configurations, different ingredient mixes, and even tinkered around with crazy new distillation processes. And sure enough, after a couple of years the solvent supply to the farm started to dry up as Geoff felt more confident about getting not-so-close friends to drink the first batches of what we now know as 42 BELOW.

This was also about the time of the explosion.

We've all heard the saying "a watched pot never boils", but I bet not many of you have heard the saying "an unwatched still can blow the fuck up in a hell of hurry if you happen to fall asleep during production". Geoff hadn't either and it's probably good now for me to tell you about Geoff's wife, Justine, who was heavily pregnant at the time.

On second thoughts, I won't go into that story, because I've just looked at the amount of space I have left to fill and it's not as much as I originally imagined. In fact, I probably should have planned this whole thing out a bit better with a proper introduction, middle part and conclusion. But I'm well on the way now and I can't really start over again because I'm actually writing this at the printers with everyone standing around waiting for me. I've known for ages that I had to do this job. But I put it off, and put it off and then just totally forgot all about it until about 20 minutes ago when the printer rang up.

I think that Geoff will probably approve of what I've written because it's generally going in the right direction. Well I hope he does anyway because there's no time for him to see it before it goes to print. I'm typing this straight into the machine that makes the printing plates. Which incidentally has a built in radio.

Now I'm going to have to digress here a little. Because this radio is tuned to a talk back show where some nature guy has been saying how koala bears actually get drunk from the juice of eucalyptus leaves and then fall out of the trees they are sitting in and crash onto the ground. But here's the thing, they don't hurt themselves because they are fluffy, round and drunk. I think maybe that's the cutest thing I've ever heard and I really hope it's true.

It also reminded me of the first time that I ever had 42 BELOW vodka, way before I even knew who Geoff was. It happened one night in the bathroom of my flat and involved a bottle of 42 BELOW vodka and some late night self surgery.

It actually all started a few months earlier with this weird growth that appeared on the side of my leg. I didn't think much about it at the time but it kept growing bigger and bigger until I was spending way too much time in the shower getting totally freaked out. So I thought I'd just fix it.

I've told this story to a few people and whenever I get to this point they always ask me why I didn't just go to a Doctor. I always tell them the same thing. Doctors are bastards. I refuse to go and see someone I don't even know, take off my pants (did I mention that this growth was quite high up on my leg) have him/her 'examine' me for 2 minutes, tell me "it's a growth, you'll need to come back and have it taken off" and then charge me $80 for the 'consultation'. Not to mention the $80 extra bucks I would have to pay when I went back to actually have the growth removed.

No I was going to save $160.

In my head I figured that cutting a piece of me off wasn't a very hard thing to do, hell I'd done it enough times accidentally, and so one Friday night when I had nothing else on; I set about getting a little surgery kit together. 1 x scalpel (art shop style), 1 x foot of slightly stretchy fishing line, 1 x sewing needle and 1 x large glass filled with 42 BELOW vodka for sterilisation. (I was actually given the vodka by that girl from earlier in the story that married the actor)

The reason I used the 42 BELOW vodka as a sterilising agent was because of its high alcohol content, which is incidentally one of the reasons why 42 BELOW is such a great mixer for high end cocktails, it was this same alcohol content that ended up playing a central role in this story. Mainly because the only glass we had to put everything in was a beer mug which I then foolishly overfilled.

Now, I don't know if anyone reading this has ever done any DIY surgery, but if you have you will know exactly the indecisiveness that falls upon you at the very last minute. There you are, standing naked in a bathroom, and all of a sudden you're having doubts. This is not a good time to have a beer mug of vodka sitting next to you.

Cut to me an hour later, pissed, still naked, but now supremely confident in my own surgical abilities. Also singing. It was at that moment that I got to work on my leg with the scalpel, and I have to tell you, it hurt like a bastard! (I'd planned on anesthetising the growth with some ice beforehand but I'd forgotten to make any and had to go ahead with my nerve ends in tip top condition).

Now here's the thing with self surgery, once you're committed you can't pull out and go to the hospital to get patched up because they view it as a self inflicted injury and send you straight to the psyche ward. I therefore had to keep going until I had completely sawed the growth out of my body.

OK, this story should have wrapped up with a nice happy ending. Instead a lot of obvious things that I should have thought about beforehand started to happen all at once.

First of all, I was having difficulty with the needle and fishing line. This was because in real life I can hardly sew a button back onto a shirt so I don't know how I thought I could sew together a gushing wound. Secondly, I had a gushing wound. This was partly due to me being a bit generous with the scalpel and partly due to the fact that the 42 BELOW vodka had now thinned my blood out considerably. Thirdly, I didn't have any bandages.

Ah frick! Now I've just realised I've only got 10 minutes to finish this ad and I've totally stuffed up the remaining space. Basically this story finishes up with the police pulling me over on my push bike for swaggering. (They actually said the word "swaggering" instead of "riding a pushbike a bit pissed". They also said a bunch of other stuff but I wasn't listening because my mind was still turning the "swaggering" word over and over in my head. Swaggering. Swaggering. Even now I don't think it's a proper police word)

Also, I woke up the next day without a hangover which I've since been told is due to the purity of 42 BELOW vodka.

Ok now I'm going to have to wrap this up in a hurry because I've totally run out of room. Basically Geoff eventually worked out how to make really good vodka and now it's all over the world and has won a bunch of awards. Also there are now three infusions. Passionfruit, Manuka Honey and Feijoa. The Americans don't get the Feijoa one.

in 1999 stefan lepionka
charlie's trading com
squeezed the juice fro
week, bottled it and s
they squeeze the juic
oranges, 500,000 app
250,000 blackcurran
9000 mangoes & 600
passionfruit. otherwis
nothing has change
they still just produc
bloody good juice wi
nothing added. charlie

and marc ellis started
pany. back then they
m 100,000 oranges a
ld it. now, each week,
from over 1,000,000
es, 50,000 grapefruit,
s, 5000 pineapples,

s. not like the others.

freedom air

Providing memorable flights without the hefty price tags.

The market

Freedom Air is New Zealand's leading value-based airline. The low cost carrier has been operating trans-Tasman services since 1995 and has recently launched new services between New Zealand and Fiji. In its eight-year history, almost 2.5 million passengers have experienced Freedom Air's special brand of no-frills travel. Every week more than 100 Freedom Air services take off, brightening up the skies with their distinctive yellow planes.

As a value-based airline, Freedom Air cuts out the added extras that traditional airlines offer, such as in-flight meals and entertainment, and passes these savings on to customers in the form of really, really small airfares. Freedom Air passengers are typically those traveling overseas on holidays, visiting friends or relatives and come from a wide range of age groups and socio-economic backgrounds.

Freedom Air currently flies from Auckland, Hamilton, Palmerston North, Wellington, Christchurch and Dunedin. In Australia, Freedom Air flies from Sydney, Melbourne, Brisbane and the Gold Coast. The airline also connects Nadi, Fiji with several New Zealand cities.

History

Freedom Air is a wholly owned subsidiary of Air New Zealand. Air New Zealand first started investigating value-based airlines in the early 1990s in an effort to keep abreast of market trends. A start-up team was formed to investigate this new breed of airline. America's Southwest Airlines is considered the grand daddy of value-based airlines and was one studied by the Air New Zealand team. At the time, value-based air travel was a growing trend in the US and Europe and has now become hugely popular all over the world. Freedom Air launched in 1995 under the leadership of Ric MacGillicuddy, followed by Wayne Dodge who led the company until 2004. During this time the company has built a very successful trans-Tasman business and has developed the value-based model to suit the needs of New Zealand, Australian and Pacific Island travellers.

During 2001, Freedom Air also launched a domestic service within New Zealand. However, after a change in strategic direction by the Air New Zealand group, Freedom Air withdrew its domestic operation in order to focus on its trans-Tasman routes. As a result, 2002 saw Freedom Air launch a raft of new trans-Tasman services. The new flights saw Freedom Air enter the main metro markets of Auckland, Wellington and Christchurch offering services to Queensland.

The Product

Freedom Air offers a unique value-based service flying direct to key holiday destinations in Australia and Fiji. It is the only airline that flies direct to the Gold Coast from New Zealand and is also the only airline that flies internationally from the provincial cities of Hamilton, Palmerston North and Dunedin. Freedom Air aims to save its passengers both time and money through its direct flights and value for money fares.

Although no in-flight meals are served, Freedom Air cabin crew offer passengers a user-pays food and beverage service, including wine, beer, soft drinks, pasta, muffins, chips and more. Passengers can also bring their own snacks on board. In-flight entertainment is served Freedom Air-style by its friendly crew in the form of fun competitions and giveaways. Throughout the year the Easter Bunny, Santa Claus and other fun characters also make appearances in-flight, adding to the fun Freedom Air experience. There's also the airline's entertaining in-flight magazine 'Freebie' to pass the time.

The Freedom Air philosophy is all about providing more people with the opportunity to travel to more exciting destinations more often. The low-cost airline is like a generic brand, delivering a high quality, reliable product without the high-gloss packaging. Although they don't add the frills that other airlines have built on top of their services, the fundamentals of the airline business still apply. Freedom Air operates to the highest safety standards and, while its prices are low, its customer service is sky-high.

Like Freedom Air's corporate colours, its experienced crew are bright, warm and friendly. While the crew's focus is always on safety, it also knows how important it is to ensure a memorable in-flight experience. Freedom Air crew members aim to create a relaxing enjoyable atmosphere in-flight, so that the holiday begins as soon as a passenger steps onboard. It is therefore crucial that the right people are recruited, and Freedom Air goes to great lengths to find the best crew members who have a genuine interest in people.

Achievements

As the first value-based airline in Australasia, Freedom Air prides itself on being an innovator in the New Zealand aviation market. It was the first airline in the South Pacific to introduce ticketless travel. This development not only simplified flight bookings for passengers but also reduced costs, assisting Freedom Air in providing lower priced fares.

Always on the lookout for ways to make its service more accessible and convenient, Freedom Air launched online bookings in 1999. Today, more than 70 per cent of its passengers choose to make their flight bookings online – a place to access the cheapest fare levels and book 24 hours a day, seven days a week. The airline's online marketing strategy won them the coveted Gold Award at the CAANZ Media Awards in 2003 for Best Use of Online. Freedom Air has received many accolades for its innovative marketing strategies, including the Supreme Award and Best Consumer

Services Award at the 2002 New Zealand Marketing Magazine Marketing Awards.

One amazing feat that many traditional airlines would deem impossible was the launch of a fully operational Freedom Air domestic service in just six days during May 2001. It is this fast acting, can-do attitude that has seen Freedom Air continue to run an extremely successful business in one of the most competitive airline markets in the world.

Recent developments

Freedom Air has recently announced that it will add a new aircraft to its fleet, increasing passenger capacity by 25 per cent. The new plane will be used to increase services on existing routes, with new opportunities also being considered. The additional leased Boeing 737-300 is expected to begin services in December 2004.

With a new strategic direction, Freedom Air will look at opportunities for new holiday destinations within a five-hour flying time from New Zealand. In line with this strategy, it has launched new services from Hamilton, Palmerston North, Wellington and Christchurch to Nadi, Fiji. More exciting holiday destinations are expected to be announced in the coming months.

Promotion

Freedom Air captures the attention of consumers through its cheeky and humorous advertising and promotional campaigns. Its current campaign reinforces Freedom Air's really, really small fares though television commercials, internet, radio, billboards and press advertising. Freedom Air's bright yellow corporate colours shine through all of its advertising and promotions, ensuring that its messages are impossible to miss.

When it comes to promotions, Freedom Air doesn't do things by halves. Recently, in a New Zealand first, Freedom Air gave away 5,000 flights on its website in celebration of its eighth birthday. The demand for the free flights was so overwhelming that the website experienced difficulties, even though the site's capacity was increased by 1200 per cent Amazingly, all the free flights were snapped up in under 15 hours, with the site receiving more than 18 million hits in that time. The promotion was advertised via newspapers, radio, PR and through event teams handing out flyers.

Known for its fun and wacky promotions, Freedom Air recently ran a radio promotion to see how many people could fit into a Volkswagen Beetle. Called the Really, Really Small Car Competition, those who managed to squeeze into the car went into the draw to win a free trans-Tasman flight.

Freedom Air also supports key community events through sponsorship and has set up a division of sponsorship called the Freedom Foundation. The Freedom Foundation works with key Trans Tasman charities to assist those who are in need of air travel. Freedom Air recognises the importance of giving back to the communities that support its services and so looks for opportunities to work with those cities. The company believes that sponsorships, such as those undertaken by the Freedom Foundation, are a small way in which it can help make a difference in the lives of those most in need within the community.

The Freedom Air website and its online travel club, Club Zoomin' is also integral to its advertising and promotions strategy. Those who join Club Zoomin' are emailed notification of special fare deals such as the famous 'Take a Mate' or two for one deal, as well as information on new destinations. The Club Zoomin' database currently has 95,000 members and is continuing to grow by the day.

Brand values

At the core of the Freedom Air brand is its commitment to provide travellers with affordable travel. Freedom Air achieves its really, really small fares by providing a value-based service. The airline encourages online bookings and does not pay travel agents commissions for booking flights. This direct booking strategy also contributes to Freedom Air's ability to offer really, really small fares.

The Freedom Air personality is fun, cheeky, humorous, up-beat and non-business. Its sun-styled logo and bright yellow colours reflect the warmth and relaxation of the holiday destinations it flies to. Its planes are painted bright yellow in line with the corporate colours and warm feelings the brand represents. Its staff are trained professionals who know just how important a friendly smile and a helping hand can be.

Things you didn't know about Freedom Air

- Freedom Air was the first value-based airline to launch in Australasia.

- Freedom Air has carried almost 2.5 million passengers in its eight-year history.

- Freedom Air initially had in-flight meals and movies, but these were transitioned to a user-pays system in 1997, making Freedom Air a full VBA.

- Freedom Air launched a domestic service in just six days.

- Freedom Air gave away 5,000 flights to celebrate its eighth birthday.

- More than 70 per cent of its passengers book their own flights online at www.freedomair.com.

- Freedom Air was awarded the Gold Award at the CAANZ Media Awards 2003 and the Supreme Award and Consumer Services Award at the New Zealand Marketing Magazine Marketing Awards 2002.

- Freedom Air flies to Nadi from Hamilton, Palmerston North, Wellington and Christchurch. Freedom Air first flew to Fiji from Palmerston North in 2000, but temporarily suspended services due to the coup in Fiji.

- In New Zealand, Freedom Air currently flies from Auckland, Hamilton, Palmerston North, Wellington, Christchurch and Dunedin.

- In Australia, Freedom Air currently flies from Melbourne, Sydney, the Gold Coast and Brisbane.

New Zealand's Favourite Brands

A celebration of the history and culture of New Zealand's most iconic brands.

ALL BLACKS®

With over 120 years of glory, the All Blacks have come to represent not just a successful sporting team, but a successful nation defined by fierce pride, gut determination and strength of spirit.

Here come the men in black

Picture this: a furore revolving around a single pair of boots. All Blacks Winger John Kirwan had adidas boots, but principal sponsors Canterbury were less than pleased.

When asked by a reporter which boots he would be wearing on the day, Kirwan calmly replied that he didn't give a damn (or other choice four letter word); he'd play in bare feet if he had to. You see, being an All Black is about sacrifice. It's about going out on a limb for your team and your country – or chopping one off – as the story of Dick "Red" Conway goes. Red amputated a broken finger so he could continue his All Blacks career.

No other sporting team anywhere in the world has quite so much tradition, quite so many stories of struggle and sacrifice, or has an entire nation, beers in hand, waiting with bated breath as a match-deciding try is scored.

Most Kiwi boys want to be All Blacks when they "grow up". And when that dream career does not happen but for a select few, they carry with them a sentimental vision of their own sons donning the black jersey and running onto the field to a thunderous roar from the crowd.

It's the Kiwi way of life, and we wouldn't have it any other way.

The moment those first spine-tingling utterances of the haka are delivered, is a moment of crystalline clarity: the All Blacks are not just another sporting team that rides a seasonal wave of glory. Nor are they just another sporting team supported only by die-hard fans. All New Zealanders, rugby fanatics or otherwise, love "their" All Blacks because they are an icon of the nation and represent the spirit and intensity of her people.

The original Originals

For a sporting team so celebrated, so steeped in tradition and inspiring great national pride, the All Blacks had a rather sketchy beginning. In 1884, after a brief game against Wellington, the first New Zealand rugby team, decked out in navy jerseys with golden ferns, made their earliest appearance on the international rugby circuit to play Australia.

For many, this team did not befit the title of the Original All Blacks and indeed there was no such thing as the New Zealand Rugby Football Union at the time. With all of the 19 players coming only from Auckland, Wellington, Canterbury and Otago, many historians have argued that the team was not truly representative of all New Zealand's regions. How then could they possibly be immortalised in the All Blacks hall of fame? As most fans of this nation's number one sport would agree, once someone plays for New Zealand, they're an All Black – in life, in death and forever.

Steaming into Sydney Harbour on the Hauroto, that Kiwi number 8-Wire personality reared its head with the Original Originals hoisting a football onto the ship's main mast, much to the delight and cheer of those waiting to greet them. In fact, there was much cheering to be done in honour of the team that set standards and galvanised the might that the All Blacks have come to be known for. During their brief foray in Australia, a total of nine games were played and nine games were won, leaving Australia with an inferiority complex that only in recent years has begun to dissipate. One Australian report recorded that "the New Zealanders seem to furnish a type of excellence required. They are a fine body of men, well-built and with their muscular powers fully developed".

NEW ZEALAND BREAKING THROUGH FROM A "THROW-IN."

The Originals

With those nine wins sitting proudly under their collective belts, New Zealand began to display a brand new kind of confidence, with rugby fervour gaining momentum. Fired with a similar passion for the sport, a young journalist named Ernest Hoben was instrumental in bringing about a unified national body and on 16 April 1892 the union became official: New Zealand Rugby Football Union was born.

Following on from the success of their forerunners, the Originals played their first test match at the Sydney Cricket Ground in 1903. Captained by Jimmy Duncan, they succeeded with a 22–3 win. However, it was the "Mother Country" tour of 1905-06 that cemented world rugby standards. Outstanding fitness, general organisation and determination were the name of the game for the Originals, and they were a force to be reckoned with. The term "All Blacks" was by now well and truly part of rugby vocabulary, and public enthusiasm for the tour was likened by Premier Richard John Seddon to the Boer War. "As indicating public interest here, information of the contests taking place in Great Britain is awaited almost as eagerly as news of the late war in South Africa," he said.

The Invincibles

A whole tour without one loss or draw, the All Blacks of 1924 were determined to avenge the single loss of the previous tour where a last minute try was disallowed. And they did it – the All Blacks couldn't be beaten with 30 games played and won. They were the Invincibles.

If the Invincibles ever had a face, it would be that of young full-back George Nepia. With his sturdy physique, Nepia was the master of the smother tackles, a powerful kicker and a fierce defender. But it was during the 1924-25 tour of Britain, France and Canada that the 19-year-old gave rugby a yardstick. In a spectacular feat of endurance, he wowed crowds by playing as full-back in all 30 matches – something that the rugby world hasn't seen repeated since.

The Invincibles set a benchmark on that 1924 tour that has since formed the basis of how New Zealand reviews All Black success – judgment is not on how many games you win, they say, but on how many you lose. And New Zealanders are the very toughest of critics; when the All Blacks lose, the entire nation not only mourns, but become instant authorities on the finer points of that loss – "They played too soft", "The bloody ref was a one-eyed South African!", "They got done in the forwards", are some of numerous retorts known to have been uttered by bereaved fans.

And so it is. Since the unbeatable Invincibles set the standard, the All Blacks have been in constant pursuit of excellence. Losing isn't prevalent, but it certainly hasn't been lacking from the pages of All Blacks history either. Fans in 1937 joked that the Springboks were the best team to ever leave New Zealand, six Tests lost in 1949, two of which were on the same day, numerous losses during the 1970s to less than mighty teams and Australia's dominance during the early and late 1990s. But true to form, the All Blacks continue to strive for success. And the proof is in the pudding – or the number of wins as the case may be. As of 2004, statistics show that since the first ever Test match, in Tests against all countries, the All Blacks have an average success rate of 72.49 per cent.

Down in History

"There is no 'I' in team", so the well-known saying goes. But those teams of All Black history would not have served well without some of New Zealand's most iconic players.

If your nickname sparks recognition with generations, you know without a doubt that it's a measure of the fame you've achieved in a lifetime. Such is the story of Colin "Pinetree" Meads, a veritable folk hero of his time. At 1.92 metres tall, the nickname was aptly bestowed upon Meads by under-23s teammate Kevin Briscoe in 1958. The name stuck, and in his 14 years with the All Blacks, Meads epitomised the golden era of rugby during the 1960s and early 70s. Coupled with solid country stock and natural athleticism, the All Blacks prototype was rugged and uncompromising – traits that often saw him villanised by opposing teams.

Of the 361 matches in which Meads played from 1955 to 1973, 133 of those were for the All Blacks. He was the first of his contemporaries to reach a half century of Tests and while that figure has become more achievable with the growing number of Tests in recent years, during Meads' career, it was not only a colossal feat, but well and above any of his playing contemporaries. Had he been a player in the modern professional era, old Pinetree would easily have exceeded a century.

Meads, with his tough farm-bred blood always did the best for his country and his best was always better than any opponents'. It made New Zealanders feel good – no matter what else happened in the world, All Blacks like Meads were doing them proud.

By modern-day contrast, Jonah Lomu is considered by many as the world's most well known rugby player. It is, perhaps, his humble beginnings and very real health concerns that bear testimony to the folklore that surrounds him.

Raised in Mangere, one of the poorer areas of Auckland, Lomu was a compelling force when he burst onto the New Zealand rugby scene in 1994. Standing 1.96m and weighing up to 120kgs, Lomu in top physical condition could run 100 metres in 11 seconds. Given space and room, he was a nightmare for much smaller defenders, and the image of him trampling over England's Mike Catt in the 1995 World Cup semifinal is one for the history books.

Considering that for most of his playing days, Lomu was under a severe health handicap, it is quite remarkable that he achieved as much as he did. His illness has also made fans aware that very often, Lomu struggled to get anywhere near the exalted heights he reached in his two glory seasons of 1995 and 1999. But in each of those seasons, Lomu was sensational, with a physical presence no one has ever quite managed to match since.

Of course, there are over one thousand other fine athletes past and present who are well worth a mention too, each with their own fascinating tale on how they became one of the privileged few to wear the silver fern at their breast. There's Buck Shelford, Sean Fitzpatrick, Fergie McCormick, Bryan Williams, Andrew Mehrtens, Zinzan Brooke and Tana Umaga to name just a few, but a thousand extra pages would be required to write their remarkable histories, such is the colossal account of New Zealand's favourite team.

The Black Jersey with the Silver Fern

It's an icon in itself, that black jersey with the silver fern. If your average rugby fanatic squeezed their eyes tightly shut, you'd bet your bottom dollar they couldn't imagine Tana Umaga or Carlos Spencer scoring a match-winning try in a pair of white knickerbockers. The minutes of the first general meeting of the NZRFU in 1893 recorded that "New Zealand Representative colours should be Black Jersey with Silver Fernleaf, Black Cap with Silver Monogram, White Knickerbockers and Black Stockings"

Perhaps washing mud and grass stains from a white garment proved all too difficult – who knows – but whatever the reason, the All Blacks have played in black shorts (knickerbockered or otherwise) since 1901.

Sponsors began to make their presence known on the uniform scene from 1993, when the familiar CCC of Canterbury appeared on the right breast of the jersey, and then to the middle in 1994 to make way for Steinlager's label. 1999 saw adidas taking on the principal supplier role, bringing with it a new look jersey with a Chinese collar.

Besides modifications to the fern in 1986 and again in 2003, nothing much else has changed. The jersey and shorts are still black, the fern is silver and the uniform will forever represent the ardent might of players past and present, the darkest hours and the brightest successes and, above all, a nation's pride in their beloved All Blacks.

Guardians of a successful New Zealand brand

Like most brands born in New Zealand, the All Blacks are unique. But, more so than others, their name is a symbol for success – not just in the arena of sporting prowess, but in the spirit and competitiveness of all New Zealanders. Naturally so, Kiwis have an intimate relationship with "their" All Blacks; they're fiercely protective, fiercely proud and at times fiercely fierce when a loss ensues. It is for that reason that the marketers of the New Zealand Rugby Union (NZRU) identify their role not as brand managers, but as brand guardians.

From hope to pride

The media is tough, and the fans are even tougher. The benchmark set by the Invincibles and subsequent All Blacks teams has meant that unrealistic expectations are often placed upon the All Blacks to not only win, but win in style. So the role of the brand marketers is not an easy one: tweaking and guiding public perception so that, win or lose, the All Blacks continue to be seen as the powerful and emotive force that they are. In more recent years, this has been particularly challenging in light of Rugby World Cup defeats. Slowly, New Zealanders were beginning to lose all hope in their most cherished national icon.

Since the 1999 World Cup loss, the NZRU has implemented a marketing strategy to shift the New Zealand psyche from hope in the team: a mood that is based entirely on results, to national pride in the team, focusing more on All Blacks efforts and commitment as well as ensuring that New Zealanders identify with this.

In the following four years, the company has focused on two key themes of the past and the present to successfully shift the Kiwi mindset so that today support for the All Blacks is at its highest point ever.

The 2000/2001 marketing campaign highlighted that All Blacks are living, breathing members of a sporting team with a colourful history. The campaign brought public awareness to the idea that one of the most important factors in the All Blacks' continual drive for success is the maintenance of that proud history.

To avoid a resulting mindset that the All Blacks were living too much in the past, this message was balanced in 2002 and 2003 with campaigns that focused on the present team, particularly on their preparations to perform.

The combined effect of both campaigns indicated to fans that the All Blacks are a team that works extremely hard to give rugby everything they've got, both mentally and physically. Every time they pull on that black jersey with the Silver Fern they're representing their country, their fans and the symbol of excellence they have come to be known for.

A goal for the future

With the new professional era of New Zealand rugby well underway, 2005 will bring with it a new set of challenges. With the two losses in the 2004 Philips Tri Nations series now on the backburner, 2005 will be one of the biggest years for rugby that New Zealand has seen. With a large itinerary of tours planned, the goal for NZRU marketers is again to unite All Black fans with the team and gain their unconditional support.

The NZRU sees the All Blacks as an asset, one that has become a genuine national icon, and one to be protected for future generations to enjoy. Few other names – and certainly no other sporting teams – have become so deeply embedded within New Zealand culture to the extent that the All Blacks have. Above all, they have inspired a very small nation at the bottom of the globe to believe they can be the very best of the best.

Long live the All Blacks.

The Haka

KA MATE! KA MATE!
KA ORA, KA ORA!
KA MATE! KA MATE!
KA ORA, KA ORA!
TENEI TE TANGATA PU'RU-HURU
NA'A NEI TIKI MAI WHAKA-WHITI TE RE
HUPANE! KA-UPANE!
A HUPANE! KA-UPANE!
WHITI TE RA!

The crucial importance of the haka within All Black rugby tradition is not a recent development. The custom of performing this imposing ritual before a match was cemented by the first "All Black" team of "New Zealand Natives" led by Joseph Warbrick. Since that time the haka has been closely associated with New Zealand rugby.

Its mystique has evolved along with the fierce determination, commitment and high skill levels that have been the hallmarks of New Zealand's national game.

The haka adds a unique edge to a game of rugby. Derived from the indigenous Maori of New Zealand, and aligning with the wider Polynesian cultures of the Pacific, it has been known to have made grown men cry. The All Blacks perform the haka with the precision and intensity which underpins their approach to the game.

Barfoot & Thompson is part of Auckland's business history and its distinctive red, blue and yellow logo is one of the city's most recognisable brands. Proudly family owned and operated, it is New Zealand's largest wholly owned real estate firm.

The Family Tree

Barfoot & Thompson is part of Auckland's business history and its distinctive red, blue and yellow logo is one of the city's most recognisable. Proudly family owned and operated, it is New Zealand's largest wholly-owned real estate firm.

In 1923 Val Barfoot started out in the commercial hub of Newmarket, establishing what is today known as real estate agency Barfoot & Thompson. Val initially bought a going concern for £75, establishing the 'V. Barfoot Land Agent'. That became known as Barfoot Bros when his older brother, Kelland, joined the firm. The Barfoot brothers were later joined by Maurice Thompson and in 1940 the business became Barfoot & Thompson, as it is known today.

Val Barfoot, 1955, Maurice Thompson, 1955

The firm quickly grew to become the Auckland market leader. Eighty years later, the Barfoot & Thompson name is part of the fabric of Auckland, consolidating its position as the city's leading real estate brand. The company has always been headed by a 'Barfoot' and a 'Thompson', reflecting the firm's pride in being family owned. The company values of honesty, integrity and service were established early on and continue to govern its business activities.

Garth Barfoot and Peter Thompson are the present directors. Garth is the youngest son of Barfoot & Thompson's founder, Val Barfoot, and with a career spanning 45 years of evolution in real estate he is the longest serving member of the team. Two members of the next generation of Barfoots also work for the company, his daughter Kiri and nephew Stephen, continuing a Barfoot & Thompson family tradition.

Garth Barfoot and Peter Thompson

Peter Thompson started out in the business almost 25 years ago, moving through a number of sales, administration and management positions in the firm. He became a director in 1997. Peter is the grandson of Maurice Thompson, the original Thompson in the Barfoot & Thompson team.

Proudly family owned and operated, it is New Zealand's largest wholly owned real estate firm.

Developing and maintaining strong roots

Barfoot & Thompson is in a unique position in the Auckland property market. As the market leader by a significant margin, it has the most complete and accurate picture of Auckland market conditions and is quite simply the expert in Auckland property. One in three Auckland residential properties are sold by Barfoot & Thompson, which means it knows more about what's happening in the market than any other real estate company. 2003 was Barfoot & Thompson's most successful year in the company's 80-year history, selling a record number of properties as well as breaking through the $6 billion barrier. This achievement is particularly impressive considering Barfoot & Thompson is a regional brand with an exclusive focus on Auckland and Northland.

Integrity is one thing that's not for sale at Barfoot & Thompson. As the market and brand leader, the company believes the onus is on them to tell it like it is. A key aspect of the firm's integrity is its commitment to clarity and transparency in external communications. The company takes care in ensuring that all communications on market conditions are a fair and accurate reflection.

Branching into the community

Involving itself at a grassroots level in the communities in which it operates is an important part of the Barfoot & Thompson culture. With 58 branches throughout Auckland and Northland, Barfoot & Thompson has a tangible presence in practically every suburban community. When you also consider the thousands of 'for sale' signs peppered throughout almost every street, in every suburb across the city and beyond, you get an understanding of the astonishing reach of this brand.

Barfoot & Thompson takes community commitment seriously. One of its specialist auctioneers has helped raise more than $1.1 million dollars for charity through gala auction fundraisers. In fact, last year Barfoot & Thompson's auction team together raised more than $2 million for charity. For Barfoot & Thompson, lending a helping hand is in the blood.

Last year Barfoot & Thompson's auction team together raised more than $2 million for charity.

2003 saw Barfoot & Thompson participate for the first time in Auckland's annual Santa Parade, sponsoring the Gingerbread House float in the city's icon Christmas event. A team of willing helpers drawn from the firm's 58-branch network were on hand to distribute tens of thousands of packets of blue, yellow and red jelly beans to the waiting crowds. The company's commitment to the Santa Parade is on-going and they are looking forward to being part of this great city event in the future.

Barfoot & Thompson is proud of its association with the Magic of Reading programme

Barfoot & Thompson is also a partner of the Starship Foundation through major sponsorship of the Magic of Reading programme at Starship Children's Health. The Magic of Reading concerns getting new books into the hands of sick children and epitomises Barfoot & Thompson's commitment to family values. The programme enables Starship Play Therapists to give a new book to each child who spends one night or more in hospital. The company also uses other sponsorship connections to bring sports heroes into hospitals to read to sick children.

Additionally, each year the Barfoot & Thompson Head Office and its 58 branches make donations to schools, community and sporting organisations.

Recent recipients include:

- Schools – Kindergarten, primary and secondary schools including Parnell District School, Kerikeri Kindergarten, Awhitu School, and Auckland Grammar School.

- Community – Auckland Rescue Helicopter Trust, Eastern Bays Hospice, Surf Lifesaving Association, Plunket, Canteen, Disabled Citizens Society.

- Sporting – Bowling clubs, golf clubs, pony clubs, rugby clubs, netball clubs, triathlon associations, NZ water polo association.

Integrity – one thing that's not for sale.

Ground strength

In line with its customer focus, Barfoot & Thompson prides itself on its team of exceptional sales staff. The achievements of Leila Macdonald, Craig Matheson and Jean Smith are a good example of the sort of people who exemplify the Barfoot & Thompson values.

Leila Macdonald

Leila is consistently Barfoot & Thompson's most successful salesperson, selling more than $89.2 million worth of residential property in the year to March 2004. Originally from Lebanon, this grandmother of five has had an outstanding 13 year career with the company. For most of that time she has been Barfoot & Thompson's number one salesperson, and never below number two.

Barfoot & Thompson's number one salesperson, and never below number two.

Working from the Remuera branch, Leila's network of contacts in the Eastern suburbs is legendary and her average sale price is $2.1 million. Barfoot & Thompson believes her results make her New Zealand's most successful residential salesperson, her track record even attracting the attention of TVNZ's *Holmes* show during 2003.

Her local profile is huge, with vendors often willing to wait until she is available to handle their property listing. A testament to Leila's superb client service is her ever growing list of referrals from past clients who have appreciated her honesty, knowledge and sheer dedication.

Craig Matheson

Anyone who's considered buying a property in Mangawhai, north of Auckland, has probably encountered Craig Matheson. On first impression you could be forgiven for not recognising him as the most successful Barfoot & Thompson salesperson in the region, but get beyond the casual look and laconic manner and you'll find a human dynamo in operation.

Craig specialises in the coastal haven of Mangawhai and habitually has more 'for sale' signs around the area than any of his competitors. Managing more than 300 listings at once is all in a day's work, seldom sleeping if there is a deal to be closed. Craig wears shorts 12 months of the year, works an average of 80 hours a week, and responds to a huge number of buyer enquiries – many of which are after hours. In 2003 he sold $11.5 million worth of property.

What makes Craig's success even more remarkable is the fact Barfoot & Thompson went out on a limb to give him a job. Having kicked a 22-year drug habit, the company supported him in getting a dispensation to hold a real estate licence and gave him a chance when scores of other employers had turned him down. His story is so impressive it made TV3's *60 Minutes* programme.

The company gave him a chance when scores of other employers had turned him down.

Jean Smith

Jean is the first woman president of the Real Estate Institute of New Zealand's (REINZ) Auckland chapter, a role that she considers to be an honour.

Her career with Barfoot & Thompson spans more than 20 years, beginning as a receptionist and rising to become the company's second woman branch manager. She has a true commitment to the real estate industry. As well as her current REINZ role, she has also served as Vice President.

Day to day, she manages the Barfoot & Thompson's busy and successful Mt Albert branch, thriving on the challenge of leading a team of 18 salespeople.

Barfoot & Thompson's head office on Chancery

Growth of the market

In line with Barfoot & Thompson's values, expert knowledge, and commitment to Aucklanders, the company makes a point of sharing its market intelligence. Key data made available to vendors, potential buyers and the financial community includes the volume of sales, average prices and the number of available listings.

Between 2002 and 2003 Barfoot & Thompson's average sale price rose 23.5 per cent, and over a five-year timeframe, the average price increased almost $100,000. During 2003, 36.5 per cent of Barfoot & Thompson sales were for $500,000 or more and 11.8 per cent of sales were for more than $1 million. Perhaps the most impressive figure yet is that the company sold more than $6 billion worth of property in the 2003/04 year – up more than a billion dollars on the previous year.

The company sold more than $6 billion worth of property in the 2003/04 year – up more than a billion dollars on the previous year

Foundation for the future

Barfoot & Thompson has 58 branches across Auckland and Northland, and more than 900 sales staff. Its distinctive blue, red and yellow brand is synonymous with the company's status as market leader. It's a fact that more New Zealanders trust Barfoot & Thompson with the keys to their home than any other real estate company.

It's a trust that has been earned over an 80-year company history. A trust that is reflected in the company values of honesty, integrity and service. A trust that has the backing of the Barfoot & Thompson families now and into the future.

Barfoot & Thompson – at a glance

- Barfoot & Thompson handles one in every three Auckland property sales.
- More homeowners trust Barfoot & Thompson with the keys to their house than any other real estate firm.
- Sold more then $6 billion worth of real estate in 2003/4.
- Meeting the property needs of Aucklanders for 80 years.
- The company is the largest wholly New Zealand owned and operated real estate firm.
- A third generation of the Barfoot & Thompson families now works for the firm.
- The company values of honesty, integrity and service are an integral part of Barfoot & Thompson's business style.

www.barfoot.co.nz

Bendon

Bendon is a Kiwi icon, with more than 50 years' successful lingerie design and marketing experience. Bendon has long been synonymous with fashion, femininity and superb fit – as well as affordable, quality products.

About Bendon

Bendon Limited is New Zealand's leading lingerie designer and marketer. Renowned for its quality product, continual innovation and commitment to design evolution, the company has a global focus. It has a major presence in the Australian market and is rapidly gaining ground in the UK and other international markets.

Premium retailers already stocking Bendon's brands include Selfridges, House of Fraser, David Jones and Myer Grace Brothers, some of whom have dedicated lingerie concept areas.

Bendon is a Kiwi icon, with more than 50 years successful lingerie design and marketing experience. Bendon has long been synonymous with fashion, femininity and superb fit – as well as affordable, quality products.

Bend On – a lingerie revolution

Bendon started making quality intimate apparel in 1947. The company was founded by Ray Hurley, a demobbed naval officer and his brother Des, a professional pattern cutter.

Called Hurley Bendon, the brothers' company revolutionised the lingerie industry with a radical new approach to lingerie design. Rather than force women's bodies into restrictive and weighty corsetry, the Hurley brothers looked at the way that the body moved and developed designs to reflect that movement. The name Bendon was a literal description of how the new lingerie could "Bend On" the body, marking a departure from the heavy wire, steel and bone foundation garments that were prevalent.

By 1966, Bendon was the market leader in New Zealand lingerie, or bodyfashions as it was then known. After another decade and a half of strong growth, Bendon was publicly floated on the New Zealand Stock Exchange in 1982. The stock exchange listing was oversubscribed in what became the year's most successful public float.

In 1987, Bendon merged with Ceramco Corporation. Pacific Retail Group is the current owner of Bendon Ltd, having acquired it in March 2002.

Bendon Limited has some of New Zealand's best known prestige lingerie brands in its very desirable portfolio, including its licensed Elle Macpherson Intimates brand, as well as Bendon Lingerie, hey sister! Fayreform, Bendon Man and the licensed Macpherson Men brand. Recent innovations include funky hey sister! sleepwear, an elegant Afterwear Collection from Elle Macpherson Intimates, and the development of Bendon Lingerie sleepwear.

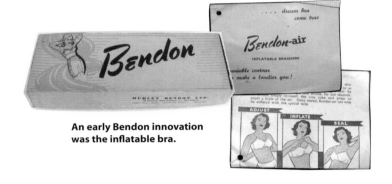

An early Bendon innovation was the inflatable bra.

Bendon Lingerie – coming full circle

In the last 10 years, three of the world's top supermodels have been associated with Bendon. Aside from Elle Macpherson, Claudia Schiffer and New Zealand's own Rachel Hunter have also fronted campaigns for the company. In 1993, Rachel Hunter, along with well-known Kiwi model Brigitte Berger, starred in an upbeat television and print campaign for Bendon Lingerie, with the tagline "It's not how the world sees you, it's how you see yourself".

The Bendon Lingerie brand, which shares its name with the parent company, is all about providing fashionable and on-trend lingerie for everyday living. It offers fresh, self-assured looks, fashion styling and lingerie that fits superbly. Virtually invisible underwear lines, smooth bra shapes and gorgeous colours make this lingerie extra special.

Bendon Lingerie recently came full circle with the release of stunning new images that reflect the company's original design philosophy. New campaigns showcase beautiful new season lingerie on a model who "bends" into a series of poses. The campaigns play on the "Bend-on" brand name – referencing the vision that originally gave Bendon Ltd its name – and presenting lingerie that bends, stretches and moulds to the body for the ultimate in shape, support and comfort.

The campaigns are also a reflection on changing lifestyle attitudes, with people recognising the value of nourishing the mind and spirit, as well as the body, through mind-body work-outs such as yoga and pilates.

Elle Macpherson Intimates

Bendon Limited is the licence holder for the Elle Macpherson Intimates brand. Founded by international supermodel Elle Macpherson, this is Bendon's premium fashion-forward brand. Launched in 1990, the brand was developed in partnership with Elle to lead, inspire and originate.

From its inception, Elle Macpherson Intimates has led the lingerie market with directional images, fashion-forward styling and the use of innovative fabric technologies. Elle Macpherson Intimates is a premium lingerie label that has become synonymous with sexy, feminine style and superb fit.

In 1990, Elle was already an Australian icon but her fame as an international supermodel was just beginning. For Bendon, teaming up with Elle – with her knockout nickname of "The Body" – was a master stroke and the first Elle Macpherson Intimates collection was an instant hit.

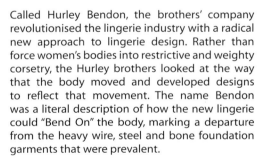

Early Bendon designs

Elle Macpherson Intimates

Bendon Lingerie

The appearance of traffic-stopping billboards featuring Elle – the person and the lingerie brand – was literally a body blow to an industry that had become a little staid. It seemed everyone stopped, looked, and fell in love with the lingerie. The Elle Macpherson Intimates brand campaigns also ushered in a new era in lingerie poster theft.

Media hysteria on both sides of the Tasman resulted in extensive coverage for the new brand. A subsequent television campaign, shot in New York by world-renowned Ellen Von Unwerth, reinforced the Elle mystique and perpetuated the sense of international brand values.

The lingerie market, post the Elle Macpherson Intimates launch, would never be the same again. And since then, Elle Macpherson Intimates has remained at the forefront of fashion with a commitment to innovation and quality. Consistently, the brand has been a leader in design, fabric selection and colour sense.

Leading-edge imagery has always supported the brand's fashionable attitude. Brand campaigns have been shot in Los Angeles, New York, Paris and London, creating a sleek, cosmopolitan image and supporting lingerie that is always romantic, sexy and individual.

Recently, Elle Macpherson Intimates has launched advertising campaigns that again demonstrate the brand's commitment to pushing the boundaries of lingerie design and marketing. Acclaimed British photographer Rankin shot an "intimate moments" campaign for Summer 03 which, for the first time, did not feature Elle Macpherson herself. The campaign gave new meaning to the word "intimate", revealing sophisticated glimpses of the latest lingerie collections. These lingerie vignettes were glimpsed through windows, doors and keyholes. The "intimate moments" campaign was further evolved through a Summer 04 campaign shot by renowned fashion photographer Mario Sorrenti.

hey sister! and Fayreform
from funky to fuller busted fashion

hey sister! is all about affordable and fun lingerie with heaps of attitude. With youthful styling, playful fashion prints and great basics to mix and match, hey sister! is perfect for the discerning younger customer.

Since its beginning in the early 1990s, hey sister! has established itself as a leading youth lingerie brand. It offers affordable fashion lingerie that plays with every mood. The brand name-checks the concept of sisterhood, and speaks of confidence, energy and cheekiness. It has a slightly rebellious edge.

Fayreform Lingerie is designed for the fashionable woman who is looking for a structured bra. The brand is committed to revolutionising the fuller-bust lingerie market, bringing indulgent femininity to supportive lingerie styling. The sensuality of beautiful designs is backed with strong, structured shapes to shape and support the fuller bust, in sizes up to 24G.

Ongoing refinements in fabric technology and manufacturing techniques have allowed Fayreform to streamline its ranges. Bra straps have been narrowed, without compromising the benefits of a supportive bra, and clever design features in fine stretch laces and meshes mean Fayreform can create very delicate and feminine looking lingerie which still provides the shape and contouring women are looking for.

The in-store experience

Bendon has its own network of retail stores throughout New Zealand. These contemporary stores blend a modern retail outfit with the warmth and intimacy demanded by lingerie customers.

Bendon opened a special flagship store – Bendon on Broadway – in Auckland in 1996. This concept store set new standards of lingerie retailing for Australasia. In 2001, Bendon opened another special concept store – Sanctuary by Bendon – at the Botany Town Centre. A real haven for lingerie shoppers, Sanctuary by Bendon again set new standards in lingerie retailing.

Bendon now has a chain of Bendon Lingerie stores throughout New Zealand. The stores are situated in New Zealand's largest and best malls, for example the Westfield Shopping Centres, as well as in premium shopping districts. Friendly, knowledgeable service is a feature of the Bendon stores, and staff are specially trained to offer the best in bra fitting and customer service.

The stores are also supported with a comprehensive marketing and promotional programme that includes special instore offers and stunning window displays to launch new season lingerie styles. And recently, Bendon has introduced stylish new packaging to wrap its lingerie offerings. The packaging includes candy striped lingerie boxes and pink and white spotted tissue paper. The lingerie boxes are a modern take on the lingerie boxes first used by the company in the late 1940s and 1950s.

Let's hear it for the boys

Bendon also caters for men, with two brands that share an emphasis on quality, comfort and fit. Bendon Man underwear is modern, masculine and uncomplicated. In a selection of durable fabrics including supersoft 100 per cent cotton knit and rib, the range is designed for both easy wear and easy care. Able to take you from work to the sports field and on to an evening's entertainment, Bendon Man underwear is perfect for any occasion.

Like Bendon Lingerie, the Bendon Man brand is virtually a household name and is synonymous with quality, comfort and enduring style. The Bendon Man range comprises briefs, fitted and loose boxers in a variety of colours, fabrics and styles.

Bendon Limited is also the licence holder for Macpherson Men. Macpherson Men specialises in underwear that is fashionable, snug fitting and ergonomically designed to mould to the body. Macpherson Men underwear offers the best in quality, comfort and signature Macpherson style.

Elle Macpherson Intimates

Lingerie trends

Bendon brands have always been at the forefront of lingerie trends. From the word go, Bendon differentiated itself by embracing new technology and fabrications. Indeed, this philosophy originally gave the company its name – creating garments that could "Bend On" the body as opposed to the rigid foundation corsetry that was the norm.

From then on, innovation became the key to Bendon's success, with its introduction of stretch strap bras and stretch bodyfashions in 1963 paving the way to its first million dollar sales figures, in 1964.

In 1968, the company launched the country's first colour coordinated slips, bras and briefs. In the early 1970s, another product landmark was the "Shevela" range of robes and dressing gowns. Shevela quickly became part of the domestic landscape, with sales statistics suggesting every New Zealand woman owned at least one of these garments.

In 1975, Bendon engineers designed the first New Zealand stretch moulding machinery for use in seamless bra cup manufacture. And in 1979, innovation was again brought to the fore with the import of a radical new computerised fabric cutting machine – the first of its kind in the southern hemisphere. The Hughes/Gerber system, capable of simultaneously cutting 200 layers of fabric, helped reduce fabric wastage and improve pattern precision and product consistency. Other firsts for Bendon included the launch of the Bendon Superbra in 1992, way ahead of the pack, and the launch of a range of innovative sports bras in 1994.

Lingerie today is a colourful business, with vibrant and feminine colours, prints and patterns to add spice to your lingerie drawer. The use of new leading-edge fabrics, especially stretch laces and meshes, have allowed the creation of seamless and smooth line lingerie that closely moulds to the body. Bendon has continually introduced these new leading-edge fabrics, a lush palette of new colours and a range of new lingerie shapes to the lingerie market.

Fayreform Lingerie

Lingerie profiles have become increasingly fashionable and in tune with outerwear in recent years. The advent of lingerie as outerwear, led by Madonna in the early 1990s, meant people were no longer afraid to show off their bras and undies. Bra straps and camisoles were made to be seen. Lower cut briefs to match outerwear trends for hipster pants and skirts, wide-sided g-strings to flatter the hips and the development of a special Trouser Knicker are among Bendon's more recent achievements. The Trouser Knicker, from Bendon Lingerie, is shaped like a snug-fitting short and is designed to give smooth lines under clothing.

Smooth line bras and contour bras have also become big sellers in the lingerie market, with women wearing tighter fitting garments which demand smooth lingerie. Contour bras, which are lightly padded to give an extra boost to the bust, have rapidly grown in popularity. And while contour bras were once the domain of A and B-cup wearers, demand has also become strong amongst C and D-cup wearers who appreciate the flattering rounded shape the contour bra gives the bust.

Bendon has also successfully moved into the sleepwear market, with stylish and comfortable sleepwear options that work well with its core lingerie business. And the Elle Macpherson Intimates brand, true to form, has taken the concept a step further with the development of an Afterwear Collection which gives women very fashionable options for at-home wear.

Afterwear is an exciting innovation that defines a whole new category in apparel, reflecting worldwide trends to easy living and easy living spaces. The Elle Macpherson Intimates Afterwear Collection delivers a delicious wealth of clever separates for knocking about the house in the greatest of style. And, if you should venture outside, these separates are more than chic enough to stand public scrutiny.

Bendon Man

Cadbury. The mere mention of the word and almost every Kiwi will be able to conjure up the vision of their favourite Cadbury chocolate and almost taste it rolling around on their tongue.

Introduction

The love for Cadbury Chocolate can connect Kiwis around the world. Cadbury has lost count of the number of mums who send overseas a block of Cadbury Dairy Milk, a Cadbury Pinky bar or a box of Cadbury Scorched Almonds to their backpacking offspring just so they know they are missed back home.

Either at home or dotted around the world, Kiwis know and love the distinctive taste of Cadbury chocolate and the brands they grew up with. Today Cadbury is still with them, evolving, innovating and creating new Cadbury chocolate delights for Kiwis to enjoy, take comfort in or just downright indulge in. Cadbury Confectionery Ltd is dedicated to delivering the number one chocolate in New Zealand for Kiwis no matter where they are.

Achievements

Cadbury is the largest chocolate producer in New Zealand and the Cadbury Group of companies is a major player in international markets with factories in Britain, Ireland, Australia, Malaysia, Indonesia, India, China, Poland and South Africa.

The Cadbury flagship brand is Cadbury Dairy Milk. In 2005, the brand will celebrate 75 years in New Zealand.

World history

In 1824, John Cadbury, a Quaker from England, set up his business in Birmingham, England. By 1831 the business had expanded from a grocery shop and John Cadbury had begun to manufacture drinking chocolate and cocoa. Little did he know how famous his company was to become!

In 1847, John Cadbury rented a large factory and his brother Benjamin came to join him, with the business then being known as Cadbury Brothers of Birmingham. This partnership lasted until 1860, after which time John Cadbury retired and left the business to his sons Richard and George who further expanded it. Richard and George dedicated themselves to making the best chocolate they could and in 1866 they introduced a new method for producing cocoa essence by pressing the cocoa butter from cocoa beans.

The resulting chocolate was viewed as the best.

Cadbury in New Zealand

In 1868 in New Zealand, a man by the name of Richard Hudson established a biscuit bakehouse in Dunedin. Hudson had a difficult life as a child; he was orphaned at the age of nine whilst living in England. He made his way to New Zealand as an illiterate child, attracted by dreams of finding a fortune in the Otago Gold.

It would turn out to be his culinary skills that would lead to his fortune however, and he soon discovered he could make and sell delicious biscuits. Encouraged by this, he set his sights on chocolate making and in 1884, Richard Hudson produced what was thought to be the first chocolate in the Southern Hemisphere.

This was at the same time that the young Cadbury brothers were establishing their Birmingham chocolate business. Fry, which had been formed in 1756, merged with Cadbury in 1918. In 1930, Richard Hudson and Cadbury combined forces to become Cadbury Fry Hudson Ltd. This gave Hudson's Dunedin business a link with one of the most important names in chocolate manufacturing and marketing.

In 1969 Cadbury Fry and Schweppes merged internationally and the New Zealand Company became known as Cadbury Schweppes Hudson Limited in 1973. A merge between this company and its Australian sister company Cadbury Schweppes Pty Ltd occurred in 1986, resulting in an Australasian operation, which saw both these companies supplying each other.

In 1990, Cadbury in New Zealand acquired the Griffins confectionery business and sold the Hudson biscuit operation. The Griffins business dated back to the turn of the century, when it was begun by George Griffin in Nelson.

In 1991, the New Zealand company became known as Cadbury Confectionery Ltd and is now the largest confectionery manufacturer in New Zealand.

Chocolate during the war

The links between chocolate and energy levels were well known, and Cadbury chocolate became an important part of the Kiwi soldiers ration packs during World War II.

The launch of Cadbury Dairy Milk

On the quest for a better tasting and better textured chocolate, George Cadbury Junior embarked on a journey to Switzerland to see how the Swiss were producing their smooth chocolate. Discovering that the trick was in the condensing of the milk, Cadbury invested in a milk condensing plant and after much recipe and method trialing, eventually discovered a winning formula in June 1904. This delicious new milk chocolate was made with full cream milk, in greater quantity than any previously known product.

The name game began and three options came up tops: Jersey, Highland Milk and Dairy Maid. After much debate, a combination of the above was chosen and Dairy Milk, with its smooth taste and texture, was unleashed on an eagerly awaiting public in 1905. This new formula was considered better than the continental milk chocolates and its taste was to take the world by storm, resulting in the discontinuation of all other Cadbury milk chocolate in 1915.

Cadbury Dairy Milk quickly became a market leader and remains so today. In 1990, Cadbury celebrated the 60th anniversary of the production of

Dairy Milk in New Zealand. To mark the occasion, it poured the biggest block of chocolate ever poured in New Zealand, weighing in at over 165 kilograms. This gigantic block of chocolate was then transported around the country in a model T Ford van, which in true 1930s style was decked out in Cadbury colours: purple and gold. Cadbury also planned a cow milking in the middle of Dunedin's Octagon, to celebrate the glass and a half logo. Selwyn Toogood was invited to perform the milking and agreed. Quaver the cow did not respond too well to his attempt and kicked him right off his milking stool!

Cadbury Dairy Milk is the company's flagship brand, but Cadbury has an extremely extensive portfolio of chocolates, with a multitude of different flavours and textures to satisfy any sweet tooth!

Cadbury manufacture and market most of the leading chocolate bars in New Zealand, including Moro, Crunchie, Dairy Milk, Caramello, Flake and Pinky, however it is constantly looking for new ideas to keep chocolate lovers stimulated.

Below is a list of New Zealand's top-selling (and much loved) Cadbury brands. See if you can spot your favourite:

Cadbury - Favourite Kiwi Brands

Cadbury Moro
Cadbury launched Moro in 1967. It proved to be a very popular product and has become the number one selling bar in New Zealand for over 30 years. The bar comes in a range of sizes.

The Moro bar is aimed at people on the go and has come to be viewed as an 'energy bar'. For this reason the Moro brand has become synonymous with action, sport and getting the energy to go out and live life to the fullest. It was the official energy bar of the 1990 Commonwealth Games. Moro has also been involved in All Black sponsorship and endorsement and currently the brand sponsors a multitude of events that epitomise its active, energetic and outgoing target market.

Cadbury Buzz Bar
Cadbury Buzz Bar began life as a delicious white marshmallow base coated with a top layer of toffee and covered in Cadbury Dairy Milk milk chocolate. This threepenny bar was so popular that it inspired Cadbury to produce a new chocolate bar: Pinky. Buzz Bar is still sold in its original form in dairies and supermarkets around New Zealand and remains a popular treat to this day.

Cadbury Pinky
In 1955, Cadbury used the popular Buzz Bar as the base theory behind their new bar, Pinky. The marshmallow was given a strawberry flavour and pink colouring and the layer of toffee was thickened to make the bar a more indulgent treat. Coated in Cadbury Dairy Milk milk chocolate, wrapped in pink foil and christened Pinky, this bar also became an immediate success with the New Zealand market and remains a popular bar today. The Pinky bar has a strong female following due to its low fat value, thus it has become a permissible treat. Pinky has a strong retro Kiwi heritage and has a very popular following with young girls.

Cadbury Jaffas
Cadbury Jaffas have an almost legendary reputation as the chocolate that people like to roll down the steps of movie theatres. To create Cadbury Jaffas, the chocolate centre must be made first. The chocolate balls are made by pouring liquid chocolate between two revolving rollers. Each roller has half the ball shape in them so when they rotate they join the two halves together to form the ball.

Thousands of these chocolate balls are then put into a big rotating drum, not unlike a concrete mixer. As the drum turns, the orange sugar syrup is sprayed on the chocolate balls. To dry, they are blasted with warm air. This process is repeated until the sugar coating is just the right thickness. The Cadbury Jaffas are then put into polishing pans and packaged.

Cadbury Crunchie
Cadbury Crunchie is one of the oldest bars in existence. It was originally launched by Fry's in 1929 in England. Crunchie has been in New Zealand since 1955 and is one of the country's top selling bars.

The Cadbury recipe for Crunchie is top secret and while many have tried to recreate the honeycomb, they have been unable to copy its unique texture. Luckily for fans of Cadbury Crunchie there is no chance of it running out of stock as the Cadbury factory in Dunedin is able to make 10,000 Crunchies an hour!

To produce the bars, the hokey pokey syrup is made first and formed into big sheets that are then left to cool and then cut to shape and size. The bars are enrobed in chocolate which is also left to cool completely before being packaged.

The famous Crunchie Great Train Robbery ad was made in the summer of 1975–76. It has become so popular that it is sometimes still screened today! In May 1993, Cadbury sent the Crunchie Steam Train out on a 21 day trip from Invercargill to Whangarei. Each time the train pulled into a station, the jingle was played through external speakers and queues of people were invited aboard to enjoy the ride and munch on Cadbury Crunchie bars and the newly launched Crunchie Nuggets.

The Cadbury colours

The Cadbury Dairy Milk packaging was originally a mauve background with red writing. At the beginning of the century, Cadbury introduced the purple colour, which has now become the Cadbury trademark.

Since 1907, the Cadbury wrapper has changed six times to keep updated with the changing fashions of packaging. Whilst retaining its basic elements of colour and logo design, the packaging has become simpler yet has maintained a classic look.

The Cadbury Dairy Milk "Glass and a half of full cream milk" slogan has become one of the most well-known and successful brands in advertising.

The Cadbury fresh milk comes from New Zealand's finest dairy herds and is delivered to the Dunedin factory.

The graphic of the milk pouring into the chocolate remains an iconic image of Cadbury and is still incorporated into designs today.

Grown in New Zealand

A brand that has truly been grown in New Zealand

Brand origins/history

The story of Cavalier Bremworth began in 1959 when Doug Bremner founded the Bremworth Carpet Company and set up a small factory in Papatoetoe, South Auckland. It was a time when fashion dictated that not only living rooms but also dining areas, bedrooms and hallways be carpeted in a commodity that had put New Zealand on the world map. That commodity was wool.

In 1964, the official Woolmark symbol was launched, and the following year Bremworth became the world's first carpet company entitled to use the Woolmark seal of quality. That same year, Bremworth also became one of the first to advertise on New Zealand's new medium of communication – television – and its dominant use of television advertising over the ensuing years helped establish the Bremworth brand as a household name.

UEB Industries, one of New Zealand's biggest corporations at the time, bought Bremworth in 1967 and proceeded to establish spinning and scouring plants around the country.

In 1972, two UEB employees, Tony Timpson and Grant Biel, left Bremworth to set up a business of their own, and Cavalier Carpets was born.

With a clear vision of what they wanted to achieve, Timpson and Biel set about capitalising on the opportunity that existed – not just locally, but in international markets as well – by creating an unsurpassed standard in carpet quality from the finest wools New Zealand had to offer.

Right from the start, when Grant Biel designed and built a tufting machine, Cavalier Carpets set in motion their founding principles of service and integrity as well as an enduring commitment to quality, which proudly is still unparalleled today. After realising that New Zealand's established yarn spinners didn't necessarily share their commitment to quality, Timpson and Biel branched into yarn manufacturing and in 1975, they established, in Wanganui, New Zealand's most modern carpet yarn spinning mill of the time.

In 1983, the company listed on the New Zealand Exchange as Cavalier Corporation and the following year merged with E. Lichtenstein & Co., one of the country's oldest and most respected merchant wool scourers.

At last, Cavalier Carpets was able to apply its own exacting standards right through from the selection, acquisition and processing of wool, to the end product.

Market conditions had changed by the mid-1980s however, and whilst UEB struggled with the harsh economic climate, Cavalier Carpets successfully steered its way through the stormy waters. In 1988, the timing was right for Cavalier Carpets to acquire from UEB Bremworth, a business and a brand of great standing that could only be enhanced by the quality and performance standards found at Cavalier Carpets.

"Consistently judged New Zealand's best"

The two businesses integrated successfully, but continued to sell under both the Cavalier and Bremworth labels until 1991, when the blue and cream Cavalier Bremworth logo was introduced. This logo was updated in 2001.

Cavalier Bremworth continued to set the standard throughout the 1990s, driven by the underlying values of quality, service and integrity.

In 2000, Cavalier Corporation closed down the E Lichtenstein & Co merchant wool scouring operation, as the margins in wool trading were insufficient to provide an adequate return on the very high level of funds employed in the business.

However, Cavalier Corporation was able to take a controlling interest in Hawkes Bay Woolscourers, which was established to operate an existing commission wool scouring business in Awatoto, Napier. In this way, Cavalier Bremworth was able to continue to apply its meticulous standards to all aspects of the production process – from sourcing wool through to the blending and processing of wool and finally to the tufting of finished carpet.

Cavalier Corporation is listed on the New Zealand Exchange and has approximately 6300 shareholders. It has a staff of more than 750, and its operations cover all aspects of the manufacturing of pure wool broadloom carpet – from wool acquisition at the farm gate, through to wool scouring, yarn spinning and carpet tufting – and distribution of that carpet.

In New Zealand, those operations include Elco Direct, a private wool buying operation, Hawkes Bay Woolscourers (92.5 per cent owned) a commission wool scourer, and the Cavalier Bremworth broadloom carpet operation which has two woollen spinning plants and a carpet tufting plant.

Overseas, it has 89.5 per cent ownership of Ontera Modular Carpets, the Sydney-based modular carpet tile manufacturer.

Brand development

"I have spread my dreams under your feet,
Tread softly because you tread on my dreams,
From a soft English afternoon Bremworth seeks out gentle greens,
golds of antiquity, the mellow browns of Tudor mansions where kings have walked.
Bremworth discovers a heritage of colour, texture, pattern
and creates a timeless carpet, a fabulous carpet, loomed for you."

(Bremworth poem used in advertising during the 1960s and 70s.)

The development of the Bremworth brand can trace its roots back to the first television advertising campaigns run by Bremworth in 1965. Technological restrictions of the time limited the creative advertising opportunities but despite this some very clear brand values were established – thus positioning Bremworth at the forefront of both quality and fashion.

As well as advertising carpet, these early campaigns also reflected aspects of New Zealand culture, and highlighted middle class social aspirations of the time. As the years passed, the campaigns began to trace a growing national identity and consciousness.

In the 1960s, development of the Bremworth brand was as much about mirroring social and cultural changes in New Zealand as it was about the evolution of a major household brand name.

In 1965, grainy black and white images featuring close up shots of carpet and the clipped, formal tones of an English or American male voice-over were the order of the day.

Technical limitations of the new medium were clearly a problem for a company selling colour, texture and style, but the rewards promised by mass-market advertising were too great to ignore.

Following an introductory series of straight product shots (featuring little else than a close-up of carpet and the occasional pair of feet), the tone and manner of the early advertisements became paternal, formal and, on occasion, highly romanticised. Product names, styles and fashion cues were clearly drawn from overseas, and in particular England.

Under the positioning line "Fabulous Carpets by Bremworth", products like "Castle Ridge" promised a lifestyle reminiscent of English country estates, while "Windermere" was brought to life by images of medieval ladies gliding through castle halls.

"Samarkand" came with a touch of the exotic, with camels and deserts featuring prominently, while "Conquero" combined interior residential shots with classic images of Spain, such as bullrings and flamenco dancing.

"New Frontier" called for images of the Sierra Mountains, a carpet traversed by cowboy-booted feet, and the memorable tag line: "Thick, shaggy, very luxurious."

The late 1960s saw the arrival of colour television, as well as the introduction of sex (but very tastefully) to sell product.

That iconic image of the era – a girl in a long flowery dress wandering through an English summer meadow – set a sultry scene that hinted at romance ahead for those choosing "Shagdrift" for their floors.

A growing self confidence as a nation saw New Zealand scenery and New Zealand bred sheep make their debut in the 1970s, as the country took less of a cultural lead from Britain, and traditional English homes were no longer considered the last word in style and sophistication.

Company milestones

1959	The Bremworth Carpet Company founded
1964	Bremworth installed their first tufting machine at Papatoetoe
1965	Bremworth first carpet manufacturer in the world licensed to use Woolmark
1967	Bremworth sold to UEB Industries
1970's	UEB established spinning and scouring plants
1972	Cavalier Carpets of New Zealand founded
1975	Cavalier built spinning plant at Wanganui
1983	Cavalier listed on the New Zealand Exchange as Cavalier Corporation
1985	Cavalier Carpet Stain Remover launched
1988	Cavalier Carpets bought Bremworth spinning and tufting plants plus name and distribution rights
1991	Cavalier and Bremworth brands merged and the Cavalier Bremworth logo launched
1992	Sisalaine, New Zealand's first "Sisal" style textured carpet produced
1995	Enhanced graphics tufter installed at Papatoetoe
1996	Knightsbridge Carpets established
2000	The Bremworth Collection range introduced
2001	Cavalier Bremworth logo updated
2002	Cavalier Corporation acquired Ontera Modular Carpets
2004	Semi-worsted spinning plant installed at Wanganui
2004	Precision patterned loop tufter installed at Papatoetoe

"Crafted from the finest grades of pure New Zealand wool"

37

If the emergence of a New Zealand identity and pride can be seen in the Bremworth advertisements of the 1970s and 80s, so too can the changing role of women.

By the 1980s, the company's advertising no longer featured solemn, authoritative male voice-overs.

Female presenters talked confidently and directly to camera, epitomising the liberated professional woman with her own disposable income. From being a passive figure adorning living rooms and gardens, women stepped into the forefront of Bremworth advertisements and started to talk carpet - woman to woman.

This new confidence was reflected in the product ranges, which now presented strong and varied colour palettes, rather than the predominantly beige hues of past years.

Fashion and style elements were emphasised by images featuring alluring models, evocative of a Vogue magazine photo shoot.

This focus on fashion reached its zenith in 1984 with one of the best known and talked about campaigns for Bremworth: a fashion show with catwalk models wearing haute couture outfits made of carpet.

Awards and Certification Milestones

1970	Ambassador Wool Shag, Shag Aragon and Windermere all medal winners at Golden State of California Exposition
1980	Timeless wins Style Award at The Australasian Floor Coverings Mart
1992	ISO 9003 certification obtained
1995	ISO 9001 certification obtained
1995	Export Commendation Award
1997	Serengeti wins IWS Golden Thread Award
1998	Barathea wins Interior Designex Flooring Award
1999	Evora wins two Golden Thread Awards
2000	"The Bremworth Collection" stand wins "Stand of the Show" award at Designex
2001	Aerolite wins Golden Thread Award and Interior Designex Flooring Award
2002	Raffia wins Golden Thread Award
2002 & 2003	Cavalier Corporation nominated as finalist in Deloitte/Management magazine "Company of the Year" awards.

"Committed to customer satisfaction"

Cavalier introduced a sense of humour when it launched its carpet stain remover in 1985, with an advertisement featuring some tricky footwork with a meatball. This advert not only appeared on television screens in New Zealand, but also subsequently aired as part of an international compilation of advertisements screening worldwide. While grandiose imagery, romantic art shots and poetry had been creative hallmarks of the previous decade, the new Cavalier Bremworth brand, like New Zealand, now exuded style, sophistication and confidence.

By the 1990s, Cavalier Bremworth raised the bar once more, with the development of one of its first "added value" promotions.

By phoning a toll-free number, customers received a free Carpet Buyers Kit packed with useful information and design ideas. Educating and informing was now an integral part of the brand proposition.

While nature, art, style and quality remained recurring themes from the start, price did not make its debut as a key selling point until the early nineties.

Interest-free and no-deposit promotions marked the economic and social changes of the era, but the Cavalier Bremworth brand continued to evolve. Alongside prize draws and finance deals, the brand advertising maintained a stylised and evocative ambience, drawing heavily upon fashion imagery as well as strong female role models.

The one-dimensional, functional advertisements of the 1960s have now been replaced by creativity that reflects the richer, more dynamic and varied society we live in, to give us advertisements that are visually sumptuous, mood-setting and tactile.

Cavalier Bremworth's latest brand campaign, launched in 2002, advances the proposition that beauty is in everything by mixing urban chic with natural beauty and art-house imagery with echoes of children's fairytales and linking the beauty of nature with life's many pleasant experiences. This new level of intimacy is expressed in the brand's current positioning line "It's not just carpet it's what you live your life on."

Product development

Just as in the past, the colours and textures of Cavalier Bremworth's carpets continue to draw inspiration from nature whilst adhering to the highest quality standards, but today its product range is far wider and more sophisticated.

The bland beige hues of the 1960s have been replaced by colourways that embrace strong dramatic shades, pastels and the hues of earth, sea and sky.

As well as offering an extensive colour palette, Cavalier Bremworth has pioneered the introduction of texture into carpet in New Zealand.

For the past decade, texture has been the hottest story in interior design, and the beauty of carpet is that it adds textural variety to a room while retaining the softness, warmth and comfort of wool. To meet the many modern lifestyle and usage needs, there are more textures to choose from today than ever before.

A loop pile carpet, for example, can be level (which means all the loops are of uniform height) or textured (where loops are of different heights). The latter can introduce a powerful design element into the carpet, providing depth, richness and warmth.

As well as textured and loop pile, Cavalier Bremworth offers a wide variety of cut-pile carpets, which are manufactured with the top of the loops cut so that the yarns stand upright. Cut-pile carpets differ in the twist and thickness of the yarn used and the structure of the carpet. For example, a chunky hardtwist creates a casual, comfortable appearance, while a fine hardtwist offers a more tailored, structured look.

As well as a wide range of colours, textures and styles, Cavalier Bremworth uses only high quality backing materials – top quality latex and closely woven jute – to ensure the carpet has superior handling qualities. This means it is easier to install and will not ruck, stretch or come away from its backing.

In the year 2000, the ultimate in luxury and fashion was launched under "The Bremworth Collection", a range of premium "breathtakingly sumptuous" pure wool carpets that delivers an enduring statement of style.

The brand today

Today, the Cavalier Bremworth name remains synonymous with
- pure New Zealand wool.
- quality without compromise.
- leadership in colour, texture and style.
- security of knowing that one has bought the very best.
- commitment to customer satisfaction.

These promises are achieved through
- the selection of only the better grades and colours of New Zealand wool.
- rigorous quality controls and adherence to our ISO accreditation.
- the development of styles and textures that lead the carpet industry.
- the establishment of the Cavalier Bremworth Warranted Dealer network to enable us to monitor dealer performance and set the benchmark for installation standards.
- the Cavalier Bremworth Customer Commitment which promises that we will put right all reasonable causes for complaint.
- our after-sale commitment, offering practical advice and tips on the care of carpet and a free carpet care kit for residential purchases.

"Cavalier Bremworth – it's what you live your life on."

Cavalier Bremworth   **www.cavbrem.co.nz**

CEREBOS GREGG'S LIMITED

Founded on a spirit of enterprise, Cerebos Gregg's products have graced New Zealand pantries for almost 150 years.

Cerebos Gregg's is part of a multi-national institution whose mission is to market and develop extraordinary brands that make a difference to people's lives. Today, Cerebos Gregg's is a dedicated and successful New Zealand business - committed to maintaining an excellent reputation in its range of high quality, value-for-money food and beverage products.

Cerebos Gregg's is home to some true Kiwi icons such as Gregg's, Robert Harris, Refresh, Raro, Whitlocks and Cerebos. Over the years the company has cultivated its position through the strength of their other familiar products such as Bruno Rossi, Civo, Special Blend and Bisto.

Brands

Gregg's – connecting Kiwis

The Gregg's brand stands for "connecting kiwis – genuine, inclusive and enjoying the good times". There is a distinct number 8 Wire personality so that the brand endures both fad and fashion.

Gregg's is the market leader in herbs and spices and instant desserts, while Gregg's Instant Coffee is simply a Kiwi institution that is now the only Instant Coffee manufactured in New Zealand.

Gregg's. Enjoyed since 1861

The history of Cerebos Gregg's is a well woven tale, richly entrenched in a passion for creativity, courage and innovation.

Lured by the prospect of gold, William Gregg emigrated from Northern Ireland to seek his fortune, first in Australia's Ballarat goldfields, and eventually across the Tasman to Otago. Amidst fervor of the gold strike of 1861, Gregg concreted his fortune not in precious metals but in the establishment of W. Gregg & Co, flourishing as a spice merchant, food manufacturer and coffee roaster.

His efforts were inherited and sustained by men like Charles Baker and D.H. Rowntree, who devoted much of their lives to guiding the company towards the 21st century. By the 1920s, this commitment to success saw Gregg's expand into a limited liability company with shares held by no less than 17 people, the majority being directors and employees of the company.

By 1925, business was booming. In a move to maximise quality control and effectively monitor product output, all operations became combined under one roof. The site at 51 Forth Street Dunedin still houses the firm's Instant Coffee processing operations after Gregg's Instant Coffee was introduced in 1960.

In keeping with Gregg's vision of maintaining quality, value and reliability, 1967 saw a relationship form with Cerebos. Cerebos was another celebrated New Zealand brand and had been a shareholder in Dominion Salt, a company established in 1948 and based at Lake Grassmere, Marlborough.

In 1972, Cerebos Foods transferred its operations from Newmarket, Auckland to a new factory site in East Tamaki where the company has remained in ever expanding premises to the present day.

The union of two quality New Zealand brands made sense, and in 1984, the two companies consolidated their triumphs by merging into one as Cerebos Gregg's.

Raro – fruity tropical fun everyday

Raro powdered beverages are a genuine Kiwi institution. What New Zealander doesn't have fond childhood memories of tall, cool glasses of Raro?

The Raro phenomenon began in 1961 when Gregg's & Co created the Rarotongan based cannery industry for juicing oranges and pineapple fruit. These products were marketed under the Raro brand name, later developing into the powdered beverage that is recognised by 98 per cent of New Zealanders.

With a goal to keep the brand forever young, in 2003 Raro Wackos were introduced to today's younger generation. By unleashing Raro into the world of weird science and tropical mismatched colours, Kiwis were again reminded of their inner child.

Robert Harris – fresh coffee to die for

With more than 150 cups of Robert Harris coffee enjoyed every minute, Robert Harris has earned its place as one of New Zealand's favourite brands.

After experiencing fresh coffee while in Italy during World War II, Mr Robert Harris introduced this unique flavour to New Zealand in 1972. Initially his coffee was made to suit his predominantly European ex-pat customers but his passion for the beverage was infectious and the Robert Harris brand was soon gracing many Kiwi supermarket shelves. Cerebos Gregg's purchased the Robert Harris business in 1990 and has continued to grow and develop the brand. To this day, no other company buys more green coffee beans for the New Zealand market and Robert Harris is still roasted and ground in Auckland.

Cerebos Gregg's tradition of innovation also led to the creation of a range of flavoured coffees which are wholly unique to Robert Harris. This innovation was rewarded when Robert Harris won the People's Choice Award for most popular fresh coffee product in 2004.

Through the franchise network of Robert Harris Cafés and hundreds of independent businesses serving this brand of coffee, Robert Harris serves over 4 million espressos a year. This passion for the industry is also evident in prestigious Robert Harris National Barista Awards in which the winner represents New Zealand at the world championships.

Whitlocks – sauces for every occasion

When Fred Whitlock and his wife started making delicious pickle and chutney products in their own kitchen during the 1870s, the homemade rustic values of a country kitchen soon captured the imagination of the people of Wanganui.

Wanganui's passionate loyalty in supporting the best local produce was what drove Cerebos Gregg's to purchase F. Whitlock and Son Ltd in 1992. Whitlock's thicker, spicier tomato sauce has been particularly popular amongst connoisseurs of fish and chips – a splash of Kiwiana to complement a great New Zealand staple.

Innovation

The company's growth throughout its near 150-year history can be attributed to a consistent emphasis on product development and refinement. Frequent initiatives to move with the times and stay constant to consumer trends have helped to create totally new market sectors in New Zealand.

Innovation continues to be the driving force behind Cerebos Gregg's flourishing history. In the 1930s, Gregg's pioneered spray-dried Instant Coffee long before the rest of the world was to know such a product existed. By preserving this innovative spirit, the company was also the first to market such products as Gregg's Instant Desserts and Jellies, Gregg's packeted herbs, spices and infused pastes; Raro and Refresh powdered drinks, and Raro Slushy and Wackos.

That good old Kiwi ingenuity became apparent in the 1960s when Gregg's stunned the nation by being one of the first television advertisers to celebrate the diversity of modern New Zealand people. The Gregg's Instant Coffee campaign, "Many faces. Different races", literally transformed the way New Zealanders identified themselves as a nation.

As a result of the honesty and truth revealed in this benchmark piece of communication, Gregg's continues to be regarded as a well trusted New Zealand brand.

Cerebos Gregg's aims to maintain its place as a market leader by continuing to create products that bring people together over coffee or around the dining table.

Company values and staff

Cerebos Gregg's strives to operate by a core set of internally developed values which are a part of each employee's daily work practice:

1. Acceptance of consequences
2. Courage
3. Creativity and innovation
4. Encouraging personal growth
5. Individual effectiveness
6. Integrity
7. Passion and intensity
8. Speed, urgency and determination
9. Team power

The company employs around 300 people throughout New Zealand. The New Zealand business head office is based in Auckland and encompasses a factory, distribution centre, sales and marketing division, Cerebos Food Service, Robert Harris café franchise division, innovation and technical development centre, operations, finance and senior management team as well as state-of-the-art coffee training facilities. Regionally, Cerebos Gregg's has offices in Wellington, Christchurch and the original Dunedin Coffee Factory, which still manufactures Instant Coffee products to this day. It is a proud fact that around 90 per cent of the company's products are made and packaged in New Zealand.

Into the Future

In creating value for employees, customers and shareholders, Cerebos Gregg's mission is to be the leading food and coffee company in New Zealand

By leveraging the strength of some of New Zealand's most trusted and iconic brands, through both marketing and innovation, the Cerebos Gregg's vision will continue to inspire creativity and deliver quality products that add value to people's everyday lives.

Positivity and passion – the Cookie Time recipe for success.

February 1983: a 21-year-old Michael Mayell stands at the table in his one-bedroom flat in Christchurch, smashing blocks of chocolate into chunks. The latest song by Culture Club pumps from the radio as the smell of home baking starts to fill the room. He's onto something good ...he can feel it!

Little did Michael know that he was in the process of creating an original New Zealand food category – individually wrapped cookies – the food category his new company was to lead in the coming years.

Michael had just returned from a six-month job in the US promoting Ski New Zealand. His return came with a resolve to become a millionaire by the age of 30. The first couple of business ideas he tried were unsuccessful, but then remembering the popularity of Mrs. Fields Hot Cookie Shops in the US, Michael realised there was nothing like those big, freshly baked, American-style cookies in New Zealand.

He asked a friend in the US to send over the Toll House cookie recipe, the classic home bake cookie recipe for North American housewives. Based on that, Michael created his original chocolate chip cookie recipe – one which was to become a Kiwi favourite. Now, over two decades later, that very same recipe is still used in New Zealand's best-selling individual cookie, the Cookie Time Original Chocolate Chip.

Soon after Cookie Time began, Michael's brother Guy joined him as a partner to help steer the fledgling business through its turbulent early years. Together they had a dynamic mix of creative entrepreneurialism and well-grounded business sense. Problems were seen as challenges, issues as opportunities, and with the benefit of youthful enthusiasm and drive challenges were fearlessly tackled head-on.

In the late 1980s Michael and Guy acquired a candy company and began the popular 'All you can eat' Cookie Time/Candy Time factory tours. Business was booming, and headlines such as "Move Over Cookie Bear" started to appear in the media. The country was beginning to take notice of the young entrepreneurial brothers from Christchurch.

Now, more than 20 years after those heady early days, Cookie Time cookies are still the market leader, the drivers and innovators of the category, and the Cookie Time brand is a much-loved Kiwi icon.

A large part of the success of Cookie Time comes from having the courage to try new things. There have been ideas such as a range of muffins and slices (branded Time Out), Batman Cookies, Pizza Time, Scout Scroggin – even selling gateaux was tried. Failure provides the opportunity to learn, and Cookie Time has learned a lot over the years. The candy side of the business also had its share of creative ideas, many of which were very successful, before the candy part of the business was sold off to focus solely on cookies. But whenever something went wrong or didn't work, Michael and Guy redefined their problems as challenges and always looked for the opportunity in the crisis.

It was this approach that gave birth to the now iconic Christmas Cookies campaign. In the early days of Cookie Time, an annual summer sales slump made December the company's least profitable month of the year. The opportunity in the crisis was to create a new Christmas product and market it in an innovative way, with university students as a national sales team. Not only were December sales turned around, but with 75 vibrant students circulating businesses nationwide with their fun and energetic delivery of festive cheer, it became a powerful branding exercise – the ultimate in experiential marketing.

Another innovative plan further established Cookie Time as a household name in New Zealand. In 1996 Cookie Time entered the world record books by baking the world's biggest cookie. The cookie was 25 metres in diameter and used 13 tonnes of ingredients, including 2.5 tonnes of chocolate and 24,000 eggs. It was so huge that it took seven years before its world record standing was finally toppled.

The popularity of Cookie Time has grown steadily over the years and now, from a factory based in Christchurch, about 16 million individually wrapped cookies are baked and 2.5 million Bumper Bars are produced each year. In fact, if all cookies are included, such as the mini Cookie Bites and Christmas Cookies, then Cookie Time bake around 44 million cookies a year.

Cookie Time is still privately owned by brothers Guy and Michael Mayell. At the factory and headquarters in Christchurch there are 75 full-time staff, with an extra 30 staff and 75 students added to the team in the period leading up to Christmas. There are 45 franchised Cookie Time distributors who service stores around New Zealand.

An enthusiasm for innovation saw Cookie Time as early adopters of computer technology and the company intranet system is now their key communication and business management tool. Managers work from home offices and the national distributor network have computers and hand-held PDAs as a standard requirement for their franchise operations.

On their retail rounds, Cookie Time distributors enter orders into the PDAs which are checked and signed on-screen by the retailer. The PDA then communicates via infra-red with a printer in the distributors van, which prints off a paper invoice for the outlet. The order is then sent via a high speed wireless network from the PDA to the Cookie Time office in Christchurch, where the order is processed. The data is channeled through to the marketing and management teams for analysis, and finally to the accounts team for processing.

With technology being a vital contributor to the success of the Cookie Time system, the company saw an opportunity to encourage others, particularly children, to embrace IT also. Michael and Guy formed the Cookie Muncher's Charitable Trust to provide opportunities for children to get involved in education through technology. The trust is the principal sponsor of eTime, a nationwide network of technology centres with the goal of inspiring and educating Kiwi kids, and encouraging them to use the technology which has played a huge role in keeping Cookie Time at the leading edge.

It is interesting to note that Cookie Time is the leader of its category, and has been for more than 20 years. Yet it has never advertised, in the traditional sense. Cookie Time have built a powerful brand on the basics:

great tasting products with all natural ingredients (there are no additives in any Cookie Time products, just the same ingredients you would find in an average Kiwi pantry), great distribution, intelligent management, strong imagery, and the creation of plenty of dynamic public relations opportunities.

Positivity and passion are at the heart of the Cookie Time brand. Mix creativity with the attitude that "success depends on your backbone, not your wishbone", and you have a Cookie Time recipe for success.

Cowells Genuine Pavlovas are the market leading brand of pavlova in New Zealand, and were the first to be commercially distributed throughout the nation.

A recipe for success

The story of Cowell's rise to fame is one of a series of happy coincidences, and opportunities taken, a story of how a business has grown from a small, one-at-a-time kitchen operation into a nationwide operation of four factories making thousands of pavlovas each week.

Cowell's Genuine Pavlovas has its origin in the first Cowell's Coffee Shop, opened by Ron and Audrey Cowell in Lower Stuart Street Dunedin in the mid-1960s. Both from the UK, Ron and Audrey were struck by Dunedin's distinct lack of coffee shops. With only one other in operation at the time, they decided to open a coffee shop themselves, manufacturing from scratch all of the items on the menu.

Audrey Cowell asked a sandwich maker how to bake a pavlova, and the response was "look in the Edmonds Book". From there, with no preconceived ideas as to how a pavlova should look, Audrey developed a large pavlova that was about 80 centimetres high. The diameter was dictated by their brand new Shacklock wall oven, and it was made so that most nights, the Cowells could bake one pavlova but, on Thursday evenings, two would fit in the oven for the busy Friday trade.

The pavlovas were garnished with fruit and cream and sold by the slice. The Dunedin Coffee Shop was definitely "the place to go" for delicious food. A whole generation of Dunedinites can remember those magnificent pavlovas sitting on the counter. Most marvelled over the height of them, and the fact that they were completely full of marshmallow from top to bottom. Many people wanted to know the secret and the Cowells lost count of the number of times they were asked.

One day, a customer asked if she could buy a whole pavlova because she was having a dinner party. Audrey's first thought was "Darn, I have to make another one!", but this small question sparked a whole new business idea, and soon the selling of Cowell's Pavlovas began.

The coffee shop was moved from Lower Stuart Street to St Andrew Street, and the fame of the pavlovas spread nationwide. Many people from outside Dunedin went to extraordinary lengths to get a Cowell's Pavlova. Selwyn Toogood (in Dunedin for It's In The Bag show) was known to make his taxi wait outside while he dashed in and bought a pavlova to carry carefully home with him to Wellington. The sales of pavlovas outgrew the tiny kitchen in the back of the coffee shop in St Andrew Street, so a separate factory was opened in Bath Street.

Ron Cowell can still remember carrying the bags of sugar up the stairs one at a time, and the pavlovas carefully downstairs to take around the corner to sell in the coffee shop. The queues at Christmas were legendary, stretching outside the door and into the street. You had to order a pavlova well in advance to be sure of getting one for Christmas dinner.

A happy coincidence

The next happy coincidence was when a young chef from Wellington called to see the Cowells. David Fox had been going round the country helping to set up the Cobb & Co restaurants for Lion Breweries, and while in Dunedin he spotted the pavlovas. He tried very hard to send Cowell's pavlovas from Dunedin to the company restaurants in Wellington, but every time, they arrived smashed. Railway bus, railways, NAC, nothing worked. He was complaining about this to his wife Virginia in Wellington one day in 1978, when she said, "Look, why don't you make them here in Wellington?"

The Cowells granted him permission for a licence to manufacture pavlovas to their recipe and technique in Wellington, and a franchise was born.

To meet the pavlova demand, the popular coffee shop was sold, and a small factory was built in Dunedin. The Cowells traded under the name of Cowell's Pavlova Kitchen – where else would you make a pavlova but in a kitchen? A second business was set up in Christchurch with Ron and Audrey's son Peter Cowell, and the Auckland franchise was started in 1980 by Marilyn Kent, a school friend of Virginia Fox.

That same year, the original Dunedin business was sold to Trevor and Evelyn Millar – regular patrons of the original Cowells Coffee Shop during their student years in Dunedin during the 1960's. A Hamilton business was opened the next year by Brian Purser and Ray Cooper who were introduced to the Cowells by David Fox. The national chain was well on its way.

Since then, there have been only minor changes in the ownership of these businesses – David and Virginia Fox retired and their business was bought by Richard Holmes in 1989. The Christchurch business was purchased by the Dunedin business in 1988 and, in a rare move all the production for the South Island was shifted to Dunedin. Three of the businesses have remained in the same ownership for more than 24 years.

Innovation is the key

Product innovation has been a driving force behind the Cowell's brand. The individual pavlova portions, Minipavs were introduced by the Hamilton licences as a retail six-pack, and have been a remarkable success throughout New Zealand. Various flavours and sizes have been introduced to meet market demand, and all of the businesses have adapted well to these changes in the 24 years of operation.

The rise of the supermarket and the subsequent demise of the corner store have had a major influence on product distribution, with the bulk of retail sales now through supermarket bakeries. In Dunedin Cowells Coffee

care home, complaining that the scrambled eggs for breakfast wouldn't scramble because there was too much yolk and not enough white!

Thankfully, irate phone calls are now a thing of the past. All eggs for the Dunedin production are separated commercially by Zeagold Foods at their poultry farm at Waikouaiti. The precious egg white is sold by the pallet, neatly packed in plastic buckets for an easier pav preparation. Having no gritty egg shells to discard and no messy yolk to sell has certainly made life a lot easier for the pavlova manufacturers.

When you're starting a new business, you make do with what you have. Cowell's were no exception here, and made great use of spare Shacklock oven parts sold by Fisher & Paykel. These parts were put together by a Dunedin company and served the company well for many years. As consumer demand grew for the tasty pavs and the humble kitchens turned into busy factories, the old Shacklock ovens were replaced by larger commercial ovens. The bigger ovens help to improve cooking quality and maximise productivity.

A bright future for the humble pav

Last Christmas, Cowell's proved that their pavs could be successfully exported in bulk shipping containers and now, the famous Kiwi brand is sold in Perth supermarkets under an Australian supermarket brand. In fact, the Australian market will soon see a lot more of the Cowell's brand as consumer demand is on the rise with our Aussie neighbours. Homesick Kiwis provide another avenue for export, with the pavlovas being sold in small quantities in Canada, USA and the UK.

There is a lot of scope for the Cowell's brand to expand across the waters, and from a modest kitchen in the back of a cafe to a booming national business, the future certainly looks bright indeed.

Cowell's Pavlova Kitchen   **Ph: 03 477 66 54**   **Fax: 03 477 66 54**

EAGLE
TECHNOLOGY

Still one of New Zealand's leading IT brands.

History

In the true sense of Kiwi ingenuity and pioneering spirit, the Eagle family has been a leader in the New Zealand technology sector for over 35 years.

In 1969 Corallie and Trevor Eagle set up punch card bureau, International Data Limited which later became part of Eagle Technology Group. Many will remember the punch card technology of those days, along with the mainframe computers which took up a lot of space and required considerable amount of airconditioning.

In the early 1970s Eagle's offerings had expanded to include consulting and educational services, uninterruptible power supplies (UPS), bank security cameras, banking terminals and communications equipment. By 1976 the company was installing ATM technology for banks and networking these machines to mainframe systems.

Eagle also secured New Zealand's sole distributorship for Prime minicomputer systems which form a large part of Eagle's history. The Prime super minicomputer was not mini by our standards today – it was referred to as "mini" because it was a lot smaller than a mainframe, but still the size of a fridge!

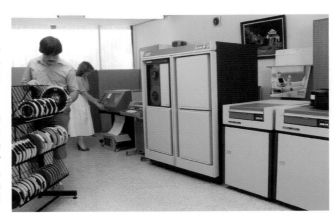

The early days with Prime computers.

Chairman of Eagle Technology, Corallie Eagle, at Eagle Technology's Auckland premises.

Keeping up with developments in the IT world was part of Eagle's vision and it wasn't long before the company was supplying minicomputers and linking these between remote offices.

In 1984, with their business activities growing significantly, the Eagles formed Eagle Technology Group which is recognised today as a trusted technology partner to many New Zealand organisations, including corporate, local body and government departments.

In 1993 Eagle supplied the technology and expertise for a customised national information system for New Zealand's health sector. The technology formed the cornerstone for New Zealand's health IT structure which is today considered an international leader.

At the time of his death in late 2000, Trevor was a leader in the information technology industry. This ensured he had the ear of government on issues such as suggested changes to the tax laws relating to research and development investment. Sadly, Trevor was not alive to see the

New Zealand government effect many of the changes he had advocated.

After Trevor's death, son Craig, who had worked in all areas of Eagle, put his own plans aside and for the next two years filled the gap as CEO. In 2003 chairman Corallie Eagle appointed Gary Langford, formerly the director of Investment New Zealand, as the new CEO. Other family members – Taryn, Brae, Chanel, Duane and Fleur – have also worked for the company. Duane Eagle, who has been with Eagle Technology for 14 years, is Eagle Technology's Business Development Manager responsible for looking after new business, product innovation and geographical expansion.

Branding

The signature gold eagle which forms the branding for Eagle Technology Group Ltd was, by virtue of name alone, the obvious choice when the company formed in 1984. A graphic design company created the original logo in consultation with Corallie Eagle, who from the beginning has made most of the decisions relating to the company's image and profile in the marketplace.

Corallie's individual style and preference for a look of both quality and endurance has inspired the branding.

As well as the stationery, signage and promotional material, the gold, black and white has extended to the decor in every Eagle office since the business began.

Eagle's current offices, located at the Epsom Stand at Alexandra Park, were refurbished in 2000 under Corallie's management at a cost of more than $2 million. Crisp white spaces contrast with quality black and gold fittings and marble floors.

Other features include cast iron stairways, superb Corinthian columns and a boardroom table measuring an impressive six metres long by two metres wide, to seat 24 people. The boardroom also boasts a cast iron chandelier restored from the original premises.

Many will remember the gold eagle sitting atop Eagle's premises in Auckland's Symonds Street. The building is still commonly referred to as the Eagle Technology building, although naming rights lapsed in 2000 when Eagle moved to Alexandra Park.

Racing

The decision to bring Eagle's Auckland head office, Sylvia Park engineering operations and New Horizons Learning Centre into one location was an easy one. However, finding the right location took more than two years.

Within the three units, Eagle had approximately 150 staff and needed a 40,000 square foot site that was centrally located, had truck access and parking for staff and up to 100 New Horizons students. The Epsom Stand at Alexandra Park not only fitted Eagle's requirements but offered parklands, plenty of fresh air, a good choice of cafes and proximity to Auckland's CBD.

Working in such close proximity to a racetrack coincides with the Eagle's passion for racehorses. Corallie Eagle had pre-established horseracing connections and she introduced Trevor to the sport. For more than 15 years the Eagles have not only owned gallopers, but have sponsored the Eagle Technology Counties Cup at Pukekohe Counties Race Day, a race attended by guests and staff from Eagle's Auckland and Wellington offices.

Sponsorship

While it is well known that Trevor Eagle represented New Zealand in swimming at the 1950 Empire Games, very few New Zealanders know that Corallie Eagle represented Auckland at table tennis. Both Trevor and Corallie's love of sport has been demonstrated in their commitment to sponsor the Iron Man contest in the 1980s, and more recently, two of the four annual Auckland Central Masters Harbour Swims: the Bay's Swim and the Rangitoto Swim.

Trevor competed in the harbour swims for many years, as did sons Brae, Craig and Duane.

Trevor Eagle presents the Eagle Technology Bays Swim Cup to Jeremy Gray, winner of the Bays Swim 2000.

Eagle Technology is also committed to supporting local activities through Auckland University of Technology Commerce Faculty, GIS in schools and numerous other community sponsored charities.

Trevor was well known for his support to science, education, community and environmental organisations. He held executive positions including Auckland area chairman of the Duke of Edinburgh Awards and trustee of the WWF New Zealand (World Wide Fund For Nature).

Trevor Eagle welcomes The Duke of Edinburgh at the Auckland Club in 1995. Left to right: Prince Philip, Duke of Edinburgh; Sir Douglas Myers; Trevor Eagle.

Another Eagle Technology Group innovation involves its partnership with Worksafe Technologies, bringing to New Zealand a Seismic Mitigation Solution aimed at keeping information technology environments operational, even through a major earthquake.

The New Zealand franchise for New Horizons Learning Centres has been part of the group since 1994. In early 2004, Eagle extended its IT training line to include Sun training, becoming New Zealand's sole Sun training provider.

In 2000, Eagle Technology established a business relationship with BST Global Inc after securing its first client in Auckland for the BST Enterprise Project and Financial Management solution. In recent years the company has ventured into international markets establishing Eagle Technology Europe Ltd in 2002. Eagle Technology has clients in South Africa, Europe, Asia, Australia and New Zealand.

Eagle today

Eagle Technology covers a broad spectrum of IT solutions including business applications and system integration solutions, geographical information systems and software development. Eagle represents some of the world's leading software and hardware suppliers such as BST Global, SAP, Epicor, ESRI (Environmental Systems Research Institute), Sun Microsystems, Microsoft, Hewlett Packard, Business Objects, Citrix and Powerware.

In 1985 when privately held consulting firm ESRI was looking for a New Zealand partner, Trevor Eagle was the first to put up his hand. US-based ESRI specialises in developing and applying a core set of application tools designed for computerised land use analysis. These applications are more commonly known as Geographic Information Systems (GIS).

Trevor Eagle

From Corallie's desk

Information technology is not only about computers, software or services. It is a combination of all three, guided by a vision of how technology can help an organisation to reach its goals. Today, as businesses concentrate on core activities to maintain a competitive edge, they require their information technology department to do even more with less.

Under these circumstances, there is a growing need for well-informed IT professionals.

Eagle has an excellent reputation in the marketplace for delivering expert services and total technology solutions. Customer loyalty is earned, and many of Eagle's customers have been with the company for many years, reflecting a high level of commitment and satisfaction from all parties.

Since 1985, when GIS was run on proprietary minicomputers, Eagle has expanded its range of skills, experience and products to offer end-to-end support for any scale of GIS application.

The company, while standing by its tried and true offerings such as GIS, UPS and enterprise solutions is constantly looking to the future.

Earlier this year Eagle's GIS team developed and launched BizPoint, a geographic information system aimed to assist businesses with workers in the field. This wireless application uses a global positioning system, is web-based and can also incorporate a tracking system.

Eagle people are experienced professionals who are continually upgrading their qualifications and are passionately focused on providing the best solution for their customers.

The company prides itself in understanding its customers' businesses and the ability to add value in assisting them to achieve and maintain their competitive edge.

Due to the diversity of the Eagle expertise, the company offers a combination of innovative and bundled solutions that are not available from any other source in New Zealand.

Edmonds Sure to Rise is one of New Zealand's most durable, colourful and recognisable trademarks. Originating in 1879, it all started with baking powder.

History

At just 20 years of age, Mr Thomas J Edmonds arrived in Lyttleton on the Waitangi in 1879. He set up business as a grocer on the corner of Randolph and Edmonds streets. He soon realised that there was need for a reliable good quality baking powder and, by drawing upon his past experience working for a confectionary firm in London, he began mixing his own concoction in a small room behind his shop.

In 1879, when Edmonds was confident in marketing his baking powder, he delivered a small batch of 200 samples around the neighbourhood, from which a small but consistent demand developed. Encouraged by this, he spent three years improving his product while other brands appeared on the market.

One day a doubting customer asked if his baking powder was any good. The grocer replied, "It is sure to rise, Madam." Struck with the aptness of his own remark he used it to design the famous trade mark with the rising sun.

Prompted by his customers and their pleasing testimonials, Edmonds placed the perfected baking powder on the market and waited for demand to develop. Three months later there had been no orders from the merchants who had placed samples of "Sure to Rise" on their shelves – the public simply did not know the brand.

Edmonds began to canvass the local Canterbury region, travelling as far afield as Rangiora. His practice was to leave a tin of baking powder bearing the distinctive rising sun trademark with almost every householder, whether they wished to buy it or not. If they were not satisfied, the householders agreed to give the baking powder back on his next visit. Apparently no tins were returned.

Soon orders for Edmonds Baking Powder increased. In 1889, Edmonds won two first prizes for his baking powder and egg powder (known as cake baking powder since 1914) at the Dunedin Exhibition.

At the New Zealand International Exhibition cooking competition in 1906, five-first prize winners used Edmonds Baking Powder. Around the turn of the century, Edmonds moved to a house in Ferry Road and built sheds behind it to manufacture baking powder on a larger scale. It was at these premises that he started making custard powder.

From the humble beginnings in the Randolph street shop, the sale of Edmonds baking powder steadily increased, in spite of fierce competition from contenders, and in 1912 over one million cans were sold. By 1915, sales were equivalent to six and a half tins for every family in the country.

In 1911 Thomas Edmonds retired, although he maintained an active interest in the business until his death in 1932.

In 1920, work began on the new factory building in Ferry Road, which was to become a Christchurch landmark for nearly 70 years. A newspaper columnist described it as 'probably the most modern baking powder factory in the world'. Thomas Edmonds jubilee booklet *Through the Changing Years* describes the new factory as "a three-storied, scientifically constructed building admitting the maximum amount of light and air. The most modern machinery is housed there and is electrically controlled, so that dust and smoke are eliminated."

Edmonds is even part of New Zealand's industrial and political heritage. During the Depression its Christchurch factory was the first to introduce a 40-hour, five-day working week.

All the cans used in the Edmonds factory were made in the company's own room from tin plate imported by the ton. The 69,000 wood cases required per year for packing Edmonds products were also made at the site.

The award winning gardens were established in 1922, and have appeared on the cover of the Edmonds cookbook since 1955.

In 1929 to mark 50 years of business, Thomas Edmonds presented the city of Christchurch with a clock tower and a band rotunda.

Recent times

In the 1980s, the production of Edmonds Baking Powder was moved to Auckland. The Edmonds gardens were bought by the Christchurch City Council, which still maintains them today.

In 1989 Bluebird Foods purchased the Edmonds business. Not wanting to tamper with such a well-known brand, the ingredient range still includes baking powder, baking soda, yeast, custard powder, cornflour and jelly. Formulation-wise there have been a few modifications including a decrease in the cream of tartar to substantiate cost savings, as well as to provide better control and functionality. Wheaten cornflour has been removed from the product to make the baking powder as well as cornflour and custard powder both wheat – and gluten – free.

The Edmonds range has been extended to include cake and dessert mixes. The cookbook range has also grown to include an illustrated version, a junior cookbook, a microwave cookbook and a range of smaller cookbooks.

2004 sees a celebration of the 125-year anniversary of Edmonds Baking Powder. It is hard to believe that the man who put his name on a humble white powder and a cookbook has been deceased for over 70 years. With such great work that went into the foundations of this product, it will certainly be a much remembered and well-used icon for many years to come.

Edmonds cookery books

The first cookery book appeared in 1907 and was a free 50-page booklet of economical everyday recipes and cooking hints. Every couple throughout New Zealand that announced their engagement was given a free copy. Housewives could apply to have copies of the *Edmonds Sure To Rise Cookery Book* posted to them free of charge.

In 1955, the first deluxe edition of the Edmonds cookery book appeared, with the glossy cover featuring the Christchurch factory.

The Edmonds cookery book is a bestseller among cookbooks and the biggest selling book ever published in New Zealand with sales reaching over 3.5 million.

Edmonds – there's no substitute

The thing I miss most about New Zealand is Edmonds Baking Powder. Australian varieties just don't cut it! The last time I was in New Zealand, I slipped a bit of Edmonds Baking Powder into a clear plastic bag to take home with me. The Australian customs officials spent quite a while questioning me about the suspicious white powder I had in my possession. The things we do for a great brand, eh?

- A Kiwi living in Australia talking about her favourite brand

Goodman Fielder New Zealand Ltd   0800 100 538   www.goodmanfielder.com.au

Emirates TEAM NEW ZEALAND

They say that no-one touched by the America's Cup is ever the same again. That is certainly true for team members, sponsors and team supporters. In New Zealand, it was true for the whole country.

The growth of Team New Zealand is a remarkable story of how a brand can expand from an idea to a household name in three years.

History

The America's Cup is the world's oldest sporting trophy, first contested in 1851 when the schooner America crossed the Atlantic and beat 15 British yachts off the Isle of Wight.

The trophy became known as the America's Cup – named for the yacht rather than the country – and the British have been trying to win it back ever since.

Over 150 years, in battles on and off the water, the America's Cup had become the epitome of excellence in a sport where sportsmanship was rarely seen. Cheating was rife, oversized egos clashed head to head and the rules were stacked against the challengers. The New York Yacht Club was determined to keep the silver trophy bolted securely into its display cabinet in their gracious city clubrooms but the challengers kept coming and the legend grew.

Team New Zealand – the emergence of a brand

In 1987 New Zealand launched its cup bid. For New Zealand, the smallest nation ever to challenge, the sentiment was: if the Aussies could do it, so could we.

With backing from merchant bankers Sir Michael Fay and David Richwhite, New Zealand made its debut.

Already, Kiwi ingenuity and technology came to the fore – rather than using wood or aluminum, New Zealand built state-of-the-art fiberglass 12-metre yachts. This upstart challenge rattled the opposition and America's Cup veteran Dennis Conner, who lost to the Australians in Newport in 1993, accused the Kiwis of cheating.

Against the odds the "Plastic Fantastic" KZ7 romped through the challenger rounds, winning 37 out of 38 matches and New Zealanders got their first taste of Cup fever.

Frustrated by delays in the announcement of the next venue and timing of the regatta, Sir Michael Fay issued an early and unusual challenge to the San Diego Yacht Club. The New Zealand Challenge abandoned the established 12-metre class and returned to the 90-foot waterline measurement stipulated in the original Deed of Gift.

The challenging yacht was KZ1, a towering carbon fibre monohull with wings extending from the deck like an aircraft carrier. For the first and only time in the Cup's history, the defender was a catamaran, Stars & Stripes, skippered by Dennis Conner. Predictably, the cat won on the water and a protracted court battle followed.

Ultimately, New Zealand lost, but once again had reshaped the event. The 12-metre yachts would never sail Cup races again and the current America's Cup Class (ACC) yachts were born.

Today KZ1 stands on the hard, outside the National Maritime Museum in Auckland's Viaduct Basin, a silent reminder - if one were needed - that New Zealand had really arrived on the America's Cup scene.

By 1992, New Zealand was recognised as a force to be reckoned with in Cup racing. Having been instrumental in the birth of the new ACC yachts, New Zealand departed from the norm with a short, wide, light Bruce Farr design sporting an unusual double strut keel and no rudder.

The distinctive NZL-20 was dubbed a "skiff on steroids' because it resembled a giant racing skiff. Skippered by Rod Davis, the Kiwis rocketed through to the Louis Vuitton Challenger finals and again took New Zealanders along with them. But controversy erupted again when their Italian Il Moro di Venezia rivals mounted a campaign against NZL-20's bowsprit. The tactic successfully stopped the New Zealand challenge dead in the water.

Having led the series 4–1, New Zealand watched in disbelief as the Italians came from behind to win by 5–4 and thus, winning the right to challenge for the America's Cup itself. For the New Zealanders it was a sad journey home.

Sir Michael Fay and David Richwhite had exhausted their Cup ambitions, so round-the-world racer Sir Peter Blake took up the banner.

Blake changed the team's name to the simple but evocative "Team New Zealand" and they set about building the team for the 1995 Cup regatta. The Silver Fern became an element of the logo and then came the masterstroke that every New Zealander could identify with – the boats' liveries were black, a traditional colour for New Zealand international sporting teams.

The team concentrated its efforts on producing superbly designed and meticulously detailed yachts. Tom Schnackenberg led a talented design team, which responded to a comprehensive and on-going brief from the racing crews.
Team New Zealand's 1995 campaign has been described as a textbook study of how to go about winning sport's oldest and most elusive holy grail of trophies. New Zealand was swept up by Cup fervour as the black boats started a winning streak in the Louis Vuitton Cup challengers series.

It seemed as if time had stopped as the whole nation sat glued to their television sets to watch the Black Magic's NZL32 and NZL38 rocket to ultimate glory. Team New Zealand won the Louis Vuitton series convincingly and continued on to America's Cup victory with a devastating

5–0 defeat of Dennis Conner's Stars & Stripes defense. It was a flawless display by an efficient, focused team that had mastered the technology, worked and trained hard leaving New Zealand grimly determined to win. It gave New Zealand a great sense of national pride and pulled hundreds of thousands of people to street parades in Auckland, Wellington, Christchurch and Dunedin.

And so began the era of New Zealand's America's Cup.

The brand and its "family"

Team New Zealand could not have existed without the backing of its "customers" – committed and loyal sponsors, each with their own leading brands.
Over the years a symbiotic relationship developed between team and sponsors. As the Team New Zealand brand grew strong, sponsors leveraged off their association with a conspicuously successful sports team. Team New Zealand in turn gained first credibility then added stature from being supported by those household brand names.

The group of sponsors' was known as the "family of five". They were seen as part of the Team New Zealand brand in its own right as sponsors' logos were displayed on a black background and always grouped the same.

51

Today, Team New Zealand is the only one of the top three America's Cup players that relies solely on sponsorship.

In the eight years that the America's Cup was in residence at the Royal New Zealand Yacht Squadron, it brought more than a billion dollars into the New Zealand economy, provided the catalyst for the redevelopment of a run-down waterfront at Auckland city, grew a thriving boat building and services industry and, because of the incredible publicity generated internationally, a small country at the edge of the south-west Pacific ocean became the holiday destination for millions.

Team New Zealand can proudly claim to be responsible for all of that.

At home in New Zealand

With the Cup safely in New Zealand, Sir Peter Blake and his team set about creating a venue like no other to stage the 2000 America's Cup. Blake requested and got financial backing from the government and the Auckland City Council to redevelop the Viaduct Basin, a run-down, shallow fishing port. His vision transformed the Auckland waterfront into a Cup village, with all the syndicates concentrated in a single area similar to pits in a Formula One Grand Prix.

While Auckland City was preparing for the influx of people, yachts and business, New Zealand began preparing its defence with Tom Schnackenberg heading design and Russell Coutts leading the sailing team.

Eleven syndicates from seven countries turned up in Auckland, which again redefined the Cup contest.

After a damaging Louis Vuitton series, the Italian team Prada was selected to challenge for the Cup. But, in a repeat of the 1995 result, Team New Zealand's black machine, NZL-60 eliminated the Italian challenge by 5–0.

Sir Peter Blake, Russell Coutts and a young Dean Barker were national heroes. A rapturous crowd greeted the black boats as they returned to the Viaduct.

Sir Peter Blake and key members of his management team stepped aside, leaving the way clear for Tom Schnackenberg, Russell Coutts and tactician Brad Butterworth to establish the framework for a new look syndicate. In the months that followed, Team New Zealand fell apart.

Within weeks Coutts and Butterworth had left to take positions with the Swiss-based Alinghi syndicate. In the vacuum that followed, a number of team members accepted offers of work with other syndicates before Tom Schnackenberg and the new directors could secure seed money from the government for rebuilding.

The sponsors returned to the fold, with a change of status for broadcaster TVNZ, and German software giant SAP joined the "family of five" structure.

By the summer of 2000–01 the black boats were back on the Hauraki Gulf to begin the extensive training and testing so critical to Cup success. The team was keenly aware that the arrival of a number of new and well-funded challengers meant that the event would be one of the most keenly contested.

They were right.

Former Team New Zealand skipper Russell Coutts and his Alinghi team won through to the Louis Vuitton Cup final and then beat another New Zealander, Chris Dickson's Oracle BMW team.

In the America's Cup regatta itself Alinghi match-tested through the challenger series and won 5–0.

Sailing to the future

Towards the end of 2003, as Team New Zealand was going through a rebuild from the water up, an overwhelming number of New Zealanders said they wanted the black boats on the water in Europe in 2007.

The results of a survey conducted in late 2003 by Colmar Brunton were remarkable in a country that traditionally is quick to disown losing sporting groups.

Team New Zealand managing director Grant Dalton says the 500 respondents were asked if they thought Team New Zealand should participate in the next America's Cup challenge in Europe. "The result shows there is overwhelming support for us to challenge again…a total of 67.4% of people want us to go."

Dalton then goes on to say, "This support is nationwide and across all socioeconomic groups. Whatever way you look at it, the survey is a massive vote of confidence in the Team."

In 2004, Team New Zealand is still on the America's Cup trail, buoyed by the support it has received from sponsors and suppliers, central and local government, businesses and the public.

2004 also saw Emirates Airline come on board as the principle sponsor of Team New Zealand, marking a change in the team name to Emirates Team New Zealand. Dalton welcomes the principle sponsor to the family fold in saying that Emirates "share with us a vision for success, a passion for excellence and a no-nonsense, practical approach to the business of winning."

In the past, strong New Zealand personalities have been associated with our challenges for the Cup – businessman Sir Michael Fay, skipper Chris Dickson, Team New Zealand boss Sir Peter Blake and skipper Russell Coutts.Now another strong personality is on board: round-the-world race veteran Grant Dalton, regarded as a hard man who will, if anyone can, get Team New Zealand to Valencia in 2007.

As the survey demonstrates, a stumble along the way can be forgiven, just so long as there is a burning desire to get off the canvas and come out swinging. Above all else, Emirates Team New Zealand and the America's Cup has come to typify the values New Zealanders cherish in their nationhood: a can-do spirit, teamwork, taking on the big guy, accepting the challenge and always striving for excellence.

Fairfax
New Zealand Ltd

Talk to Fairfax - Talk to New Zealand

Fairfax New Zealand Ltd, New Zealand's largest media company, has a strong focus on innovation and leadership. Fairfax New Zealand Ltd established its operation in New Zealand on the 1 July 2003 with the purchase of the publishing assets of Independent Newspapers Ltd (INL).

INL had evolved out of the Wellington Publishing Company Limited, which was founded in 1906 to publish Wellington's morning daily newspaper, *The Dominion*. Through a series of acquisitions it went on to become New Zealand's largest media company.

These assets include nine daily newspapers including *The Dominion Post*, *The Press*, *Waikato Times*, two national Sunday papers, a stable of magazines with particular strength in the lifestyle category, a magazine contract publishing business and an internet operation. Fairfax New Zealand Ltd also publishes over 50 community newspapers throughout the country.

These latest assets join those of the parent company John Fairfax Holdings Ltd. Their mastheads include the prestigious *Sydney Morning Herald*, *The Age* and *The Australian Financial Review*. Fairfax is a highly competitive media company with a strong performance ethic, serving its communities through high quality independent journalism and dynamic venues for commerce and information.

Profile of Major Titles

Sunday Star Times
The *Sunday Star Times* is New Zealand's only national broadsheet newspaper with a readership of 702,000**. *Sunday Star Times* is a newspaper which breaks and backgrounds stories of national significance, at the same time providing a quality leisure read for an audience which has time to take it in. It could best be described as adult, contemporary, relevant and news worthy. The recently launched *Sunday*, a glossy magazine inserted into the broadsheet format, has proved very successful.

Sunday News
Sunday News is the national Sunday tabloid newspaper of New Zealand. The paper's position statement is "No.1 for Sport and Entertainment." Established in 1964, the paper has become a Sunday ritual for thousands of Kiwis. On a typical weekend 521,000** New Zealanders relax with the *Sunday News*.

The news pages include lively backgrounds on the latest news, often giving readers a different perspective on big news events and popular current affairs. Some of the country's most outspoken politicians and commentators write on its comment pages.

The Press
The Press daily newspaper has the largest circulation and most comprehensive coverage of news and advertising in the South Island of New Zealand.

The Press provides more than local, regional, national, and international news. It caters to special interest groups such as farmers and business people, and every publishing day provides pages of features covering such diverse subjects as health, opinion, food, real estate, wine, entertainment, computers and technology, gardening and more.

The Dominion Post
Wellington is more than New Zealand's capital city. It is a vibrant and dynamic economic, cultural and social community. This concentration of energy is reflected in Wellington's morning newspaper, *The Dominion Post*.

The Dominion Post provides thorough coverage of local and international news, as well as special features that inform, educate and entertain its readers. Employment, motoring, real estate, entertainment and special retail-living sections cater to the needs of readers and provide advertisers with a sound platform to communicate with their target consumer groups.

Waikato Times
The Waikato Times is a vibrant, energetic evening newspaper with a Saturday morning edition, which serves Hamilton city and the greater Waikato area. It is Waikato's most popular and well-read daily newspaper. A valuable and respected information source, with two updating editions daily, the Waikato Times keeps Waikato people informed on the latest international, national and local news with an emphasis on Waikato stories. The paper has a strong sports and racing section and special sections devoted to farming and business news.

The Southland Times
The Southland Times has played a major role in the life and times of the province since its first edition was published in 1862. Not only has it been the principal provider of information to generations of Southlanders, it

---

Fairfax New Zealand creates, builds and operates mastheads and brands that are market leaders.

As vigorous, ethical competitors, Fairfax New Zealand benchmarks itself against competitors, both in New Zealand and leading companies abroad.

Fairfax New Zealand has a commitment to serving its communities through high quality independent journalism. It aims to produce compelling material that effectively surprises its audience and is an integral part of their daily lives.

Circulation : 41,009^
Readership : 104,000*

Circulation : 99,123^
Readership : 261,000*

Circulation : 92,436^
Readership : 222,000*

Circulation :26,749^^
Readership : 58,000***

Circulation : 20,566^^
Readership : 42,000***

Circulation : 18,425^^
Readership : 42,000***

Circulation : 10,296^^
Readership : 24,000***

Circulation : 14,329^^
Readership : 31,000***

Circulation : 29,557^^
Readership : 61,000***

Circulation : 209,143^
Readership : 702,000**

Circulation : 110,759^
Readership : 521,000**

Circulation :217,695^^^
Readership : 933,000**

Circulation : 77,195^^^
Readership : 659,000**

Circulation : 76,731^^^
Readership : 377,000**

has also over the years been one of the region's largest employers - and continues to be so.

In spite of the growth of other competitive media, the *Times* can still boast by far the best circulation and readership in the region.

The Daily News
The Taranaki region is located on the West Coast of the North Island and is the major energy and dairy region of New Zealand. *The Daily News* is the local paper and has a comprehensive cover of local, national and international news and photographs. It is one of only eight morning newspapers in New Zealand and one of the largest provincials.

Manawatu Standard
The Manawatu Standard is a regional newspaper, based in Palmerston North. The newspaper has a circulation of more than 20,000 which serves a diverse readership, including a strong tertiary education sector. The newspaper's emphasis, particularly on the front page, is generally strong on local coverage, because this is what makes *The Manawatu Standard* different to other print media.

The Nelson Mail
The Nelson Mail has served the Nelson region with a daily newspaper continuously since 1866 and is one of New Zealand's oldest and most respected provincial newspapers. While much emphasis is placed on local news gathering, the newspaper employs a team of 34 journalists to ensure a mix of national, international news, business and sports coverage, features and utilities.

The Timaru Herald
The Timaru Herald is a provincial newspaper with a strong emphasis on local news. It also provides coverage of national and international events and publishes special features, including the weekly *Farm Review*, a specialist farming publication. Strong sport, fashion, entertainment, real estate and classified sections make *The Timaru Herald* the leading medium in the region.

The Marlborough Express
The Marlborough Province is famous for its wine and seafood, giving it the well-deserved title of "The Gourmet Province". With a population of 43,035 people, there are 16,302 households in the Marlborough and Kaikoura regions. Based in Blenheim, *The Marlborough Express is* delivered to homes

throughout the province - Kaikoura in the south, through to Blenheim, Picton, The Marlborough Sounds and west over to Rai Valley.

NZ House & Garden
Every month this sumptuously presented magazine invites readers to step into some of New Zealand's most outstanding and original houses and gardens and meet their inspiring owners. *NZ House & Garden* reflects a wide variety of homes and lifestyles.

Cuisine
Cuisine magazine is a bi-monthly, glossy lifestyle magazine with an editorial mix of wine, food and travel. *Cuisine* has nearly trebled its circulation in five years, which currently stands at 76,731 copies.

Cuisine's editorial mix reflects its readers' interests. *Cuisine* readers love the good things in life; they love to cook, entertain at home and dine out frequently and they love to travel. *Cuisine* has twice been acknowledged as one of the top three food magazines in the world in the highly-regarded World Food Media Awards.

The TV Guide
With a circulation of 217,695, *The TV Guide* is one of New Zealand's most popular magazines with the highest circulation of all the weekly titles. This bright and brash New Zealand institution has earned its reputation as being "the best thing on TV" and offers readers the most comprehensive television listings available.

Stuff
Fairfax's award winning interactive national news website, www.stuff.co.nz

* Nielsen Media Research NRS Jan-Dec 2003, Average Issue Readership 15yrs+
** Nielsen Media Research NRS Jan-Dec 2003, Average Issue Readership 10yrs+
*** Nielsen Media Research NRS 3y/e Jan-Dec 2003, Average Issue Readership 15yrs+
^ Audit Bureau of Circulation 6 months to March 04
^^ Audit Bureau of Circulation 12 months to March 04
^^^ Audit Bureau of Circulation 6 months to December 03

Tel: +64 9 970 4000   Fax: +64 9 970 4045

Fairydøwn®

ENGINEERED FOR EXTREMES FAIRYDOWN ADVENTURE

*"I don't think there's much doubt that your bags are
the best that can be obtained anywhere in the world."
- Sir Edmund Hillary*

Mill in the Valley

The Ellis family crash-landed in New Zealand early on New Years Day in 1874 when their vessel, the Surat, struck rocks along the Catlins coast on its final leg from England. Three weeks later the family made their way to Dunedin with virtually none of their possessions.

After a few years working at a local woolen mill, Ephraim Ellis and his brother in law started a factory in Kaikorai Valley manufacturing flock from textile wastes in 1877. In 1882, Ephraim's son Arthur was taken from school at the age of 13 to begin working in the factory. These were uncertain times and it wasn't until 1891 that the Ellis family business improved enough for contemplation of the future. During this time, the flock trade continued to be vulnerable with kapok used as a replacement for flock as it provided much better returns.

In 1901 a brief and unsuccessful foray was made into wire mattress manufacturing, however flock and kapok mattresses were still much more successful. A bold move was made to not just sell the mattress filling to retailers but also to sell the finished product.

Mechanisation provided greater efficiency for mattress manufacture and eventually spelt the end for the manufacturing retailers. In 1911 Ephraim withdrew from the business, forcing Arthur to pay his father for his two-thirds share in cash. This was seen by Arthur as a bit of a rough deal; he had worked incredibly hard to develop the business on no wages in his junior years and minimal pay until he was well into his twenties. Arthur was dealt a further blow 10 years later when he discovered he had been left out of his father's will.

A passion for the mountains

Arthur Ellis and his wife Agnes had six children including Roland and Norman who both worked in the family business. When Arthur was in his mid fifties he began steadily handing over his shares to the brothers. Roland was a man of contrasts, generous to the community and people in need but frugal and hard on his staff until they proved themselves worthy.

Far from the frivolities of the Roaring Twenties, Roland discovered a love of the mountains and in 1927, took part in the third ascent of Mt Aspiring with four other Otago climbers. This was the first unguided ascent and during this period Roland constructed an original alpine tent and became intensely interested in alpine apparel. While waiting out a storm on the Bonar Glacier during the climb of Mt Aspiring, Roland came up with the idea of replacing their heavy woolen blankets with a down-filled sleeping bag. In 1928, the first bag was created; a shell fabric made from light cotton sateen sourced from England and filled with eider down from Northern China.

This was the birth of the Fairydown Adventure brand.

Arthur Ellis Ltd continued to manufacture mattresses adopting modern techniques and construction methods. The Sleep-well brand name developed with slogans such as "New Zealanders slumber on Sleep-well". After importing sewing and embroidery machines in 1925, manufacture of down quilts began. By the late 1930s the quilt room employed more than 100 women. Additional products such as pillows and camp beds were also developed during this period.

Sleeping bag manufacturing began during this period with Norman Ellis taking a special interest in the manufacturing process and introducing

some innovative technical breakthroughs. However, sales of the early sleeping bags were limited to the hardy mountaineers of the time and production was a minor "fill in" job between quilt seasons. Arthur Ellis Ltd became known throughout the South Island by the 'Sleep-well' and 'Fairydown' brands that were associated with quality, superior workmanship and style.

By 1939 Arthur Ellis Ltd was in sound shape having weathered the depression years well. The company had played a major role in keeping most staff employed; boosting morale and provided extra support when needed.

In 1953, Arthur Ellis Ltd became a public company. This change lead to the development of the new Christchurch factory built in Hornby, and saw the beginning of mattress production in 1957. Sleeping bag production remained in Dunedin with 2000 made in 1953 increasing to 5500 in 1955. In 1960, a down plant was installed in Hornby to relieve pressure on Dunedin.

"The company has always been careful to maintain as high a standard in the hidden interiors of its products as in the visible exteriors."

– Roland Ellis, 1959

Fairydown at Camp 9

In 1951 the New Zealand Garwhal expedition which included Ed Cotter, Earle Riddiford, George Lowe and Ed Hillary summited seven new peaks up to 22,180 feet in the Himalayas. Down sleeping bags and clothing were supplied by Fairydown and proved more than satisfactory. Roland was instrumental in then securing Ed Hillary and Earle Riddiford a place on Eric Shipton's 1951 Everest Reconnaissance Expedition. Ed and George were subsequently included in the successful 1953 expedition. Hillary and Tenzing used Fairydown sleeping bags at their camp at 28,000 feet the night before they climbed to the summit. The testimony of Sir Edmund Hillary put Fairydown and Arthur Ellis Limited in the world spotlight and helped the company secure previously undreamed of export markets.

"You'll be pleased to know that Tensing and I used your bags in Camp 9. It would be an exaggeration to say we were warm in this camp – or the South Col, as we had only a single bag in order to save weight, but I found a single bag was quite sufficient in Camp 7 and below – wearing, of course, our down clothing. As a matter of interest, Tensing gave me the unsolicited testimonial that his New Zealand bags were the best he had ever used. I don't think there's much doubt that your bags are the best that can be obtained anywhere in the world."

- Sir Edmund Hillary

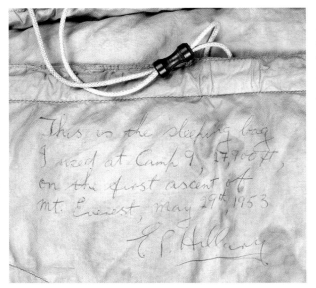

Roland's son Murray shared his father's interest in mountaineering and spent many seasons climbing at Mt Cook and in the Otago mountains. With his engineering background and outdoor experience he was selected in 1957 to join Hillary's section of the British Imperial Trans Antarctic Expedition. The intention was for Hillary's team to act in support of Sir Vivian Fuchs's vehicle crossing of Antarctica.

After assisting in the construction of Scott Base, Murray and another engineer, Jim Bates, made use of the winter months by modifying farm tractors (originally intended only for unloading the ships) to be suitable for long-distance polar travel. Hillary's team eventually stole the show, reaching the South Pole over two weeks before Fuchs.

The expedition caught the imagination of the public; support increased further when the clothing and the original Everest bag were put on public display throughout New Zealand.

With a growing reputation, the international mountaineering community placed orders for Fairydown products. More bags were developed to cater for the wider market and sales went up to 9000. Christchurch began sewing sleeping bag cases which were then sent with feathers to Dunedin for finishing. Due to Hornby's readily available labour and purpose-built site, sleeping bags were all shifted to Christchurch. During this time, down blankets were also developed and manufactured.

In 1964, Arthur Ellis was tragically killed in a motor accident and his grandson Murray took over as general manager of the company.

"Tensing and I visited Arthur Ellis and Company in New Zealand during August 1971. We were impressed with the excellence of their manufacturing processes and the continuing high quality of their sleeping bags. I have used their sleeping bags in the Antarctic, the New Zealand and European Alps and on innumerable occasions in the Himalayas. They excel at sea level or at 28,000 feet on Everest, and I don't think there is much doubt they are the finest bags that can be obtained anywhere."

– Sir Edmund Hillary

The 1970s marked a decade of milestones for Arthur Ellis Ltd In 1973 the company listed on the New Zealand stock exchange and in 1977 Arthur Ellis Ltd celebrated its 100th birthday. With a gala dinner at the town hall, staff efforts were not forgotten with each member receiving two pewter goblets each and a copy of *Mill in the Valley*, a book covering events of the last 100 years.

By this stage Fairydown was well established as an outdoor brand, built on the reputation of its sleeping bags. In 1980 Murray's son David joined the business and introduced modern fabric designs, adjustable harness backpacks, tents, ski clothing and Entrant fabric in sleeping bags. The 1980s was a time of new innovation for Fairydown which was now shining bright as the leading New Zealand outdoor brand.

Changing hands

Saying goodbye to David Ellis, the last family member to work in the company, the Arthur Ellis family's involvement ended in 1989 when the company was sold to Northern Feather. This Danish company invested extensively in the Hornby site – upgrading the factory, and adding a world-class down conditioning and computer filling system.

Alongside the duvet and sleeping bag lines, four highly experienced machinists worked full-time to produce down jackets for alpine use – a complex and prestige product without much profit margin.

Due to capacity constraints, exports started slowly. Throughout the 1960s, a fair amount of exploration took place but very little was actually realised. To compensate, Fairydown sleeping bags were very favourably mentioned in the Whole Earth Catalogue, a bible for North American environmentalists.

With favourable exchange rates, business boomed to the North American market. The Fairydown sleeping bag range continued to develop and by the early 1970s a wide range of products was offered for all seasons. Synthetic fibre was also introduced into the sleeping bag range.

Northern Feather experienced troubled times during its ownership and in 1991 the company was sold to Donaghys Industries, bringing it once again back under New Zealand ownership. This switch in ownership brought with it a change of company name to Sunshine Ellis Ltd, signaling the presence of the camping brands, Sunshine Leisure and Great Outdoors. However, the name change was not popular and in 1994 the company was returned to Arthur Ellis Ltd and has remained so until today.

The move to offshore manufacturing

During the 1990s, and after many years of competing against primarily New Zealand manufactured brands, the market saw an influx of international brands targeting the New Zealand market. In order to compete with this trend, 1998 saw Fairydown Adventure begin offshore manufacturing in Asia. By 2003 all Fairydown adventure products were manufactured offshore, allowing more freedom with design and technical developments.

Innovations in manufacturing are still today an integral part of the Fairydown brand with developments in sleeping bag manufacturing remaining the most important and enduring. Quality of materials, innovative design and manufacturing remain uncompromised.

50-year anniversary

In 2002, in celebration of the 50-year anniversary of the first ascent of Everest, Peter Hillary for the second successful time reached the summit of Everest, this time using the latest Fairydown 'Everest' sleeping bag at camp 9. During this anniversary year, there were many formal and informal events held to celebrate this historic event, including an exhibition held at the Auckland museum where the original 'Twenty Below' used by Ed Hillary at camp 9 was on display. This bag is still on display at the Arthur Ellis Head office in Christchurch.

Ensuring a bright future

With fast paced international product development becoming forever stronger and marketing sophistication in the outdoor sector becoming savvier, the need to step up was essential. In 2002 the company once again saw a management change and this time a separation from Donaghys Industries. The new management style and vision; lead by entrepreneur Hugo Venter, this vision was to be a company at the forefront of product development, design and marketing.

A frenzy of activity ensued for the brand in both design and marketing. The Fairydown logo was re-designed but remained the solid identity for all sleeping bags, backpacks and tents. 2003 saw the launch of the Zone brand, the new 'identity' for Fairydown clothing. The brand has been welcomed into the market and in the short time since launch, there has been large expansion in its market share.

The New Zealand and Australian markets make up the majority of turnover for Fairydown Adventure. The goal to grow and develop export opportunities has a strong focus. Today the brands are exported to Korea and the UK, with development under way in Japan.

Expedition List

Year	Expedition	Year	Expedition
1951	New Zealand Garhwal Expedition	1990	Peter Hillary Ascent, Nepal
1953	British Mt Everest Expedition: Edmund Hillary, Sherpa Tensing Norgay achieve first successful acsent of Everest	1991	Brigette Muir First Female Attempt, 7 Summits
		1992	New Zealand Cholatse Expedition NZ Kathy Basalaj World Record 100 Women Link up
1954-89	Australian Antartic Exploration	1993	Robert Anderson Solo Ascent Everest Gore-Tex Fairydown Southern Traverse
1957-58	British Trans Arctic Expeditions		
1963-66	Victoria University Antarctic Expedition	1996	Eco Challenge Team Event, Canada Keith Murray, International Adventure Racing Team, 1st placing Southern Traverse Fairydown Team, 1st placing
1967	Hillary's Antarctic Expedition		
1969	Hillary's Himalayan Expedition	1996-99	Fairydown Tongariro Mountain Classic
1972	South West Face Everest	1997	Coast to Coast Longest Day Andrea Murray, 1st place, new record 12.08 Veteran, Russell Prince, 1st placing Mt Everest Seven Summits Challenge, Brigette Muir Eco Challenge Team Event ; Australia Keith Murray, International Adventure racing team, 1st placing
1977	New Zealand Everest Expedition		
1978-79	Caffyn Soto Kayak Circumnavigation of New Zealand		
1981	Whitbread Round the World Yacht Race	1998-99	Antarctic Ice Trek Expedition Peter Hillary, Jon Miur, Eric Phillips
1982	Caffyn Solo Circumnavigation of Australia		
1985	New Zealand Alpine Club Everest Expedition, Caffyn Solo Kayak Circumnavigation of Japan Australian Mt Shivling Expedition, Tibet	2000	Eco Challenge Team Event; Patagonia Keith and Andrea Murray, John Howard, Neil Jones, 1st placing
		2001	Fairydown Adventure Kepler Challenge
1988	American/New Zealand Expedition, Tibet New Zealand Himalayan Kayak Expedition, Tibet	2002	50th Anniversary Everest Expedition, Peter Hillary Fairydown Adventure Kepler Challenge
1989	New Zealand Everest Expedition North Face, Tibet		

Tel: +64-3-3497077   **Fax: +64-3-3499884**   **www.fairydownnz.com**

Feltex
CARPETS

From the University of Otago to the Ritz-Carlton in California, one of New Zealand's best known brands has been chosen for some of the world's most prestigious projects.

Carpet maker to the world

Established more than 70 years ago, Feltex Carpets has built a brand with a solid reputation for providing innovative, high quality and stylish floor covering solutions. The carpets are the result of a philosophy orientated to quality and dedication, which applies to every aspect of the company's operations.

Today, Feltex produces more than 25 per cent of all carpet in New Zealand and Australia and is one of the world's dominant producers of natural wool carpets.

The Feltex operation includes a wool scouring plant, six spinning mills, three tufted carpet mills, a woven carpet mill and offices in New Zealand, Australia and the US.

Finding its way into five-star hotels, cruise ships, offices, hospitals, theatres, schools, universities, banks, offices, houses of parliament and homes, the Feltex brand is the global carpet of choice in New Zealand, Australia, Asia-Pacific, Japan, USA, and the Middle East.

But there is no area in which the comprehensive skills and innovation of Feltex are more evident than in the technically demanding design and production of aircraft carpet.

Feltex is an accredited supplier to Boeing Airbus Industrie and is constantly updating its skills and systems to meet the demanding specifications of the world's leading carriers.

After more than a decade keeping the feet of New Zealanders warm, 10 looms were installed at the Lower Hutt plant and Feltex produced its first carpet in the early 1940s.

Later in that decade, a factory to produce woven carpets was built at Christchurch, supplemented by the purchase of wool scour capacity at Kakariki near Fielding.

The company grew substantially in the 1970s and 1980s through the strategic acquisition of other carpet makers.

In the 1970s Kensington Carpets was purchased followed by Stevens Bremner, a tufted carpet maker located at Foxton, in 1980.

Later in the 1980s, Feltex built a plant to make woollen spun yarn at Fielding and purchased an additional yarn plant at Dannevirke.

In Australia, the company began in the 1920s manufacturing felt floor coverings and Wilton carpet under the name Sydney Felt and Textiles Ltd.

Production of the first Axminster carpet started in Victoria in the 1940s, followed by the first tufted production in the 1950s. These operations and those of Redbook, Invicta and Minster Carpets became part of Shaw Industries – the largest carpet manufacturer in the world.

In May 2000, Shaw decided to exit Australia and Feltex made a decision that would confirm it as a major carpet brand by purchasing all of Shaw's Australian operations.

A complete range

The purchase was a turning point for Feltex.

Prior to this, the Feltex brand was associated with quality wool rich carpets and yarns made almost exclusively from New Zealand wools.

With a can-do attitude to customer requests, and total quality control from fleece to the floor, the brand had developed a reputation for being one of the most versatile manufacturers of quality carpets and yarns in the world

The May 2000 purchase gave the company the capability to broaden the Feltex range and include carpet manufactured from man made fibres, building a brand that covered the full spectrum of carpeting needs.

The merging of the operations resulted in efficiencies across the business, including rationalisation of the product offer, a greater focus on the brand portfolio and improvements in customer response times.

A pattern of growth

For a globally-recognised brand, Feltex certainly had humble beginnings.

In 1929, Feltex started its New Zealand operation manufacturing felt slippers.

A strong brand presence

The Feltex brand has achieved more than 60 years of growth in established markets. Despite recent competition from alternative flooring finishes, the company has developed an increasingly stable brand presence in both New Zealand and Australia.

A new dimension in carpet

Customer
Services
0800 100 008

Feltex
CARPETS
COMMERCIAL

meet the needs of virtually any project. An almost unlimited number of colours and intricate designs are available in tufted and woven carpets made from wool, wool blends and man made fibres.

The Feltex ranges

Feltex has developed a number of carpet ranges designed to meet the needs of specific markets.

Some are marketed under the Feltex brand, others are branded independently and designed to provide strategic support at retail level.

Feltex Reserve

Manufactured to the highest degree of design and craftsmanship, the Feltex Reserve Selection range of carpets features woven premium pure wool Wilton and Axminster, as well as tufted plush pile carpets.

In the past decade, the average size of the market in Australia has been 49.5 million square metres per year. In New Zealand, the average was almost 9 million square metres per year over the same period.

The market is split approximately 30 per cent commercial and 70 per cent residential, with the market size in any one year influenced by the age of the carpet and need for replacement.

The residential replacement cycle is usually from five to eight years, while the commercial cycle can be as long as 10 to 15 years.

Influences on the commercial market include the volume of new construction, general economic climate and one off events.

Carpet sales are boosted by events such as the construction boom associated with the Sydney 2000 Olympics, the introduction of the GST in Australia and the Australian First Home Owners Grant.

Feltex supports its customers

About 70 per cent of Feltex carpet is sold for use in the residential market. Some of these sales are for new homes, but the majority are for people who are redecorating their homes or replacing existing carpets.

Residential sales are made through retail buying groups and independent retailers who sell both Feltex and competitor brands.

To maintain a high profile and strong market presence, the brand provides a range of in-store support including prominent display units, carpet samples and other point of sale material.

Feltex retailers are also supported by a simplification in the purchase process through call centre ordering, electronic commerce and provision of carpets that have been pre-cut prior to delivery.

In the commercial market, sales are often through a tender process or direct contact with major buyers and commercial flooring contracts.

The company's commitment to the Feltex brand values of excellent service, timely delivery and cost competitiveness has built many successful long term relationships

Whether using stock carpets or custom designs for specific projects, Feltex prides itself in providing superior service and flexibility of choice. In this market, Feltex works with architects, designers and other specifiers to

LIVE WITHOUT COMPROMISE.
CARPET ACCORDINGLY.

Reserve

Feltex Classic

An exclusive range of the highest quality pure wool carpets, Feltex Classic offers more than 200 colours, textures and designs to suit almost any mood, preference and style of decor.

Invicta and Kensington

A spectacular range of quality wool and wool-rich carpets, the Invicta and Kensington ranges are textural and tonal.

Redbook

Renowned for its universal comfort and appeal, Redbook carpet provides practicality and comfort while meeting the demands of family living. Redbook brands include Performance Plus 11, Soft Touch and Luxura, each of which combines exceptionally soft fibre with leading stain protection warranties.

Minster

Minster is a hard-wearing selection of nylon and polypropylene carpets that combine quality and value with comfort and style. Minster includes the Market Street range and offers more than 500 colours and designs.

Commercial

This is arguably the finest, most comprehensive range of commercial carpets in the world. With Feltex offering the latest designs, colours and textures in a wide variety of weights, yarn combinations and styles, customers can choose from an extensive stock range, or custom design carpet to suit their individual needs.

Investing in the brand

The Feltex philosophy is simple: to create the finest range of residential and commercial carpets around the globe, with quality, technical expertise and unparalleled craftsmanship as the cornerstone of the company's existence.

With this philosophy and an ongoing investment in superior technology, skilled people, service excellence and a commitment to satisfying customer needs, Feltex has created a brand that has won respect not only in New Zealand, but also worldwide.

Fisher & Paykel

innovative living

Fisher & Paykel Appliances designs, manufactures and markets a range of innovative household appliances that are developed with a commitment to technology, cutting edge design, user friendliness and environmental awareness.

Founded on a spirit of enterprise, the journey of Fisher & Paykel Appliances began in 1934, when Maurice Paykel and Woolf Fisher joined forces to import domestic refrigerators into New Zealand. A new government imposed regulation of the time, requiring that all appliances be manufactured within the country did little to hinder their entrepreneurial strength and, soon after, the Fisher & Paykel manufacturing story began.

The company initially manufactured the designs of other appliance companies under license, but New Zealand's geographical isolation, teamed with the pioneering spirit established by the company's founders, quickly resulted in innovative manufacturing that challenged conventional appliance design.

After many years of optimising conventional designs, Fisher & Paykel engineers began to build appliances with improved performance. Incorporating sophisticated electronics from the emerging computer industry with a new generation of electric motors from the space industry, smarter, and more efficient appliances were produced.

Fisher & Paykel is now seen as the innovator in the appliance industry. Already a household name in New Zealand and Australia, Fisher & Paykel is now gaining favour as a premium brand, delivering innovative design and technology in over 40 countries worldwide.

The electronic control of smart motors, along with other ground-breaking technologies in design and manufacturing, has resulted in over 400 international patents that recognise Fisher & Paykel appliances as unique. Innovative systems such as Smart Drive® autowashers, Active Smart® refrigerators, AeroTech™ ovens and DishDrawer® dishwashers give Fisher & Paykel a place in many international markets from Asia to Europe as well as the home of appliances, the US.

Fisher & Paykel can proudly attach its name to a number of world firsts in appliance development, such as flexible manufacturing and the use of pre-painted steel for product cabinets. Over the years, the company's pioneering approach to manufacturing has lead to the design and development of its own production lines for making appliances. This particular division of the business now constructs manufacturing plants and machinery for other appliance companies throughout the world.

Today, Fisher & Paykel has state of the art manufacturing facilities in Mosgiel and East Tamaki in New Zealand and in Cleveland, Australia. The design and development of all appliances is completed on site by the company's own staff.

Brand development and positioning

From initial research right through to design development, manufacturing, and product implementation, the Fisher & Paykel brand is proudly unique and intrinsically complex. Its history of progress to date spans 70 years, with much of its early development shaped by the spirit of Kiwi ingenuity.

In New Zealand, the brand personality has been shaped by a heritage of market isolation and what once was a large and significant family business. The Fisher & Paykel brand is considered by many as an adopted family member in most New Zealand households; a brand that delivers stylish appliances that are reliable, competent and practical.

The Quantum strategy is confined to the New Zealand and Australian markets where the Fisher & Paykel brand offers a wide range and more mainstream positioning. The Quantum strategy was initiated in 1998 in order to identify the best in technology and design offered by Fisher & Paykel. Those products that meet the stringent benchmark are identified with the Q badge as a mark of particular excellence. This enables the marketplace to easily classify those products in the extensive line-up offered in New Zealand and Australia.

Brand values

Fisher & Paykel's brand values reflect the way its products enhance and assist people in their everyday lives.

Mirroring the pioneering minds of its founders, innovation is the nucleus of the Fisher & Paykel brand. The success of the company's products is a result of the evolutionary deliverance of ground-breaking technology together with user friendly designs that are directly relevant to consumers.

The key values or "DNA" of Fisher & Paykel and its brands can be described in four simple words:

Style creates desirability. It is reflected in Fisher & Paykel's product designs and in the way the company evolves in response to changing market needs.

Integrity is about building relationships with customers. It reflects the trust behind Fisher & Paykel's solid reputation, and the way in which consumer values are reflected in product design.

Care reflects the way Fisher & Paykel looks after its customers, its community, and its environment.

Innovation is the heart of Fisher & Paykel - from product development to customer care.

Fisher & Paykel and the environment

With New Zealand's worldwide reputation for its well-preserved environment, Fisher & Paykel sees a commitment to environmental conservation as an integral part of company culture. From the elimination of ozone-depleting

Type Tested
Lic 6080

Water Conservation Rating

AAA
AA

WATER SERVICES ASSOCIATION of Australia
http://www.wsaa.asn.au

chemicals in 1994, through to the ongoing optimisation of appliance efficiency, Fisher & Paykel's philosophy has been to quietly initiate eco-friendly manufacturing practices and techniques.

In a ground-breaking move in 1993, the company piloted an appliance recycling project to gain insights into this type of process. Now, more than 10 years later, this initiative extends far beyond the salvage of some 25,000 appliances per year, to the re-using and pulping of packaging, as well as the recycling of waste from Fisher & Paykel factories.

With an established policy for continual improvement, Fisher & Paykel appliances are constantly evolving to meet new energy efficiency standards. The company's key product platforms – Active Smart® Refrigeration, Smart Drive® Washing Machines and DishDrawer® Dishwashers – are all designed to assist the reduction of the use of precious energy and water resources.

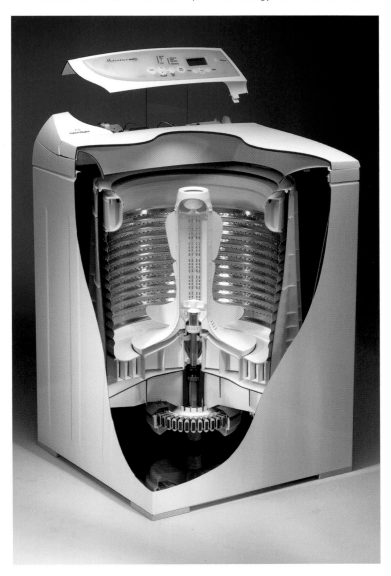

Smart Products

The entire Fisher & Paykel range is characterised by form and function. Stylish, sleek and streamlined designs are adopted to blend seamlessly with any home décor while sophisticated and practical technology is implemented to meet the demands of busy lifestyles.

With the kitchen now a major focal point of the home, Fisher & Paykel cooking products are distinguished by practical designs and a minimalist approach to style. Consumer research and innovative technology have resulted in a superior range of ovens, cooktops, and rangehoods - all offering the convenience of fingertip control. While most cooking products are based on standard European convention, they are delivered in a more robust format with larger capacities.

Adding life to food through sophisticated technology, Fisher & Paykel refrigeration products are run by an advanced electronic intelligence that monitor temperature conditions and selects the best way to preserve freshness, nutrition and flavour. A sophisticated sense of style is apparent both internally, with practical features such as solid shelves, and externally through soft curves and a range of finishes to complement the kitchen design.

A world first in form and function, the DishDrawer® is a whole new concept in dishwashing. Ergonomically designed to offer the same effortless operation as opening a kitchen drawer, the unique size of the single DishDrawer® gives consumers the flexibility to design kitchens the way they want. Skilled Fisher & Paykel designers have employed sophisticated electronics and a host of new technologies to manufacture a product that not only gets dishes hygienically clean but is economic and sensitive to precious resources.

The direct-drive wash system, used in Fisher & Paykel's Smart Drive® autowashers is a world first in laundry technology. Manufactured with sophisticated electronics, these autowashers have taken fabric care to a new level by simplifying the washing process. Fisher & Paykel autowashers remove the toughest dirt and stains while remaining sensitive enough to handle the most delicate of fabrics. The mechanically simple wash system results in greater reliability while the electronic controls provide an easy to use interface, offering many more wash options.

From milkbars and family picnics to shopping lists and kitchen cupboards,
Hansells is one of New Zealand's true heritage brands

History

Hansells has been a Kiwi favourite since 1934 when Lionel "LB" Maunsell identified a niche in the New Zealand market for a range of food flavourings and essences. Industrial chemist Dr. Hanson was hired to assist LB in the research and development of these revolutionary products, and soon after, with a clever union of the two men's surnames, the company "Hansell's Laboratories" became a reality.

For a company that today has an annual turnover of $70 million, Hansells had surprisingly humble beginnings in the backyard of the Maunsell homestead, Milford House. The first Hansells factory was the product of a converted poultry farm and went through many subsequent alterations until it reached its current facility, housing more than 19 individual production lines and a warehouse for nationwide distribution.

In the company's formative years, Hansells were pioneering innovators of their time, with the execution of successful sales and marketing campaigns long before the introduction of television in the early 1960s. One of LB's notable innovations was his alliance with Aunt Daisy, a popular radio personality of the time. With the help of this "first lady of advertising", LB was able to project his brand to kitchens all over New Zealand.

That very modern concept of subliminal marketing also made an early appearance, when LB established New Zealand's first marching team. Marcher's uniforms were tailored with stylised headwear featuring the very distinctive Hansells "H" emblazoned upon their uniforms.

With deteriorating health, LB retired shortly after World War II, handing over the reins of his booming business to son John Maunsell. John continued on in his father's name, cultivating the business right through into the early 1980s when Hansells was sold to a group of private New Zealand investors.

Brand identity

The Hansells brand identity has ebbed and flowed over time, with an aim to always meet with consumer conscience and demand. In its 70 year history, the company has had a total of eight logos, each uniquely identifying an epoch in time.

The original logo bears testimony to the underlying scientific processes involved in the formulation of the brand's range, with the word "Laboratories" featuring prominently on company insignia. This element of the logo was very quickly dropped as it did not appeal to the grocery market in which the Hansells growing range of products was positioned.

1934

1944

1954

1964

1968

As the company became more diversified, in 1945 the name was simplified to "Hansells" – meeting with the simplistic rationing mindset of post-war New Zealand. To appease consumer and trade demand, 1963 saw the introduction of 'Hansells' minus the apostrophe. This change evolved from the fact that grocers, bakers and customers referred to the 'Hansells' product range in the possessive form. To both reflect and reinforce this change, the laurel wreath was introduced as a powerful symbol of a winning brand.

Subsequent updates have remained consistent with the latter whilst adapting to current style, design and typographical trends.

Product range

Essences

LB was a resourceful businessman and was quick to turn what was considered a product weakness into a successful marketing story. As essences were emulsion-based (a combination of oil, water and alcohol), they were generally cloudy in appearance. Unable to change the formulation process for his essences, LB instead built an ingenious brand positioning story around the proposition "Hansells Essences – Cloudy for Strength".

Although there has been a marked shift towards easy to prepare meals and convenience baking, the simple art of cooking has been enjoying a renaissance in recent years. The Masterton manufacturing plant still produces around one million bottles of essences and food colouring per year.

Baking Ingredients

Originally marketed under the King brand, Hansells has now redesigned the popular baking ingredient range with a contemporary look under the Hansells brand as well as tamper-evident packaging. Combined with the essence range, Hansells provides a comprehensive selection which will see further additions to stimulate young New Zealanders' interests in the culinary arts.

Jungle Juice

For many Kiwis, Jungle Juice is synonymous with growing up in the 1970s and 80s. New Zealanders over the age of 25 will recall catchy advertising jingles and the many lively characters associated with this juice phenomenon.

Jungle Juice contained flavouring and colouring sachets that were typically added to a half-gallon container of water along with a cup of sugar. This was usually the same vessel that Kiwi dads would carry their beer home in when the pub closed at 6pm.

Hansells had initial reservations about the brand name as the term was also a reference for an illicit alcoholic concoction brewed in the Pacific Islands during World War II. These concerns were soon set aside. Hansells was a firm believer in market research and, with positive target market feedback, the brand was launched in 1971 with resounding success.

Vitafresh was to eventually supercede Jungle Juice as it offered the convenience of a complete mix of flavour, colour and sugar in one sachet and coincided with the age of the one and two litre plastic jugs. Jungle Juice and the half-gallon jar are now consigned to a well earned retirement.

Vitafresh

First introduced in 1970, with the convenience of a flavoured beverage in a ready-to-mix powdered form, Hansells saw a rapid rise of this brand. Today, this category is worth nearly $30 million per annum in New Zealand retail sales.

Vitafresh has undergone many facelifts over the years but the underlying proposition of a value-priced, thirst-quenching drink for the whole family, with the added benefit of Vitamin C, has not changed. Kids love Vitafresh because of its great refreshing taste and parents love it for its economical value and easy preparation. Over 20 million sachets are produced annually to satisfy this demand.

Thriftee and Quench

Cordial-based drinks have always been popular with New Zealanders and Quench and Thriftee are no exceptions.

Quench was first launched in 1963 and although now retired from the New Zealand market, it is still being produced to satisfy a large export demand into the Pacific Islands.

Thriftee was introduced in the 1970s as a diabetic/sugar-free alternative to Quench.

Make-A-Shake

Milk and the goodness of dairy based drinks have always been part of New Zealanders' everyday nutrition. Many romances have started in the dairies of rural towns and behind those counters were Make-A-Shake dispensing units, with a range of flavours to tempt customers.

In fact, consumers were so spoilt for choice that when asked "what flavour would you like?" the response was usually "anything". Not so surprisingly, Hansells in turn produced a flavour called "Anything". Although today, milkshake bars are likely to be found only in rural New Zealand, Make-A-Shake still remains a firm favourite on shopping lists across the nation.

The King brand and Old Fashioned Soup

The King brand has an original heritage in the heartland of Otago under the Dunedin-based company, Lane Latimer. Hansells acquired this company in late 1987 and subsequently absorbed the manufacturing of King products into the Masterton facility.

As soon as winter sets in, soup sales are guaranteed to climb. Although the modern convenience of "heat and eat" soups have definitely made their presence in the market, there is a large proportion of consumers who still like to make soup the traditional way; many winter time meals have been made around the cereal-based King Old Fashioned Soup varieties. Sales continue to climb with over 300 tonnes of soup mix being produced annually. The production of winter soup mix also compliments the summer demand for Vitafresh for optimum utilisation of manufacturing resources.

Weight Watchers

The Hansells association with the Weight Watchers brand goes back to 1967 when Hansells became the first licensee in New Zealand. It has been a long and profitable relationship for both parties, with steady growth in this category. More recent expansion has seen the launch of over 20 lines into Australian supermarkets.

Products produced and sold under the Weight Watchers brand include desserts, sponge puddings and custards, drinks, muffin mixes, sweeteners, instant soups and gravies.

Hansells Today

Hansells continues to display steady growth and is a dominant fixture of the New Zealand and Australian food manufacturing market. Having expanded through organic growth based on its founding brands, Hansells now has an annual group turnover of $70 million with a staff of nearly 300.

With successful acquisitions of smaller food companies in the mid-1990s, Hansells today owns and operates a snacks division based around the Krispa potato chip and Aztec corn chip brands with the manufacturing plant located in East Tamaki, Auckland. In addition the Hansells Group operates a separate company known as PLC New Zealand Limited, specialising in supermarket house brands. The PLC Company has its main office in New Lynn, Auckland, concentrating on the hot filling and retorting of various beverages, as well as the production of salsas, jams, mayonnaise and dressings.

Although the original Masterton plant remains part of the true heritage of Hansells, the marketing and sales head office is now located in Auckland. The company proudly retains its private Kiwi ownership, with a company culture and management style to match its distinctive range of iconic brands based on true New Zealand family value.

Improving lifestyles and optimising wellbeing in New Zealand for 100 years.

The market

With our fast-paced lifestyles and restricted time for exercise, achieving good health and wellbeing can sometimes be a challenge.

The frenetic pace of a 21st century lifestyle often demands a challenging balancing act between work and healthy living. More often than not, the latter takes a back seat. Consequently, many New Zealanders are now looking for ways to counteract their busy lifestyles and enhance healthy living.

Healtheries is a successful Kiwi business and one of New Zealand's most trusted brands. Growing to become the country's leading marketer of health foods, supplements and beverages, it has continually proven to be the guardian of health and wellbeing in all three categories.

New Zealanders have been relying on Healtheries products for 100 years and today almost every supermarket, health food store and pharmacy in the country is a Healtheries stockist.

Serving New Zealand for 100 years: a history of success

Providing New Zealand with healthy lifestyle choices has always been at the heart of the business that is Healtheries.

From a humble miller of flour staples 100 years ago, the company has since developed an extensive product portfolio of health foods, supplements and beverages that is second to none in Australasia.

The key to success? Throughout Healtheries' 100-year history, the company has maintained a proud record of keeping its commercial finger on the nation's nutritional pulse.

A century ago, Healtheries had that same customer focus as it does today. It's an attribute that has formed the backbone of the company's achievements across 100 years of business.

At the beginning of the 20th Century, New Zealand was emerging from colonisation, a new nation in its own right, with growing prosperity and a sense of pride in its achievements. As they grew into nationhood, New Zealanders also were acquiring a new worldliness. Immigrants began introducing new tastes and were demanding new ingredients for their ethnic dishes.

Against this background of cultural and social change, two flour millers began a speciality flour business in central Auckland in 1904. In addition to common wheat flour, Healtheries also stone-ground wholemeal and ryemeal flours. For five decades the business provided staple and fine flours for the nation.

With New Zealand emerging from decades of deprivation caused by global recession and war, Healtheries again began to diversify. In the 1950s and 60s, under the direction of a new owner, the company steered a new course, reorganising its food range and adding glucose to its milled products.

By 1979, Healtheries employed 90 people, manufacturing more than 400 product lines. It was exporting more than one million product units every year to more than 20 countries including the UK, Singapore and Australia. In recognition of this, Healtheries received a New Zealand Export Award in 1981. Since this milestone achievement, exports have grown to such an extent that they now represent 40 per cent of the company's sales – half that figure accounted for by sales to Australian key grocery and health food outlets.

In 1982, with the opening of new laboratories, Healtheries was the Southern Hemisphere's biggest manufacturer of vitamin and mineral tablets and capsules with the capacity to produce 500 million tablets a year.

At the dawn of a new millennium, the company continued to grow and in 1994 Healtheries moved to Mt Wellington, Auckland, consolidating its manufacturing, warehousing and office activities in dedicated modern premises.

Present managing director Sarah Kennedy was appointed in 1997 and by the end of the decade, seven out of ten dollars in company revenue was earned through sales in supermarkets.

As Healtheries entered the new millennium, the company remained a clear leader in New Zealand, with a monopoly on 60 per cent of the supplements market.

With such a history of dedication to consumers, Healtheries' position as a favourite New Zealand brand was confirmed in 2000. A *Readers' Digest* survey, "A study of trust in New Zealand society" resulted in a triumph for Healtheries, who won the vote as New Zealand's most trusted supplements brand.

In 2004, Healtheries and its 220 staff celebrate 100 years in business. The business remains an entirely owned New Zealand company dedicated to providing products that help people enhance their optimum health. The company's annual sales exceed $50 million and bear a portfolio of more than 750 products.

Products for nutrition

Health and wellbeing is the guiding light that signals the company's direction, and the Healtheries product range in the 21st century reflects the much wider palate of the New Zealand consumer.

Today the Healtheries brand adorns more than 750 different products spanning many health and wellbeing categories, including vitamins and minerals, garlic and herbal supplements, cereals, rice wafers, natural foods and an extensive range of herbal and fruit teas.

In many of these categories Healtheries is New Zealand's market leader.

Quality is the watchword at Healtheries. Products are manufactured from the finest ingredients under rigorous quality control. A highly qualified team of technical and research staff integrate the latest international scientific research with proven and tested natural ingredients. Supplements are formulated in conjunction with a leading naturopath and large technical team to ensure therapeutic doses are continuously delivered.

As a benchmark for consumer trust and excellence in manufacturing, Healtheries have also procured license to contract manufacture for many well known brands.

Recent developments that shape the future

Healtheries has a three-fold vision for the business as it progresses toward 2020 and beyond.

Firstly, the health and wellbeing of New Zealanders is the company's prime motivation in achieving this vision - Kiwis are known as a relaxed and open race of people, active and health conscious, innovative and ready to adapt to new ways of living.

Healtheries will continue to assist New Zealanders to appreciate and enhance healthy lifestyles. One aspect of this means the company will remain committed to trialling and developing new products and bringing them to the forefront of the consumer market in New Zealand.

Secondly, Healtheries is committed to expanding its export growth. Being a similar consumer market to New Zealand, Australia is a prime target for growth as the company reverses the commercial migration trend.

Healtheries' third vision is to cultivate the business in a direction that makes it capable of taking a lead position in global health and nutrition markets. This requires both flexibility and a focus on the way the business operates, its inner processes and people, and the activities that keep Healtheries competitive and in the global spotlight.

In the community

Healtheries has served the New Zealand community since 1904, thriving on the commitment to provide Kiwis with products they can use with confidence.

A key element is a commitment to reinvesting in the communities in which the company operates.

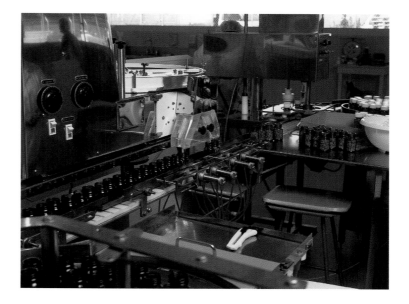

This commitment manifests through financial support for charities that raise awareness of key health issues affecting New Zealanders, and by the donation of resources and expertise to organisations that help promote healthier lifestyles.

Osteoporosis New Zealand
Healtheries provides much needed sponsorship to Osteoporosis New Zealand, through donations from calcium product sales and awareness raising activity.

New Zealand Breast Cancer Foundation
A long-term principal supporter of the New Zealand Breast Cancer Foundation, Healtheries makes a donation from every sale of a range of Womens supplements.

The Coeliac Society of New Zealand Inc.
Eating out can be a nightmare for coeliacs (people who are allergic to gluten). To help educate food providers, Healtheries has funded the Coeliac Society's major communications. In 2002, Healtheries funded a brochure for restaurants asked to cater for coeliacs, and in 2003, a brochure on guidelines for preparing gluten-free food. Healtheries has been involved with the Coeliac Society since the 1970s.

Things you didn't know about Healtheries

- Enough Healtheries tea bags are bought each year to stretch from Auckland, New Zealand to Brisbane Australia, if laid end to end.

- Since its beginnings in 1904, the company has continuously manufactured some of its original flours - including wholemeal and ryemeal.

- The best-selling New Zealand supplement is Healtheries Garlic, Vitamin C, Zinc and Echinacea with Olive Leaf tablets, ideal for avoiding winter colds and flu.

- Healtheries products are some of the most progressive in the world. Every year the company devotes a significant portion of its turnover to researching trends and developing new products.

interislander

With its unique geography of land mass cleft by a 19-kilometre stretch of water, New Zealand depends heavily on the bridge created by ferries to efficiently transport rail, road freight, passengers and motor vehicles between islands. Sailing 365 days a year and up to 13 times per day, Interislander vessels have become a part of the landscape, well woven into the fabric of things that make up the real Kiwi experience. For New Zealanders, the memory of one's first ferry trip remains vivid and spans generations.

History

The roll-on roll-off ships that connect Wellington and Picton originally had the vital role of linking the freight spine of the country, bringing together the two sections of the main trunk rail line and carrying trucks and commercial vehicles. That need is as vital today, but passenger and private vehicle business has grown to share priority and purpose. The demand for domestic inter-island travel has shaped the business such that it has become an integral part of everyday life in New Zealand.

Carrying over one million passengers a year, the ferries have left an indelible mark on the life of ordinary New Zealanders. The ferries and their sailing patterns are now a familiar part of the scenery in Wellington Harbour and Queen Charlotte Sound. Yet back in 1962 there was nothing commonplace about the launch of the inter-island service.; it marked a revolutionary change from what had gone before.

In 1924, a Royal Commission of Inquiry into New Zealand's railway service contended that an inter island rail ferry service would have to be established sooner or later to provide rail transit to span the length of the country. Railways worked quickly once the government go-ahead was given. The first ferry, Aramoana, was built in Dumbarton, Scotland, and arrived on 26 July 1962. Aramoana's arrival marked a significant moment in the nation's transport history. The rail system now extended almost the entire length of the country. For the first time in New Zealand, a vehicle or railway wagon could be driven aboard a vessel in one island and driven off in the other without having its load disturbed. The service dramatically stimulated inter island traffic and South Island tourism. Over 40 years later, Interislander is an icon of everyday New Zealand life.

The purchase of the business by Toll Holdings in late 2003 is seeing Interislander embark on a new era of improvement. Alongside modernisation of logo and image, a multi-million-dollar refurbishment of the major passenger vessel, Arahura, has recently been completed. The objective is to restore Arahura to its former glory as New Zealand's major passenger vessel, rejuvenating the service facilities for which Interislander ferries are renowned.

Brands and logos

The launch of Aramoana in 1962

Interislander, the operator of both The Lynx fast catamaran and Interislander conventional ships, identifies itself as an integral part of New Zealand, linking the North and South Islands. Interislander often evokes nostalgic memories of family holidays, mates getting together and journeys travelling to big events or occasions. New Zealanders have a strong desire for images and things of which they can be proud and call their own. For Wellingtonians and residents of Picton in particular, Interislander ferries are a regular sight, part of the harbour and part of daily life. In this capacity, Interislander ferries have reached iconic status.

Toll recognises that Interislander vessels are icons in New Zealand, and wants to ensure that they reach their full potential, providing a uniquely Kiwi experience for New Zealanders and international tourists alike.

In 1986 Interislander was rebranded incorporating the form of a dolphin, inspired by Pelorus Jack, the dolphin who for more than 20 years, accompanied ships across Cook Strait. According to Maori history, Pelorus Jack (also known as Tuhirangi) guided Kupe, a Maori voyager, across the ocean to New Zealand. Pelorus Jack then escorted Kupe and his party safely through the outer Marlborough Sounds to the West Coast of the South Island. Pelorus Jack was an icon to Cook Strait travellers from 1888 through to around 1912. At all hours of the day and night, Jack would respond to the call of the ships' engines and soon would be riding the bow waves.

The latest 2004 evolution of the logo known as the "dolfern" keeps the legend alive with the friendly, free-spirited dolphin depicted leaping energetically from the water. The ripples behind him form the familiar shape of a New Zealand Silver Fern – an icon embodied with national symbolism designed to evoke feelings of national pride and cement Interislander as a truly New Zealand icon.

The logo is fluid and animated, arousing a sense of journey and movement across the strait. The mostly blue colour scheme is sympathetic to the scenic beauty of the voyage and respects the heritage of previous designs. This ensures the immediate recognition of New Zealand's most memorable maritime identity.

The brand represents fun, family and relaxation. It is a name that instills memories held dear by generations of New Zealanders, travelling for Christmas and Easter holidays - and develops associations with summer, sunshine, adventure and family. A key trigger to recognition of the Interislander brand is the song which accompanied the well-known TV commercials, "Cruising on The Interislander," sung by The Warratahs, a local Kiwi band.

The Interislander — Pre - 2004

interislander — 2004 Onwards

Over the years, what is so well known as "the Interislander" has actually been represented by six vessels, each bearing in name the reference to the fundamental link the service provides

Aramoana	"Pathway Over The Sea"	Service years:1962 - 1983
Aranui	"Great Pathway"	Service years:1966 - 1984
Arahanga	"The Bridge"	Service years:1972 - 2000
Aratika	"Direct Path"	Service years:1974 - 1999
Arahura	"Pathway to Dawn"	Service years:1983 - present
Aratere	"Quick Path"	Service years:1999 - present

:The Lynx, though it is a more recent addition to Interislander's family, is a well-known service amongst the New Zealand public. The Lynx is most commonly identified by its original television commercial, featuring seagulls being swept off the vessel's bow because of the incredible speed. This advertisement is still noted as one of New Zealand's longest running and most memorable TV campaigns.

The Lynx TV advert with Boris the seagull

Due to its catchiness, the creative concept was on-sold to other fast-ferry operators overseas, who could relate to the message it portrayed. The original advertisement concept came about because Interislander had no visual material of The Lynx vessel itself: its actual appearance was a mystery to all but its architects and builders. Interislander had received design specifications, but could not accurately portray the vessel visually. This is why in this original advertisement you only see the front tip of the bow!

Interislander has had four versions of The Lynx throughout its history:

Condor 10	Service years: 1994 - 1999
Condor Vitesse	Service years: 1999 - 2000
The Lynx	Service years: 2000 - 2003
Incat 046	Service years: 2003 - present

Interislander ferries are well equipped with navigation, emergency and rescue equipment, and have highly-trained and experienced crews. This seaworthiness makes them a vital rescue service in unpredictable seas. The highest profile rescue was of passengers from the Union Steam Ship Company's Wahine. On 9 April 1968 the Wahine hit rocks at Wellington's harbour entrance. Despite very heavy seas, Aramoana made her way with all her speed to aid the sinking Wahine. The stricken ship listed heavily as Aramoana arrived, but the Cook Strait ferry stayed nearby and launched two motor lifeboats, aiding the rescue. Wahine eventually sunk, claiming with it the lives of 51 people. Thanks to the efforts of Aramoana, 682 officers, crew and passengers lived to tell the tale.

A total of ten vessels have been part of the inter-island ferry fleet over the years. The operation has changed hands and names numerous times – but the service remains one of New Zealand's most important and well-loved experiences. Comprising just one vessel back in 1962, the operation has grown enormously. In its first year, Aramoana carried 207,000 passengers and 46,000 vehicles. Today, Interislander carries over one million passengers, 230,000 vehicles and over 40,000 commercial vehicles annually across the fleet.

Interislander is focused on providing passengers with a world-class service, extending from booking through to disembarkation. The travel experience and service offerings for passengers are being constantly fine-tuned. While in the past the main entertainment was provided by the spectacular views, today the vessels offer a wide range of attractions, from a choice of bars and cafes, video games and a play area for children. Interislander passengers can even catch up on the latest box office smashes at the onboard movie theatre. Interislander ferries now feature heavily in the travel itinerary of international travellers, offering them an unspoilt view of the magical Marlborough Sounds. It is a privilege to share this territory with them.

Interislander is constantly evolving to ensure that its service meets the needs of the New Zealand travelling public. It is proud to offer a service which is so readily recognised as part of the tapestry of great New Zealand holidays. We hope the romance continues for years to come.

Tel 0800 802 802 (within NZ)   Tel +64 4 498 3302 (outside NZ)   www.interislander.co.nz

All beer is good, some beer is better.

History of the brewery

The West Coast of New Zealand is a vast, rugged land; one of legends, greenstone and moas, gold miners and rain forest, glaciers and Monteith's beers.

In the mid-1800s the West Coast was a wild and desolate place, with mountains towering over the coastline and only a series of glacial river mouths for harbours. But gold had been found, drawing 30,000 adventurers from around the world eager to challenge the wilderness rainforest and high mountain passes. These prospectors always welcomed a satisfying beer at the end of the day. Thankfully there was plenty of choice, with over 300 pubs on the Coast – 84 of them on one Hokitika Street!

Once the gold dried up, many of the prospectors left the coast in search of fortune or alternative lifestyles. The few that stayed found the West Coast to be a paradise and to this day, tourists from around the world flock to see the marvels on offer. This beautiful land has another unique attraction that is of great interest to both tourists and locals alike: the Monteith's Brewery.

In the late 1920s a group of quality breweries, led by the family-owned Phoenix Brewery, combined their expertise and brand portfolios to form the Westland Brewing Company. The new venture, located in Greymouth, was led by William Monteith, head of the largest merging brewery, Phoenix Brewery.

The new site was originally established as a bottling operation for the Westland Brewery with its five smaller partner brewing operations – Davie's Crown Brewery, Omoto Brewery, Pearn's Brewery, Mandl's Brewery and Monteith's Phoenix Brewery – all shipping large wooden hogsheads, holding approximately 250 litres of beer, to the Greymouth site for bottling.

Over the years, new facilities were added to the Greymouth site as the older turn-of–the-century style breweries were closed down.

By the 1960s the Westland Brewery had grown to include Morley's Brewery in Westport and Harley's Brewery in Nelson, bringing the number of breweries contributing to the history of the Greymouth brewery to seven.

The late 1960s also marked a significant business step for the West Coast brewer when it joined with the then Auckland-based Dominion Breweries. Keen to grow its well regarded West Coast brews, the Westland Brewery signed a supportive business agreement enabling it continue to produce

its popular Westbrew Golden Lager, Tira Pale Ale, Westland Extra Stout, Westbrew Bitter, Monteith's Special Stout and Westland Golden Draught.

Fifteen years later, and to the delight of Coasters from as far afield as Westport to Haast, Westland Breweries rediscovered the Monteith's recipe and again started brewing its well-loved Monteith's Original Ale.

As the 1990s approached, beer consumption in New Zealand began to fall, placing pressure on remote brewers such as the Westland Brewery. So much so that by the mid 1990s the only surviving beer brand at the Westland Brewery was Monteith's Original Ale. With a need to change clearly apparent, and an opportunity to match public interest, Westland Brewery changed its name to Monteith's Brewing Company. History clearly showed that Monteith's was the core of what had been Westland Breweries.

Throughout the 1990s the Monteith's Brewing Company became renowned for the production of high quality beers. In 1999 Monteith's enjoyed its greatest success to date, receiving Grande Gold for Monteith's Original at the prestigious Monde Brewing Awards in Brussels, and being voted Best Brewery in Australasia at the Australian International Brewing Awards the very same year.

Trying times

Despite its successes, the start of the 21st century proved extremely trying for the West Coast brewery. Following a complete review of its brewing operations in 2001 DB Breweries (formally Dominion Breweries) announced the closure of the Monteith's Brewery. The results of the review showed that the cost of keeping production on the West Coast was no longer viable for DB Breweries as it struggled to meet ever increasing brewing requirements created by a brand that continued to experience an exponential growth in popularity.

Three days later the Monteith's Brewery was re-opened as DB Breweries responded to angry calls from West Coasters and loyal consumers throughout the country. Unsurprisingly, customer and community reaction to the announced closure highlighted the passion and loyalty associated with the Monteith's brand, its products and the importance of the brewery to the West Coast region.

Nowadays

Monteith's has gradually grown and evolved from being a modest regional brand, to become the leading craft beer brand on the New Zealand market. Monteith's is fundamentally about different beer styles and occasions.

The Monteith's family of fine beers now consists of five core variants, with each offering its own unique taste experience. It also adds limited releases to the mix from time to time, highlighting its continued dedication to brewing innovation and expertise.

Monteith's Original Ale

Monteith's Original captures the soul of the traditional English pale ale. This richly hopped beer dates back to the early 1700s, providing an intriguing blend of herbal aromas with just a hint of blackberry, a big smooth malty body and a clean hoppy finish.

Monteith's Celtic Red Beer

Monteith's Celtic is true to the spirit of Irish-style ales – a heritage of burnt red beers traditionally brewed in the Emerald Isle. Its distinctive red hue is derived from kiln-roasted barley producing a distinctive smoky aroma and chocolate maltiness. The beer is lightly hopped for an invigorating dry finish.

Monteith's Golden Lager

Monteith's Golden is a refreshingly smooth lager brewed in the classic Munich style. The Bavarian capital was renowned for the emergence of its malty lagers and their unique style. Monteith's Golden faithfully recreates them with rich nutty malt characters, balanced with mellow hops for a memorable taste experience.

Monteith's Pilsner Beer

Monteith's Pilsner traces its history back to the last major beer style introduced to the world. Pilsner-style beers burst forth from the Czech town of Pilsen. Holding true to these Bohemian origins, Monteith's Pilsner delivers a complex malty character with a fresh herbal aroma. It has a dry finish with an explosive hop tang.

Monteith's Black Beer

Monteith's Black is a real West Coast classic. Five premium malts have been blended together to produce a delightful complexity of flavour and a distinctive dark chocolate aroma. The mouthfeel is full and rich without being heavy, and well balanced with a crisp hopped finish that lingers on the palate.

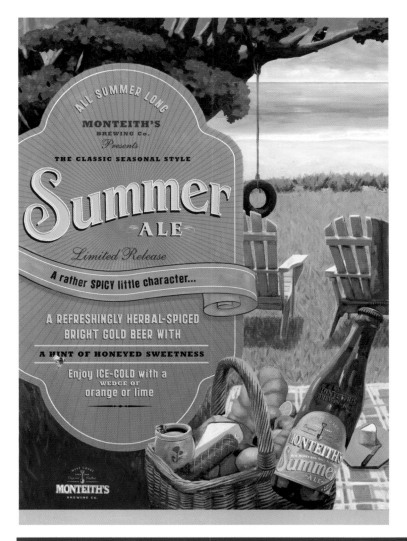

Monteith's Radler

Monteith's Radler is a refreshing fruity lager beer. Radler, the beer style, originates from Bavaria. It was first created in the early 1920s by the owner of a Austrian Gasthaus, Franz Xaver Kugler. In search of an invigorating brew, he developed an easy drinking lager bier with a citrus twist - flavoured with lemon and lime. The perfect treat for the many cyclists (Radler in German) and mountainhikers who visited his alpine guesthouse.

Limited releases

From our ever popular Rata honey and spice flavoured Monteith's Summer Ale, to a crystal clear Monteith's Kristallweizen or a rich and spicy Monteith's Oud Bruin, Monteith's is consistently providing different flavour experiences to introduce drinkers to a number of new and unique beer styles.

Drinker connections

Along with Monteith's limited releases, the beer brands involvement with the Hokitika Wildfoods Festival and the Monteith's Wild Food Challenge provides drinkers with unique occasions on which to enjoy their favourite Monteith's beer.

Hokitika Wildfoods Festival

The Hokitika Wildfoods Festival is by far the biggest event on the West Coast, with over 30,000 visitors from around the country and abroad swarming to Hokitika to celebrate the weird and wonderful tastes of the Coast.

Monteith's involvement with the event spans the past decade. It is an ideal association with the local initiative which is now recognised as one of New Zealand's foremost festivals.

Monteith's Wild Food Challenge

The Monteith's Wild Food Challenge is New Zealand's pre-eminent beer and food matching competition with restaurants around the country, creating a unique two-course meal utilising a variety of wild food and complementing it with a beer from New Zealand's finest craft brewery.

Now into its seventh year, the challenge has helped develop the appreciation of beer, further enhancing the role that beer plays in today's society.

The Path Ahead

True to its West Coast heritage, Monteith's continues to inspire great beer drinking occasions. By matching New Zealanders' thirst for new beer styles and drinking occasions with its strong coast heritage, Monteith's continues to be a favourite choice for beer drinkers throughout New Zealand.

The National Bank
The thoroughbred among banks

Origins

The National Bank was founded in London in 1872. It was formed with the aim of "extending to the colony of New Zealand the additional banking accommodation which the rapid increase of the population and remarkable development of the mineral, pastoral and agricultural resources of the colony so urgently demand'."

The National Bank first opened for business in New Zealand in 1873, with branches in Auckland, Wellington and Christchurch. Soon afterwards, it took over the 13 branches of the Bank of Otago, which provided a relationship with the rural community that remains strong to this day.

Growth

During its first 100 years the National Bank focused on building its strength in the personal, rural and small business markets, and in the process, built an enviable reputation for the quality of its service.

In more recent times it has grown its customer base and its range of services significantly, through mergers and acquisitions. Today, The National Bank is one of New Zealand's leading banks, consistently rated among the best for customer service. It is the bank of choice for the hundreds of thousands of New Zealanders whom it has helped to succeed, in both their business and personal lives.

Brand icons

The National Bank is one of New Zealand's most widely recognised brands. A contributing factor to that recognition is that it has consistently incorporated some key, distinctive symbols in its external communications – the National Bank horse, the 'Thoroughbred among banks' strapline, The National Bank green colour, and its theme music of Vivaldi's *Four Seasons*.

The black thoroughbred has been a big feature of The National Bank's television advertising since the early 1980s when a series of advertisements showing it in movement against a variety of backgrounds were shot, using the "thoroughbred among banks" strapline. These advertisements also introduced the Vivaldi Four Seasons music that has since become inextricably connected with The National Bank brand.

These key brand icons are incorporated into the bank's identity in a number of ways. Vivaldi's *Four Seasons* is used for the bank's 'hold music' as well as on television advertisements. The National Bank green colour is the predominant colour in all National Bank branches and signage, as well as communications such as print advertising, brochures and posters. The 'Thoroughbred among banks' strapline is used extensively in customer communications, along with the bank's distinctive logo featuring the black horse and shield. These key elements of the National Bank's brand identity symbolise the commitment to quality that is at the heart of the Bank. Together, they make up a brand identity that is instantly recognised throughout New Zealand.

Supporting our community

The National Bank is run by New Zealanders, for New Zealanders. It has always taken an active role in supporting the communities it serves. The bank's sponsorship programme is designed to reflect its commitment to quality and excellence, and it forms a significant part of the way people see the National Bank. That's why the bank supports some of the things that are most important to New Zealanders.

The thoroughbred among banks.

The National Bank

"During its first hundred years the National Bank focused on **building its strength** in the personal, rural and small business markets – and in the process, **building an enviable reputation** for the **quality of its service.**"

Over a decade ago, The National Bank was the founding sponsor of Daffodil Day, which raises funds every year to help the Cancer Society fight cancer through research, prevention and education. It's an event that all staff get involved in and over the years National Bank people have raised millions of dollars to help fight this disease.

The National Bank is the principal sponsor of New Zealand Cricket. It sponsors both the Black Caps and the home International Series. It also fosters the development of young talent through a number of initiatives, including KIDZ coaching.

The National Bank Cup is New Zealand's premier domestic netball competition. The Bank is the official bank of Netball New Zealand, and it supports netball at all levels. It is also a principal sponsor and official bank of the New Zealand Symphony Orchestra, one of New Zealand's cultural icons.

The National Bank's position as the most preferred bank for New Zealand farmers is reflected by its sponsorship of The National Bank Young Farmer Contest, which helps to develop the country's future rural leaders. The Bank also supports the rural community through a range of other activities, including A&P shows, Calf Club Days and the Mystery Creek Fieldays.

Into the future

Technology has had a huge impact on banking, not just in back office processing but also in the choices customers now have in how they do their banking.

But in the midst of this technological change, the human element in banking remains as important as ever. As we move into the 21st century, the focus for bank staff has moved from providing transactional services, many of which can now be done electronically, to working with customers to add value and help them manage their finances better. As always, the emphasis remains on quality service.

After a long period of ownership by Lloyds Bank (now Lloyds TSB), the National Bank moved into a new era. On 26 June 2004 it became part of ANZ National Bank Limited. Although now part of the wider ANZ Banking Group, with all the opportunities and advantages that holds for staff and customers alike, the National Bank continues to operate as a separate and quite distinct brand.

The success in building one of New Zealand's most recognised brands has been built on a foundation of consistency and a deeply held commitment to core values. However banking may change in the future, those values will remain the cornerstone of the National Bank.

Nestlé is one of the world's most universal brands. Worldwide, Nestlé confectionery brands include names such as Kit Kat, Milky Bar and Smarties, but here we tell the story of brands with backgrounds under the Southern Cross.

Nestlé have long imported chocolates into New Zealand. Think Nestlé, and the first response is "chocolate", think for a little longer and you'll undoubtedly remember.

Nestlé Scorched Almonds

In the 1930s until the advent of television in the 1960s changed people's habits, families generally stayed home in the evenings and followed radio quiz shows and series. Pubs closed at 6.30pm until 1967, dining out was rare and an evening out usually meant a trip to the suburban cinema. Many couples booked permanent seats for a Saturday night. Here was an opportunity for Nestlé and hence the genesis of Nestlé Scorched Almonds.

A night at the movies was a treat. That treat included patronising the prominent cinema vestibule counter before the film and during the interval. Boys marched down the cinema aisles as the lights went on for the interval, bearing big trays of ice creams and confectionery and served the customers that did not wish to leave their seats.

Nestlé sold chocolate assortments in cinemas, but looked for a lower-priced, great tasting product that could be shared as an evening treat.

Nestlé Scorched Almonds – roasted almonds coated in famous Nestlé milk chocolate – were launched.

Boxed from the start (so handling in the dark did not cause melting) and in a small enough pack to be convenient, Nestlé Scorched Almonds were a hit.

Later as volumes grew, an inner bag was added to protect our product and maintain quality and freshness.

There has always been a commitment to produce a delicious product at a not-too-expensive price - a gift for sharing that has grown from a cinema base to become "the perfect little gift".

A packet of Nestlé Scorched Almonds expresses thanks and appreciation in a touching, sentimental way – not flashy, but a sincere gift in the form of a delicious chocolate and almond treat. Nestlé Scorched Almonds are an appropriate gift at the foot of the Christmas tree, a welcome tribute on Mother's Day and other days of celebration, or perfect for a special treat. Viewers never tire of the television commercial showing a charming little girl at Christmas wrapping up precious Nestlé Scorched Almonds for everyone she loves and keeping some for herself as a special treat.

Inevitably, other chocolate scorched almond products have followed Nestlé's success. How does Nestlé hold its premier position? Strict quality standards in the selection of the best grade almonds – all even in size, evenly roasted and always with a generous coating of Nestlé chocolate for a delicious, melting taste.

Quality is an unchanged criterion over the years, but four elements have evolved:

- What started out over 50 years ago as mainly a product for sale in cinemas is now prominent and very popular wherever confectionery is sold. Displays of Nestlé Scorched Almonds are everywhere: food

stores, corner dairies, fuel stations, specialist confectioners and the newly dynamic cinema groups. This success goes well beyond New Zealand as Nestlé Scorched Almonds are exported to enthusiastic "little gift" lovers in Australia, the US and Canada.

- It is difficult to overstate the positive loyalty Nestlé Scorched Almonds holds as "the perfect little gift". Over 60 per cent of Nestlé Scorched Almonds are bought as a gift (A.C. Nielsen Research). Over half of all Nestlé Scorched Almonds are sold in the October to December months, indicating just how integral the brand has become to a traditional Kiwi Christmas.

- Packaging has always shown the coated almonds, but today's graphics are more eye-catching, standing out on crowded shelves to say "buy me - I'm the perfect little gift".

- Popularity breeds siblings in the Nestlé family. Original milk chocolate coated Nestlé Scorched Almonds have been joined by dark chocolate-coated almonds and almonds coated in Nestlé Milky Bar.

Delightful!

Nestlé Pixie Caramel

Put a team of chocolate enthusiasts together and the ideas flow.

Flavours abound– mint, strawberry, orange, honey and other palatable essences.

Various ingredients to add to chocolate come to mind: rice bubble, biscuit and hokey pokey. Yet the universal favourite partner for chocolate has to be caramel, and a caramel bar was very early on seen as a key development for Nestlé in New Zealand.

The search was for a long-term, promotable bar for individual consumption, not a tablet variation but a product standing proud with a distinct identity.

In the early days Nestlé Pixie Caramel sold for a sixpence. That may not seem much for the youngster to spend in today's free spending economy, but back in the 1950s, Nestlé Pixie Caramel broke into the market because the 'chewyness' of the caramel centre meant that demolishing each bar took some time – and that meant value for money.

Value for money remains at the heart of the brand today with Nestlé Pixie Caramel positioned as "the longer lasting chew".

This slogan has been featured consistently over the years and is one of the most powerful tag lines in the New Zealand confectionery marketplace. As Nestlé Pixie Caramel's franchise grew, we decided to invest in television advertising on the "longer lasting chew" theme. Filming took place in the old Auckland Distructor site in Freeman's Bay. Readers will remember the iconic TV commercial, depicting an honest Kiwi hero delaying his last moments in front of a villainous looking South American firing squad by enjoying a "longer lasting chew" Pixie Caramel bar.

Heards

In 1986 Nestlé acquired Heards Limited, a company that had a strong brand history in New Zealand.

Mr Leonard Heard established the Heards business in 1914. He made a small range of boiled sweets in a building in Henley Street, Parnell, Auckland, above what is now the Stanley Street motorway access.

The Heards brand label and sweet production steadily grew, and in 1921, the family firm moved about 400 metres to larger premises on Parnell Road where Heards were to supply chocolate products as well as candy.

In 1948 Heards was formed into a limited liability company, going public in 1950.

Manufacturing moved to a new factory at Waiuku, South Auckland in 1975. Nestlé became sole selling agents for Heards Limited in 1976 and the brand continued to flourish. The sales agreement between Nestlé and Heards included an option for Nestlé to purchase Heards Limited should that company wish to sell in the future. That decision came about after 10 further years and Nestlé bought the company in 1986.

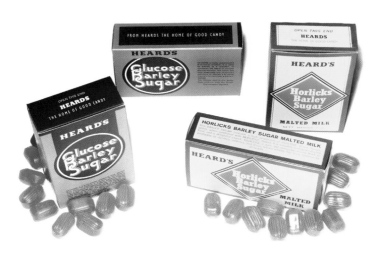

The Heards confectionery range was wide but the most prominent product became Heards Barley Sugars that has today become a staple in vehicle glove boxes right around New Zealand and an energy-sustainer everywhere.

A major sales period for Heards Barley Sugars is the 40-Hour Famine charity fund event. The 40-Hour Famine is a major national fundraiser for the aid of developing countries. Schools, church and community groups sponsor young people to go without solid food for the 40-hour period.

Barley Sugars are allowed as part of the famine to lessen hunger and provide a much needed energy burst, making this is a major consumption event for Heards Barley Sugar.

The Heards range of products extends from Barley Sugar, Malted Barley Sugar, Refreshers and Butterscotch to popular Heards lollipops and Milk Chews. As the very appropriate slogan for Heards says, "Thank Goodness."

Black Knight

Licorice has a long and distinguished history, being used for medicinal purposes as far back as the 7th century B.C. Egyptian alchemists, Greek physicians and Chinese herbalists all valued the licorice root as both a medical remedy and as a sweetener. Today the root is a key ingredient in the Black Knight licorice we know and love.

Black Knight licorice was the brainchild of an early New Zealand licorice manufacturer in Wellington, Keith Cuncliffe.

The original black knight was King Richard I of England, famous as a warrior King in France and the Holy Land. Keith Cuncliffe had a large bronze statue of the Black Knight on this desk and decided on Black Knight as a licorice brand because he wanted a name he respected and could look up to. As easy as that!

Since that day, the Black Knight brand has become a household name and the range is extensive enough to suit various consumer tastes and needs. Varieties include Luxury Medley, Licorice Cannonballs, Licorice Straps, Twists, Super Twists and Allsorts – all available in packages ranging from 250 grams through to one kilogram, for the ultimate licorice indulgence.

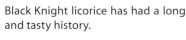

Black Knight licorice has had a long and tasty history.

We treasure our heritage and the strong brands we work with.

This is a great opportunity for us to salute the skilled people who have developed the products, created the packaging and marketing moves that have made these brands the household names they are today.

Tel: 0800 830 840   Fax: 09 367 2819   www.nestle.co.nz

Recording the triumphs and tragedies of New Zealand for over 141 years.

The market

Almost every single New Zealander will have some kind of memory associated with *The New Zealand Herald*.

Whether it was as a delivery boy or girl getting up without fail at 5am on wet wintry mornings, as a bargain hunter devouring the classified section every Saturday, or as a traveller returning home from their OE and re-connecting with all of the goings on by reading it cover to cover.

From farmers to cafe goers, stately homes to state houses, *The New Zealand Herald* is a celebrated brand read by a staggering 1.08 million New Zealanders a week*– more than any other daily newspaper in the country.

Typically, these readers live "north of the Bombays", in Greater Auckland, home to 31 per cent of the national population. But it is also the major morning paper in Hamilton, is widely read in all the other provincial cities in the North Island and can be found for sale in towns throughout the whole of New Zealand.

* SOURCE: NIELSEN MEDIA RESEARCH AP15+ Jan-Dec 03

The history

The New Zealand Herald began publication in November 1863 at a time inauspicious for two reasons: it was Friday the 13th and two other newspapers were already competing for readership among a population of only 12,000. But the new paper shrugged off the shadow of superstition, adopted an editorial viewpoint congenial to the colonists and then quickly delivered on good reporting.

For the 141 years since, the history of *The New Zealand Herald* has been a mirror held up to history of the country.

The founder, William Chisholm Wilson, had been part owner of one of the other two Auckland papers, *The New Zealander,* but set up on his own because of differences on editorial policy towards the war then raging in the Waikato where British troops were fighting Maori on land issues.

The New Zealander had adopted a sympathetic tone toward the Maori cause. Wilson supported the army, an opinion shared by most Aucklanders of the time. The first issue of *The Herald* – six broadsheet pages for threepence – therefore attracted heavy reader and advertising support and circulation quickly built up to an estimated 3000.

They were stirring times! The new daily newspaper promised – and delivered – comprehensive foreign news coverage, which included the

American Civil War. Although news travelled by sea in those days and was slow in coming; Abraham Lincoln was assassinated on 15 April 1865, and *The Herald* got the news on 9 July.

Closer to home, British troops were moving against Waikato iwi in 1863. Within a week of the first issue, *The Herald* reported a scoop from the critical Battle of Rangiriri, won by the British but at the cost of 47 dead and 81 wounded. Rangiriri is 84 kilometres south of Auckland, yet it took the reporter three days to get the news back.

William Wilson died in 1876 and his sons, William and Joseph, formed a partnership with Alfred Horton who had taken over the other Auckland newspaper, *The Southern Cross*. The two companies merged and from January 1877, except for one brief period in the 20th century, *The Herald* has had Auckland mornings to itself.

In 1925, the partnership was formed into a company, Wilson and Horton Ltd. As many of us will remember, for 108 years, *The Herald* was printed in Wyndham Street, in the heart of downtown Auckland until the 1970s when the printing presses were moved to Ellerslie.

By 1934, the country's leading daily was selling 62,000 papers a day. This nearly trebled over the following 20 years to 170,000 and, rising fast, reached 215,000 by the 1990s.

Ownership changes occurred when Brierley Investments took a majority shareholding in 1994, followed the next year by a 30 per cent stake in the company by the Independent News & Media. Then in 1998, Independent News & Media moved to 100 percent ownership and linked *The Herald* with a large global newspaper chain.

Achievements

The Herald's greatest achievement is that it has faithfully recorded the triumphs and tragedies of New Zealand for over 141 years.

A quick flick through the archives leaves an indelible impression of a nation that has grown, sometimes painfully, from pioneers to leaders on the global landscape. Headlines as "Wahine disaster", "Queen Elizabeth visits" "Walker Wins Gold" show the human side of New Zealand's history, while recent headlines such as "Lord of The Rings Academy Sweep" show how far the country has come.

We now take for granted that if anything happens, anywhere in the world – or even on Mars – it will be captured in all its technicolour glory. But this has only been made possible by *The Herald*'s commitment to technological innovation, which has given a string of firsts to its credit. For example:

• Twenty years after the newspaper's first issue, the company bought a high-speed rotary press in England and astounded the local newspaper world by printing 12,000 copies an hour, compared with 1200 an hour produced by the previous flatbed press. (Nowadays, anything less than 70,000 copies an hour would be considered slow.)

• Political cartoons were introduced in 1903, drawn by Trevor Lloyd. His successor was Gordon Minhinnick who from 1930 became the best known and most influential cartoonist in New Zealand newspaper history. His career spanned almost 60 years, providing much angst to politicians during this period!

• *Herald* photographers began taking pictures from the air in 1915 from the flying-boats based at the Walsh Brothers flying school in Mission Bay. This enabled readers to be places they couldn't be – above derailed trains,

wide-spread floods and even, somewhat forlornly, the broken mast of Team New Zealand in 2003.

• The first of what became daily pictures on news pages appeared in 1925, followed by wire photographs in 1949. Photographs now whip across the world in minutes using electronic pictures and text.

• *The Herald* was also early to adopt spot colour and then full colour. Three computer-controlled Goss HT70 colour presses were installed in 1995 at a cost of $100 million. Suddenly, photographs of human endeavours became more poignant, car advertisements became more colourful and the mouth watering food recipes were to die for!

• In 1998, the massive Saturday edition became *The Weekend Herald*, with enough news, comment and reviews to keep readers busy for the entire weekend.

But perhaps the newspaper's greatest achievements have sprung from the influence of its editorial campaigns on New Zealand society. In the very first issue they began with a bold declaration: "*The New Zealand Herald* will claim for itself the glorious privilege of independence." At that time, newspapers had been forced to close down because their outspoken reporting had incurred government displeasure. *Herald* editors have consistently campaigned to preserve press freedom ever since.

In more recent times campaigns on behalf of readers have led nationwide discussion, and in some instances led to political and policy change. Most readers will recall "The Knowledge Wave" series, the "Our children" campaign and more recently an exposé on leaky homes which sparked major changes to New Zealand's building codes.

All these endeavours came not without recognition. *The New Zealand Herald*'s long history of achievement culminated in winning a triple crown of journalism awards in 2000. It was named the Qantas Newspaper of the Year, the Commonwealth Paper of the Year, and the Best Paper in the inaugural Pan Asian Newspaper Publishers awards.

The product

In a diverse multi-media market, *The New Zealand Herald* is the only single source of a full range of international, national and regional news, background coverage and comment available. This makes it the most influential newspaper in New Zealand.

The Herald's links with other newspapers in the Independent News & Media international chain provide it with rich resources to complement its associations with news agencies and other sources around the world. In fact, so isolated were New Zealanders 20 years ago that the 'World News' occupied just one page. Now it has its own section.

Because of its size and regional spread, the paper also has an extraordinary commercial daily impact – especially the Weekend Herald which peaks at 220 pages, 70 per cent of which carry classified and display advertisements.

There is probably not a single New Zealander who hasn't got a job, a flatmate, a house or even a second hand fridge from *The Herald*! As a result, *The Herald*'s massive readership makes it a magnet to advertisers. In the Classified Customer Contact Centre alone, 70 inbound and telesales service representatives are available to process sales and advertising opportunities, as well as offer a comprehensive service ranging from sales and information right through to booking ads; this results in the placement of around 19,000 classified ads a week. The huge volume of daily advertising in turn allows more space for editorial content. This has enabled *The Herald* to employ a large, highly professional journalistic staff to keep in touch with the pulse of the nation and to paint an editorial picture of daily events in New Zealand and around the world.

So vast is the editorial the newspaper is now divided into sections to give readers easy access to general news, business, sport, classified advertisements and a wide range of other subjects. On an average Saturday, it carries some 200 pages and attracts an average readership of 723,000*.

*SOURCE: Nielsen Media Research, National Readership Survey, Jan-Dec 2003, All People 15+

Recent developments

Over the past five years, the most dramatic development in news dissemination in the country has been the arrival and expansion of the online edition of *The New Zealand Herald*, nzherald.co.nz, now the main vehicle for keeping in touch with local events and by Kiwis living or travelling abroad. It is consistently the country's top-rated online news service, according to the ratings agency, AC Nielsen.

During 2003, an average of 724,000 unique readers visited the site each month and this number is continuing to grow strongly in 2004. Almost all the stories and pictures from the print edition of *The Herald* appear on the site, and it is updated throughout the day, seven days a week, by a team of online journalists.

The team not only adds breaking stories (every 15 minutes on weekdays) but updates background information to complement running stories. It is a widely used national archive with all stories published since 1998 accessible.

Promotion

The CEO of a famous computer company predicted some 20 years ago there would only ever be four computers in the world! Similarly, others have predicted a paperless world. Yet neither has happened. Newspapers and magazines have found a niche in people's lives where they welcome the rich variety it brings – and never more so than with *The New Zealand Herald*.

With the plethora of competitive news sources available and the ongoing pressures on people's spare time *The Herald* has maintained a strong brand by promoting the depth and breadth of information that's on offer. Encompassing everything from lifestyle coverage to cutting edge investigative reporting, the simple slogan "There's a lot more to it" was developed. Ever since its launch in 2001, the campaign has encouraged people to read more of *The Herald*, and to read it more often. As well as this, it has changed the way in which people judge their news source. Away from just the simple reporting of facts, *The Herald* has maintained relevance by interpreting and providing people with information that helps make their lives easier and more enjoyable. The campaign has demonstrated the diverse range of areas in which *The Herald* can provide this information and shows the depth with which key stories and areas of interest are covered.

Advertisements composed with wry humour and sharp observation has garnered *The Herald* attention not only from its target audience but also from international advertising and newspaper award juries.

For example, in the 2000 PANPA awards, *The Herald* beat out all the newspapers in the Pacific Area to win the coveted Best Newspaper of the Year (over 50,000 circulation). And more recently, in 2002 at the INMA awards (International Newspaper Marketing Association awards), *The Herald* was presented with the "Best in Show" award and five first-places in what the judges noted as being "one of the strongest showings ever".

But most of all, the marriage of smart, savvy marketing, coupled with 141 years of unrelenting dedication to technology and strong editorial content, has assured *The Herald* a place not only in this book, but in the hearts of all New Zealanders.

Brand values

It wasn't so long ago that because of its conservative values and defence of the freedom of the press, *The New Zealand Herald* was both affectionately (and not so affectionately) called the "Granny Herald".

However in the late 90s, *The Herald* repositioned itself both internally and externally to reflect the daily role it plays and the relevance it has within peoples' lives. Today, it provides over 1 million New Zealanders a week with not just news and current affairs, but information they can use. This, in effect, enables people to live their lives better. Whether it's interpreting events that allow people to make more sense of the world they live in, by giving them the most extensive guide to employment opportunities or giving them a great recipe for a herb pilaf, *The Herald* delivers information, insight, interpretation and opinion across all manner of subjects

With brand values based around honesty, leadership and optimism, *The Herald* aims to make New Zealand a better place. It tackles issues head on and doesn't hide behind what's easy or popular. It aims to champion change, unite people around a positive future for New Zealand and believes that the positive will always be more influential than the negative.

So by maintaining the integrity, balance and judgement of a newspaper while evolving its relevance in peoples' lives and relentlessly keeping up with the times, the "Granny Herald" has finally been buried.

Things you didn't know about *The Herald*

- *The New Zealand Herald* is one of a stable of newspapers, owned by parent company Independent News & Media PLC, including daily papers published in Whangarei, Tauranga, Rotorua, Masterton, Wanganui, Hastings, Dannevirke Levin and Oamaru.

- The Herald has had only 15 editors in 141 years, with the longest serving editor being William Berry (1875–1903) who was at the helm for 28 years.

- The ninth editor, Sir Leslie Munro (1942-1951), became New Zealand Ambassador to the US and permanent representative to the United Nations. During a distinguished UN career he became president of the UN Security Council, and then Secretary-General of the International Commission of Jurists. When he returned to New Zealand, he was an MP for nine years.

- In the early hours of the morning, as the country sleeps, the country's biggest daily newspaper is distributed over thousands of kilometres to nearly 100,000 delivery points by a national network of trucks, cars, buses and aeroplanes.

The Weekend Herald

"Throw yourself into the Weekend"
The Weekend Herald. There's a lot more to it.

The Weekend Herald made a grand entrance to an empty stage in 1998, cementing a place as New Zealand's first true weekend newspaper. Aucklander's embraced this new phenomenon with enthusiasm making the publication an overwhelming success. It is now the New Zealand Herald's flagship issue.

Six years later the *Weekend Herald* continues to maintain it's position as the New Zealand Herald's highest circulating daily, boasting sales of approximately 230,000 copies each week.

The key to the *Weekend Herald*'s success has been the continued understanding that their readers are the lifeblood of their paper. Not that sustaining this position in reader's hearts and minds has allowed them much time to reflect. The overall focus of the paper has been to continually evolve; staying in touch with what readers want, whilst maintaining their high standards of editorial integrity.

Minor updates have been a constant focus, keeping the paper relevant and contemporary, easy to navigate and always striving to reflect the weekend feeling we all love. 2003 saw an exciting addition of the new weekend magazine: *Canvas*. This magazine provides in-depth feature stories on current topics and personalities for those wanting a more relaxed read intermingled with regular columns spanning all aspects of our modern lifestyle.

2004 has been a huge milestone for the *Weekend Herald* with a complete renovation of the entire weekend paper based on extensive research with current readers and potential readers.

The most dramatic makeover was the overhaul of the *Time Out* section. From humble beginnings as a relatively small section of the paper it has truly come of age as a magazine in its own right. The resident authority of the latest in music, movies and television and the inside story on Auckland's glamour, gossip and nightlife, it has extensive coverage that lasts the weekend distance and beyond. The ultimate users manual for New Zealand's largest and most cosmopolitan city, *Time Out* is Auckland's one stop shop guide for the city's weekend. If it isn't in here, it isn't happening.

The end product of this proud but brief history is a user friendly, entertaining paper with a litany of essential news and views that engage and inform. Despite many evolutions, groundbreaking stories remain the *Weekend Herald*'s main currency, backed by magazine sections that are constantly expanding to provide a broader mix of topics and contributors.

46 Albert Street, Auckland City   Tel: 09 379 5050   www.nzherald.co.nz

PROGRESSIVE

Stocking pantries since 1929.

The market

Characterised by constant change, the market in which Progressive Enterprises Limited (PEL) operates is one of fierce competition and multi-dimension. Supermarkets are the largest component of the market and where 95 per cent of shoppers buy their groceries. In the year to April 2003, New Zealanders spent $9.8 billion in supermarkets – an average of $151 for every household, every week. New Zealanders visit their supermarkets regularly, on average nine times a month.

The supermarket companies compete fiercely on price, quality and service, in a high-volume, low-margin business. But each department within every supermarket faces further competition from outside. Across New Zealand, there are more than 12,000 retail outlets and 10,000 food service operators in direct competition with supermarket departments.

As a result, supermarkets are constantly evolving to meet new expectations and demands – from the introduction of self-service in the 1950s, to today's 24-hour provisions and mini supermarkets at petrol stations. The one certainty in this constantly evolving market is that fierce competition will continue to drive new ideas.

that a review post-merger by the expanded company has seen the service extended to the Foodtown brand, www.foodtown.co.nz.

In 17 June 2002, Progressive Enterprises bought the Woolworths business, increasing the merged companys' market share to about 45 per cent. In the following two years, a strong customer focus was the core of business activities with a launch of the Foodtown Woolworths onecard rewards programme in 2003 as well as several store re-brandings during 2003 and 2004.

Achievements

PEL's major achievements revolve around meeting the needs of its customers. In July 2002 the PEL of today came together with the acquisition of Woolworths New Zealand Limited. With it, Woolworths brought to the group more than 70 supermarkets nationwide, increasing the market share of the business to 45 per cent. The acquisition has resulted in PEL growing to become one of the biggest companies in New Zealand with an annual turnover of more than $4 billion.

In 1998, Woolworths launched its innovative online grocery shopping site, www.woolworths.co.nz. In a fast-paced, 21st century New Zealand, this site proved to be a trailblazer in business-to-consumer online retailing. The site immediately tapped into the modern lifestyles of New Zealanders, saving them time by addressing modern requirements

PEL has since moved to achieve greater efficiencies – and thereby lower costs and better prices – by opening a state-of-the-art distribution centre in Mangere, South Auckland. The $28 million centre is the biggest grocery distribution centre in New Zealand. The 60,000 square metre building is the size of 10 rugby fields and, at peak times, one million cartons are trucked through its giant despatch doors. Serving 153 supermarkets in the North Island, the centre operates 24 hours a day with 300 staff working three shifts to monitor and despatch 14,000 product lines.

In June 2003 Foodtown and Woolworths launched the innovative onecard rewards programme. The Foodtown Woolworths onecard superseded the Foodtown card and immediately captured a huge audience with its promise of "bigger savings and better rewards". Today there are in excess of 1.3 million Foodtown Woolworths onecards in New Zealand.

History

The PEL brands have been part of many New Zealand communities since 1929 when Woolworths opened its first New Zealand store in Cuba Street, Wellington. Woolworths was initially a general merchandise retailer and remained so until the 1950s when the company made its first foray into food retailing by opening a Food Fair store in Panmure, Auckland.

In 1958 the first Foodtown opened in Otahuhu, South Auckland. The Otahuhu market proved a success and a second Foodtown was opened in Takanini, South Auckland in 1961. Opening specials included a box of Weet-Bix for "one and nine pence" (19 cents), a 16 ounce tin of Watties peaches costing 21 cents and 10 pounds of potatoes for 29 cents.

The first Countdown store opened in Christchurch in 1981, established by Rattrays Wholesale, also owner of the Super Value franchised markets.

In 1992 Foodland Associated Limited (FAL) from Perth, Western Australia, purchased the Countdown and Rattrays business. This was followed by FAL gaining a majority share holding in Progressive Enterprises Limited, including General Distributors Limited, trading as Foodtown.

In 1993, the Countdown/Rattrays, and Foodtown businesses were all brought together under the Progressive Enterprises Limited umbrella.

Prior to the launch in 1998, online shopping introduced a pilot site in 1995 with a small group of users. It was early days for online shopping in New Zealand but Woolworths was a key player in developing online commerce relationships with customers. The Woolworths site has proved so successful

The product

The primary brands operated by PEL are Foodtown, Woolworths and Countdown.

Foodtown and Woolworths

In 2002, when Foodtown and Woolworths stores joined forces under the Progressive Enterprises umbrella, it was with a very strong commitment to PEL customers. The aim has always been to deliver customers with an altogether better product, service and prices – every day and in every category. Foodtown and Woolworths stores pride themselves on providing a depth and breadth of range for food lovers that are delivered with commitment and passion.

The Foodtown and Woolworths onecard rewards programme brings "bigger savings and better rewards" to more than 1.3 million card-holders nationwide. Customers also benefit from a number of other outstanding brand initiatives. One example is the Master of Wine Bob Campbell's Wine Ratings which guides customers to the best wine buys in a range of price categories.

The Foodtown Magazine is a prestigious food and lifestyle magazine that offers inspirational ideas and practical information on food, wine, travel, home and garden, health and other lifestyle issues.

There are also a number of other store formats provided under the Woolworths banner. These include Woolworths Quickstop and Micro convenience stores located at Gull service stations throughout the North Island. Offering a range of up to 3000 grocery lines, they provide local communities and motorists with a top-up supermarket for groceries, meals, and food on the go – 24 hours a day, 365 days a year.

Countdown

Working under the maxim "You can count on us to keep prices down", Countdown is ideal for the budget-conscious shopper who values service and convenience. Countdown stores have great opening hours, pleasant shopping environments, ample parking and they pack your groceries in free bags. All new or refurbished stores follow the modern, large-store format with wide aisles and a new look and layout that is far superior to its pack-your-own competition. The brand has pioneered the "power aisle" concept at PEL - a huge central aisle dividing the grocery departments to improve store-wide access and allow for a more expansive view of specials on offer.

Nationwide, in May 2004 there are 69 Woolworths stores, 28 Foodtown stores, 52 Countdown stores, 18 Woolworths Quickstops and 8 Woolworths Micro stores.

SuperValue and Fresh Choice

SuperValue and Fresh Choice are a franchised brand of stores offering a good range of products at competitive prices.

First established in the South Island in the early 1960s, SuperValue is a supermarket brand with considerable heritage.

Fresh Choice is a South Island-only brand that is focused on providing a pleasant, modern shopping environment for customers to enjoy.

There are 32 SuperValue and 9 Fresh Choice stores in New Zealand.

Recent developments & points of difference

Online shopping

We live in a technological age where shoppers' free time has become increasingly thin. To meet this growing need, the Foodtown and Woolworths brands operate an Internet-based online shopping service.

Any time of the day or night, those with internet access can order online and have their groceries delivered at their convenience. The service was pioneered by Woolworths and launched commercially in Wellington in November 1998. Today both Foodtown and Woolworths online shopping are available nationally.

Celebrate New Zealand

The Celebrate New Zealand initiative is a long term nation-building programme designed to raise the consciousness of the nation about all the good things embodied within our fine country.

During the month of February Foodtown, Woolworths and Countdown supermarkets promote New Zealand-produced fresh products and packaged goods.

There is also a range of in-store promotions across all brands and customers can join in and win classically-New Zealand prizes. Other initiatives include the latest eco-friendly reusable shopping bags, special newspaper supplements focusing on New Zealand supplier success stories, a staff scholarship programme and in-store demonstrations of New Zealand products.

Eco strategy

PEL recognises the importance of being a responsible retailer that is considerate of the environmental impact of its activities. The company has in place a number of initiatives that are helping staff and customers to reduce rubbish and to encourage recycling.

Operating in all Foodtown, Woolworths and Countdown supermarkets nation-wide, Pack 7 is designed to reduce waste by encouraging supermarket staff to pack a minimum of seven items in customers' shopping bags.

Re-useable calico and green eco bags are also available to shoppers. Customers are encouraged to bring the bags back into the store whenever they shop, helping to reduce the number of plastic bags issued. The 6oz recyclable calico cotton bags have a convenient shoulder strap while the ECO bags are made from non-woven polypropylene with a rigid bottom and shorter handles. During the Celebrate New Zealand programme, PEL also launched recyclable plastic "art" bags, featuring works by local artists from all around New Zealand.

In addition, PEL recycles plastic bags, plastic and cardboard. The company has implemented award-winning energy conservation measures that substantially reduce power and materials used throughout the business. Particular attention is paid to refrigeration, air conditioning, hot water and lighting.

Signature Range and Basics

PEL is proud to sign its name to Signature Range, the group's premium brand available across all stores. Signature Range products are supplied exclusively to PEL, which ensure the freshest products and highest quality is always maintained. This is backed with a full replacement guarantee.

Basics offer a comprehensive range of everyday, lower priced grocery products offering exceptional value, bringing truth to the Basics by-line - "Quality guaranteed at the lowest prices".

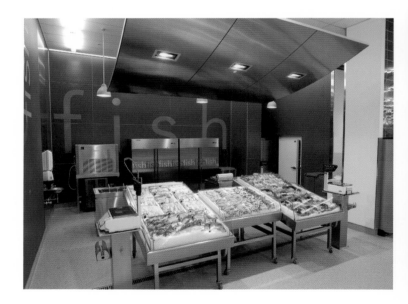

Foodtown Auckland City - A new way of shopping

Foodtown Auckland City - New Zealand's most modern and most customer-focused supermarket is the first of its kind, designed specifically for modern city living.

Foodtown Auckland City never sleeps. In order to serve the vibrant urban environment it inhabits, it is open 24 hours a day seven days a week.

This is a store ahead of the rest, with design and layout intended to make shopping easier and more enjoyable. The service excellence focus has driven not only the store design but the way the supermarket operates.

In respect to its location and the city clientele it serves, the store layout enables customers to shop swiftly should they choose to do so. Each fresh department is complemented by a department specialist providing expert advice on products in their particular sections.

Features include a store-within-a-store concept within such sections as fresh food, the fromagerie, wine, 2 Go meals, bakery and fresh salads, international foods and health and beauty.

Brand values

The brand values of Progressive Enterprises Limited are people focused.

Progressive People
From shop floor to boardroom and check-out aisle to bakery, PEL people are encouraged to strive for achievement both on the job, and outside work. Staff members are able to nominate their co-workers at any level for recognition by the Progressive People programme. A selection of staff members are awarded this honour every year.

Supporting young Kiwis
PEL has a youth focus with core values of safety, prevention, early intervention and a commitment to promoting and enriching the lives of young New Zealanders.

With more than 170 stores reaching into households nationwide, the business has a unique platform to provide support for a range of organisations at community, regional and national levels. Through support for Variety - The Children's Charity, Inzone and Plunket, PEL is dedicated to supporting youth organisations that make a difference that last a lifetime.

Employer of CHOICE

The acronym CHOICE describes PEL's motivation to provide the best possible working conditions for its staff.

C - Committed team work – people working together for the common good of all stakeholders in the business.
H - Honesty and trust – key elements in building teamwork.
O - Openness and respect – core ingredients for personal growth and to foster co-operation.
I – Involvement and interest – in the tasks at hand and those of fellow staff members.
C - Consistency and quality – attributes that are mandatory in the service industry.
E – Enjoyment in a day's work.

Things you didn't know about Progressive Enterprises Ltd

- PEL employs more than 18,000 New Zealanders.
- More than 1.3 million Kiwis have a Foodtown Woolworths Onecard.
- Foodtown is 45 years old, with the country's first supermarket opening in Otahuhu in June 1958.
- The first Countdown was opened at Northlands, Christchurch in 1981.

the paint the professionals use

"Cast a glance down any New Zealand street.
Chances are, every building will have been touched by Resene."

Resene had humble beginnings in 1946 when an Eastbourne builder, Ted Nightingale needed an alkali resistant paint to cover his concrete buildings. There was nothing of this kind available at the time, so in typical Kiwi style he developed his own – in a cement mixer in his garage! In response to demand from other builders, Nightingale commenced producing his paint on a commercial basis under the brand name Stipplecote. As well as Stipplecote, Nightingale manufactured a range of admixtures such as No Bond and Curecrete, which still being on the market today, have lasted the test of time.

As demand for his paint products began to supercede the space in his garage, Nightingale established Resene's first factory in an old stable in Wellington at the close of 1946. From his new factory, he launched the first waterborne paint in New Zealand in 1951 under the brand name Resene, a name derived from the main ingredient of paint: resin. This launch was followed in 1952 by company registration under the name Stipplecote Products Ltd and a move to a larger factory in Kaiwharawhara, Wellington.

In the years that were to follow, Resene have forged an enviable reputation of excellence and quality – a reputation that is the cornerstone of the company's continued success. Marked by innovation and good old fashioned Kiwi ingenuity, Resene have developed a range of paint and specialist coating products for residential and commercial buildings, as well as marine, heavy industrial and automotive use that are second to none. Many products have been developed as a creative answer to a client's problem. Most have set new standards for other manufacturers. All are the result of intensive research and testing.

With manufacturing operations in Wellington, Tauranga, Fiji and Australia, Resene is undeniably a leading force in the South Pacific paint market. And while Resene is New Zealand owned and operated, it also enjoys close links with international material suppliers, such as Rohm & Haas, Du Pont (US), and Bayer, Wacker and B.A.S.F (Germany).

"Our eyes see over nine million colours. Colour has hue, intensity and luminosity. It makes a statement and demonstrates confidence and capability."

colour systems. As a result of this early discovery, Resene developed the truly innovative Resene Total Colour System. Based on sophisticated technology this system provides the necessary protection against the elements.

When it comes to colour, paint is about fashion. Colours come and go with changing trends, so flexibility in colour tools and scheme development is paramount. The Resene Total Colour System offers this flexibility through a wide range of services, from tools such as colour charts through to special colour matches and complete scheme development by specialised staff. All services simplify the colour selection process for professional specifiers, commercial and retail customers alike.

Sophisticated tinting technology enables Resene to produce durable colour options that remain vivid long after they have been applied, including the integral tinting of a wide range of textured and specialist coatings. The Resene Total Colour System is a world first, providing innovative tinting options with a full range of decorative and protective coatings.

Resene has embraced electronic imaging technology to simplify development and confirmation of colour schemes. With the launch of Resene EzyPaint, a downloadable virtual painting programme available free from the Resene website, www.resene.co.nz customers can design colour schemes and order testpots from the comfort of their own homes. A sophisticated full electronic rendering service is available for specifiers – Resene RenderRite – enabling them to see the finish before the painting has even started.

The elegance and robustness of the Resene Total Colour System has attracted international attention and its sophisticated tinting technology is licensed in many countries around the world including Europe, the United States, South Africa, Zimbabwe, the Dominion Republic and China.

"What we are doing is setting standards for ourselves, meeting them and then surpassing them. We are seen as the company that gets it right."

The key to Resene's reputation is its solid commitment to excellence and quality, monitored through controlled testing in Resene's registered laboratory. Resene not only provides extensive architectural colours and services, but also the quality products required to achieve the optimum finish. All products are backed by a technical team who are committed to maintaining product quality through the research of improved technologies to enhance product performance, application and safety. Evidenced by exports of paint technology, Resene paint is recognised as world class.

Resene leads a colour revolution in New Zealand that started in 1969 with the introduction of the British Standard Specification (BS) 2660 colour range. New Zealand's harsh marine environment and high levels of damaging ultraviolet rays quickly expose the limitations of overseas

Resene is well known for leading the development of environmentally sustainable surface coatings in New Zealand, from the underpinning innovation of waterborne paints to the removal of lead from all of its products more than 30 years ago. In 1996, Resene launched New Zealand's most comprehensive range of Environmental Choice products – products that comply with rigorous standards set down by an independent government auditing body. Today, over 70 per cent of the Resene product range bears the Environmental Choice "big tick" logo. This includes two 'firsts' for the New Zealand paint market - a range of patented low-odour products and waterborne enamels. Resene's commitment to this program and the continuous development of low-risk products ensures that safer, professional quality paint is available to everyone. Resene quality is assured every step of the way with its internationally recognised quality systems and ISO 9001 accreditation that allow Resene to guarantee its products for consistency and performance.

"If Resene gives a product the mark of approval, then professionals in the building industry will use it. There isn't any higher recommendation."

Innovation and meticulous attention to quality, along with the ability to problem-solve has assured Resene the respect of New Zealand's architectural and building industry professionals. This reputation is reflected in the company's sponsorship of the New Zealand Institute of Architects – Resene Awards Programme at national and branch levels. This programme recognises quality, innovation and excellence in colour and architectural design – the same principles that drive all Resene actions. Resene is a leader in providing professional advice, high quality products and the best colours – the three vital ingredients in any successful coating project. Architects, specifiers and contractors recognise this and endorse the product range through their ongoing commitment to the brand.

Working hard to stay ahead of market trends, Resene has an international reputation as a leader in paint research and technology. The Resene product range includes paint and specialist coatings for residential and commercial buildings. To help building professionals keep abreast of new

developments in the product range, Resene has an innovative range of architectural services and reference materials, including technical and specification manuals, the Total Colour System, samples and online information. With strong working relationships with paint contractors and the wider construction industry, Resene has intimate knowledge of their businesses facilitating the development of products and services to suit their needs.

"It certainly was the right move. Having our own chain of stores gives us a tremendously strong base and control of our own destiny."

The Resene ColorShop is where New Zealand meets Resene. More than 55 stores around the country confirm the commitment to servicing all customers in the best way possible. Resene is the only New Zealand company with its distribution focused on a nationwide chain of specialist paint stores. Today, the ColorShops are staffed by trained retailers who excel in understanding not only the specifications of Resene's wide product range, but also product innovations and technology advances.

The Resene ColorShop's most sought-after role however, is that they can offer colour and paint advice to all who walk through their doors looking for inspiration. A high percentage of New Zealand's population are homeowners and the popular do-it-yourself approach prevails, meaning valuable reputations can be quickly won or lost in a country with a population of nearly 4 million people. This has led to a consistent level of quality and durability across all Resene products which far outweighs competitive offerings. The Resene ColorShop brings Resene to the doorstep of its customers – ensuring they remain its strongest supporters.

An increasingly sophisticated New Zealand consumer market requires even greater sophistication from manufacturers – and the paint market is certainly no exception. With a history of innovation and excellence, Resene today continues to meet and exceed the requirements of its clients. Resene paint and colour technology is exported to other countries around the world, and its chemists are internationally respected for their development of superior quality products. With over half a century of experience, and three generations of the Nightingale family at its helm, Resene has certainly shown just how far a little Kiwi ingenuity can go.

From any perspective, it's a bright future ahead.

innovation

inspiration

imagination

www.resene.co.nz

Tel: 0064-4-577-0500   **Fax: 0064-4-577-0600**   **www.resene.co.nz**

RJ's is proud that it's the only New Zealand company specialising solely in licorice products. Today, they produce one of the largest varieties of licorice products in the world.

The History Of RJ's Licorice

"Although not a long one it is a successful one."

In 1983, Roger Halliwell was approached by the receiver's of Granny's Licorice Ltd to assist in identifying whether the company had a future. Halliwell immediately reduced staff numbers from 70 to 17 and halved the range of products manufactured to effectively turn around the Granny's Licorice profit. After six months, Halliwell was completely caught up in the excitement of making confectionery and decided to buy the assets. Over the following five years, he concentrated on developing a quality product to boost the Granny's brand identity. Hard work was rewarded when Halliwell was approached by Arnott's in 1988, with an offer to buy the business.

During the five years following this sale, there was little change in the traditional licorice market, motivating Halliwell to go back to the drawing board. "I had the time to plan a strategy to realise my vision for licorice confectionery," he says. In 1994, the chance appeared for Halliwell to repurchase the former land and buildings of Granny's Licorice and so, the RJ's licorice brand was launched.

RJ's is named after Halliwell's son, Regan James who returned from overseas to help set up the business. In partnership with Dixie, Halliwell's wife, they all agreed on a mission to take a traditional licorice market and turn it into a category highlighted by innovative and uniquely different products.

New machinery was purchased from North America and was re-modelled to meet their personal requirements. Manufacturing eventually began in May 1995 with the Licorice Logs the first product to hit the market.

Developing RJ's into the brand Kiwis know and love

Luckily for RJ's, New Zealanders love licorice. Each year, RJ's produces approximately 2 million kilos of licorice, 90 per cent of which is sold to the New Zealand market. With RJ's having a 48 per cent market share, New Zealanders are enjoying over 3.5 million kilos of licorice products per year.

The main ingredients of licorice are flour, sugar, glucose, molasses, treacle, licorice extract and caramel. As a branding concept, many of RJ's traditional licorice products are referred to as herbal. This is because RJ's only uses authentic licorice extract which comes from the root of the blue flowering snow pea plant (glyceriza glabra). This extract is 50 times sweeter than sugar – in fact strangely, it is so sweet that it is bitter. Licorice extract also has a wealth of medicinal qualities and has been used for that purpose for centuries.

Product development

The Licorice Logs, like many of RJ's initial products, were originally presented in a basic clear plastic container with a label. Later this progressed to individually wrapped logs in clear film and eventually printed colour film was used.

With dedication to brand development and positioning, RJ's soon saw their brand progress to become the Number One Licorice manufacturer in the New Zealand market (AC Nielson). There was no time to rest on their laurels however, especially with one of the world's largest food manufacturers as their major competitor.

Quality and innovation

The key to RJ's reputation is a strong focus on superior quality and innovative licorice products. You only need to visit their factory to understand this – it is spotlessly clean. Reflected in the licorice products manufactured, the RJ's staff prides themselves on their preparation hygiene and quality work environment.

To be a market leader, RJ's has to continually maintain its competitive edge. One product that has proven to be a step ahead of competitor offerings is the Licorice and Raspberry Choc Log. With an eye always directed at the international market, RJ's knows that they're the sole manufacturer of this product worldwide.

More recently, "soft eating" licorice has increased in popularity to become one of the fastest growing licorice products in the New Zealand grocery market.

Product presentation is an area of quality that RJ's place a huge emphasis upon. From a point of sale perspective, quality packaging is vitally important, especially when the brand is lined up in a supermarket next to competitor confectionery. A substantial amount of money is budgeted each year for graphic design so that visual package designs are kept stylish, up-to-the-minute and adaptable to international markets.

Innovation comes not only from the people involved in RJ's, but also through product development and the machinery that assists in making such development happen. Much of the machinery has been made or adapted by local engineers. "I believe in purchasing the best quality machinery available to provide a product point of difference, be it in cooking, packaging or taste", says Regan.

Flexibility is another of RJ's many secrets to success and as customer satisfaction is important, the company offers quick response time to market needs. RJ's provide customers with unique, personalised products upon request, are able to meet short timeframes and are open for market feedback; any customer – be they retail or consumer – can speak directly with Roger or Regan. These points of difference are what set's RJ's apart from its competitors.

Location

Some people say, "Why Levin?" Prior to purchasing the original Granny's Licorice factory, Roger investigated many locations to determine which would be the most suitable for RJ's.

Levin was at the top of the list as Roger and Dixie's family had grown up in the town and was the place where they had spent a large majority of their working lives. What better place to work than a familiar environment?

The large factory premises, consisting of 20,000 square feet, were initially purchased to allow for growth over a ten year period. However, with business booming, RJ's outgrew this in seven. The attraction of low overheads in Levin for a building this size meant external financial assistance was kept to a minimum. In 2003 the need to extend the existing plant became necessary and RJ's doubled the size of the factory, increasing the manufacturing capacity by over 200 per cent.

Employing staff in Levin also proved to be of benefit for both RJ's and the town. Roger's earlier business and community involvement in Levin meant that there were plenty of eager people wanting to work in the RJ's team. Staff numbers now total around 40.

Keeping it in the family

From the outset, RJ's was to be a family business. The company vision clearly indicates this: "To grow and maintain a strong family business to provide for its future generations."

There are currently five family members working in the business. Roger acts as managing director, his wife Dixie as the director and son Regan as general manager. As with many small businesses, the general manager looks after the complete running of the business, from manufacturing through to sales and marketing. With such a multi-faceted role, it became apparent that another person was needed to remove pressure from Regan and in 2001, Regan's sister, Amy Law, was appointed as national sales manager.

Based in Auckland, Amy is able to focus completely on RJ's sales within New Zealand and takes over the day-to-day marketing of their products.

This has allowed Regan to spend more time focusing on their export business.

RJ's have been inundated with requests for their licorice from many parts of the world, and to date, have not had to go searching for business. Export

currently makes up approximately 10 per cent of sales with capacity to reach as high as 80 per cent. "The key is to ensure we can maintain supply and focus to our New Zealand business whilst slowly growing our export business," says Roger. RJ's currently has key customers in Australia, United States and the United Kingdom making up around four containers per month.

This continual growth of RJ's has lead to further pressures on the human resources. To compensate Sean Wilde, son-in-law of Roger and Dixie, recently joined the business as factory manager. It is Roger's dream that some day his two daughters, Angela and Jacqui, will also be an integral part of the business.

Mirroring the family orientation at top level, RJ's employees see themselves as a team; like a big family unit, they are the company's greatest asset. Staff members are encouraged to make suggestions on any area of manufacture and RJ's endeavours to make use of those suggestions. As a result of the "big family" feel within the business, RJ's workforce is a very stable unit, with few staff leaving.

RJ's makes a point of immersing each staff member in all processes involved in the production line. This enables the staff to have a clear understanding of all job positions and gives each member the opportunity to find a niche they find challenging and enjoyable.

Outside the factory, RJ's takes an active role in the community and always has a number of sponsorships running. A major sponsorship of RJ's is the recently constructed Levin hockey turf. Named The Halliwell Turf, Levin now has a world-class sporting asset. Other recent sponsorships include local rugby teams, and a golf tournament. RJ's are also a key sponsor for the Kidcare Foundation which was established to provide support to at risk children.

To the future and beyond

Licorice has, and always will be, known as a traditional confectionery. While RJ's aims to keep that tradition alive, they also have plans for further innovations to add a new dynamic and dimension to a very well known brand. With strong family values, lateral thinking and creative minds, RJ's will take its licorice well into the future. WATCH THIS SPACE

RJ's Licorice Ltd   Tel: (06) 366-0270   Fax: (06) 368-5731   www.rjlicorice.co.nz

SKYCITY

Fun is a serious business – we know that.

From a night out at the movies to a flutter on the blackjack table to a meal in the Southern Hemisphere's tallest building, the name SKYCITY has become synonymous with fun and entertainment in New Zealand, and more recently, in Australia.

With gaming and entertainment properties in Auckland, Hamilton and Queenstown in New Zealand, as well as Adelaide and Darwin in Australia, SKYCITY also has a 50 per cent interest in Village SKYCITY Cinemas, New Zealand's leading cinema chain.

So it's rather easy to forget that only eight years ago, SKYCITY's physical presence was a single construction site in Auckland. The proposed 328-metre Sky Tower was the subject of local controversy, and its doors were yet to be open to the very first customer.

In 2003, 12 million customers visited a SKYCITY property, enjoying attractions ranging from movies, accommodation, conference facilities, restaurants and bars, casino gaming, live entertainment and theatre, adventure tourism, shopping and special events.

And Sky Tower? It has become the most distinctive feature on the Auckland skyline, New Zealand's leading visitor attraction (one in every two international visitors to New Zealand enjoy the views), and a source of considerable local pride. Aucklanders have voted Sky Tower the best symbol of their city every year since 1998.

SKYCITY itself is now a diversified, trans-Tasman entertainment group, with a track record of performance, profit and dividend growth that makes it one of Australasia's most successful companies.

It's a serious business, the business of fun!

History

SKYCITY's success is based on a singular vision: to create fun and entertainment for its customers. This means having a very clear focus on understanding customer needs, and delivering exactly what they want.

When SKYCITY first opened in Auckland in 1996, the entertainment experience was decidedly American in flavour – hardly surprising given that for the first two years SKYCITY was managed by US-based casino operator Harrah's. Soon came a realisation that the "Las Vegas of the South Seas" model wouldn't necessarily work, and customer research confirmed these instincts.

When SKYCITY Limited took over the operation from Harrah's in 1998, there was a shift into offering a broad-based, locally-relevant range of entertainment offerings. While retaining a focus on providing exceptional customer experiences and service, SKYCITY wanted to ensure the entertainment facilities and products had a uniquely local flavour.

A range of significant changes to the SKYCITY experience were instigated: from the art on the walls, to the Asian-Pacific flavours in the restaurants; the performers offered on stage, the product range offered, and the sponsorships and events SKYCITY became associated with, all amounting to a distinctive Kiwi flair.

As the number one venue for top line events like Rally New Zealand, local Super 12 celebrations, the comedy festival, and the world premiere of 'Whale Rider', SKYCITY has become the local entertainment 'hub'. Today, visitors experience award-winning seafood cuisine alongside appearances by some of New Zealand's top entertainment and sporting celebrities.

Achievements

It's tempting to measure achievements by citing awards won: SKYCITY was New Zealand Company of the Year in 2001, and was named one of the world's best small companies by Forbes Magazine in 2002 and 2003.

Now one of New Zealand's top ten listed companies by market capitalisation, SKYCITY has been very successful in financial terms - delivering shareholders six consecutive years of growth in profits and dividends.

However, there are other achievements of which SKYCITY is just as proud. Wherever one of SKYCITY properties is based, they aim to be a cornerstone enterprise, a company on which people can rely upon to play its part as a community and business leader.

This philosophy is behind the work SKYCITY has done to promote tourism on both sides of the Tasman: working co-operatively with other major tourism operators and government, taking a leadership role to promote local economic development and helping to establish new tourism ventures.

It also underpins an involvement in a wide range of community sponsorships including the SKYCITY Starlight Symphony, Starship Children's Hospital, New Zealand Special Olympics and in Adelaide our support of the McGuinness McDermott Foundation.

SKYCITY has also been a long-time supporter of Auckland rugby and, more recently, Waikato rugby. SKYCITY Community Trusts in Hamilton, Auckland and Queenstown have now distributed nearly NZ$12 million to grass-roots community groups.

The product

SKYCITY's focus on the deliverance of exceptional customer experiences has been vastly successful - setting them above other casinos in Australasia that have focused more exclusively on gaming.

However, like any restaurant worth its salt, SKYCITY needs to keep its menu of entertainment offerings original and fresh – a prerequisite to keep customers coming back. This is achieved by continually creating exciting products, as well as an ever-changing programme of promotions and live entertainment events.

SKYCITY is particularly interested in the investment of innovation: in 2001 SKYCITY partnered with Waitomo Adventures Limited to develop Sky Jump – offering customers the opportunity to plummet 192 metres from the top of Sky Tower in 25 seconds, and helping to consolidate an urban adventure tourism industry in Auckland.

SKYCITY is also dedicated to investing in the people of New Zealand - over three quarters of its 4,500 staff members deal with customers on a day-to-day basis. The quality of personal interaction the staff has with customers is of vital importance in ensuring a satisfying customer experience. Through staff recognition, reward and training programmes, there is a positive emphasis on industry-leading customer service, being a responsible host, and supporting confident, friendly people who really enjoy dealing with customers face-to-face.

Recent developments

SKYCITY Entertainment Group continues to evolve rapidly, based on customer feedback and demand, as well as anticipating new trends in the entertainment and gaming sector.

SKYCITY Auckland has recently undergone a major refurbishment and extension, reaffirming its credentials as the city's leading accommodation, conference and entertainment venue.

2003 saw a redevelopment of the Sky Tower entrance and retail area, the launch of a hip new casino and bar plus the refurbishment of the four-star SKYCITY Hotel. New Zealand's largest convention facility (seating 1,500 people for dinner) opened in April 2004, with forward bookings through to 2007. 2005 will mark the opening of SKYCITY Auckland's second hotel, the five star SKYCITY Grand, taking room numbers on site to 660.

Village SKYCITY Cinemas will soon include selected Gold Class theatres – luxury viewing facilities with large, padded armchairs and footrests, alcohol and food service throughout the screening and wine coolers to keep drinks chilled – another move made in response to customer feedback and research.

In 2000, SKYCITY's purchase of a casino in Adelaide marked an initial foray into Australia. With foresight, Adelaide Casino was considered as a place where SKYCITY could make a difference: it offered fond memories for many people, but was well past its prime in terms of decor, customer numbers and the quality of its product range.

SKYCITY aimed to replicate its successful approach in Auckland to redevelop the Adelaide Casino. In 2001 parts of the complex were refurbished and re-branded as SKYCITY Adelaide.

SKYCITY invests much time into a greater understanding of its customers. 2004 marks the first stage of an A$70 million redevelopment to propose a broader range of entertainment offerings to meet local customer demand. SKYCITY'S initial focus is on celebrating and reinvigorating the heritage site, with the introduction of new food and beverage outlets on the street front. The next phase will see the creation of a bistro-style restaurant, a cocktail bar featuring live entertainment, a terrace bar, private function facilities and new gaming areas.

Similarly, in February 2004, SKYCITY announced it was acquiring the Darwin Casino (subject to regulatory approvals). Already a solid business, SKYCITY aims to improve the offering to deliver a broad-based gaming and entertainment facility, again, based on the successful Auckland model.

Promotion

SKYCITY knows that while component products and facilities are individually very attractive, together they form an exceptionally compelling whole.

SKYCITY has had a clear vision from the outset: to be New Zealand's leading entertainment brand, and progress towards achieving that goal is implemented through a consistent focus on the customer experience.

Keeping an ear to the ground to sound out customer demand is important. That's why greater customer choice is vital for SKYCITY promotions, offering customers a choice when they visit. Yes, that flutter on the blackjack table will feature, but so will the opportunity to eat at a world-class restaurant that offers international cuisine with a local flavour, and the chance to catch a theatrical or live music performance.

Also on offer is an integrated customer loyalty programme, SKYCITY Action. Action rewards regular customers for the dollars they spend, and tailors those rewards to meet what SKYCITY knows to be their particular interests – whether that's food and beverages or shopping and gaming. It's an internationally acclaimed, award-winning programme that is now in place at all SKYCITY locations.

Brand values

Creating an exciting, compelling and entertaining experience for customers isn't just a marketing tactic it's the very core of SKYCITY'S corporate strategy – a thread that runs through everything they do. It is a vision shared by everyone, from board members right through to front-of-house staff.

The primary challenge is to ensure that every one of SKYCITY's customers in New Zealand and Australia leaves wanting to come back for more, wanting to relive the experiences they've just had, and sharing those experiences with others.

Things you didn't know about SKYCITY

- SKYCITY employs around 4,500 staff from more than 70 cultural backgrounds.

- More than 12 million people visited SKYCITY across Australia and New Zealand in 2003.

- SKYCITY operates 75 per cent of the cinema screens in New Zealand.

- Our Auckland site is home to the largest commercial kitchen in the country.

- The Sky Tower is the most popular paid visitor attraction in the country.

- After Air New Zealand, SKYCITY is the largest tourism operation in New Zealand.

SKYCITY Entertainment Group Limited, 86 Federal Street, PO Box 90643, Auckland

SKYLINE

THE GARAGE COMPANY

Providing quality homes for cars and people since 1956.

The Skyline Garage founder Lindsay Cook had a vision to produce quality garages with an affordable price – ideals that hold true to this day.

Since its establishment in 1956, Skyline has become a household name, producing buildings that are designed to serve a dual purpose - to look attractive and withstand the harshest of conditions.

Lindsay Cook's concern for detail and his concept of building packaging has given Skyline a reputation that is second to none. Offering a wide range of buildings including the popular Gottage, a garage and a dwelling all in one, Skyline's superior quality and value is the culmination of nearly 50 years of experience, innovation and dedication to the industry.

Whether customers require extra storage, accommodation, an office, workshops, carports or out buildings on farms, Skyline has the answer.

All buildings are made to order and are complemented by a large range of colour schemes, wall claddings and many other options for the discerning customer.

Each building is individually custom-designed to meet the requirements of a variety of lifestyles. Heights, widths, depths and roof pitches can all be varied to accommodate almost anything a customer wants to house – including the kitchen sink.

The end result is a building that's both functional and attractive, adding value to any property. With the individual's needs in mind – and quality at the forefront – it should come as no surprise that Skyline customers come back for more, year after year.

sheds are also experiencing substantial growth as houses become more confined and storage is at a premium.

Skyline's main objective has been to increase production in order to keep up with demand. Today, Skyline's market leadership is maintained by commitment to research and development as well as the use of quality building materials.

Achievements

Skyline, "The Garage Company", has firmly established itself as the original mass producer of garages.

During Skyline's lifespan, there have been over 100,000 Skyline buildings constructed, most of which have been in New Zealand. Skyline is proud of the fact that it has been able to offer customers a cost-competitive option when the necessity for storage or accommodation becomes apparent.

With unceasing innovation and meticulous attention to design detail, Skyline has set a lofty benchmark for competitors to follow. This benchmark still exists today with Skyline producing the best quality garages available in the market place.

Of great importance to the success and subsequent achievements of the company is the fact that it has remained a family business, maintaining family morals and dedication to the industry. For the Skyline business, the Cook family have created a network of nearly 50 distributors throughout New Zealand as well as jobs for over 300 people – many of whom have been long serving staff and instrumental in the initial establishment of the Skyline brand.

The market

Through ingenuity and innovative design, Skyline originally created its own niche in the construction market for affordable buildings to provide storage and accommodation.

Over a period of 50 years, this market has grown and changed in a dynamic fashion. The market now includes several competitors and a far wider range of products. Despite plenty of competition, Skyline is still a dominant force in the market place with more homeowners between the ages of 25 and 50 now needing accessory buildings. In fact, when people talk about garages and sheds, the name Skyline is the one commonly passed between lips.

With almost 50 years in the market, Skyline certainly knows how to keep abreast of changing consumer trends. In this time, Skyline has shifted the focus towards the provision of accommodation style buildings under the brand name Gottages. Garden

The product

From the inception of the Skyline brand, the product has always been recognised as a superior quality, affordable building that is able to withstand the test of time.

Each building that is produced in the factory comprises of up to 1000 components. Every building is individually produced to customer requests and dealt with as a separate order.

Perhaps the most ingenious innovation in the Skyline system is the way the buildings are packed for transportation to their final destination. All the equipment needed to construct a standard double garage is contained within a single package constructed of timber, which is then used in the garage. These packs are usually no larger than 4.8 metres long and 1.2 metres wide with a height of one metre, and a weight of little more than one tonne.

In Skyline's formative years, it was a regular occurrence for these garage packs to be delivered on a domestic trailer. Because every component can be contained within a carcass,

this reduces transportation costs and saves the builder time when construction begins. As a product, a Skyline building takes the hassle out of dealing with several different suppliers for various components of the building.

Skyline truly is a one-stop shop.

As each building produced is treated as a single order, the Skyline product range is extensive. However the Skyline brand is associated with four main product lines: garages, Gottages, garden sheds and carports.

Thousands of these products are sold through the distributor network each year, and although the basics have stayed the same, the look of the range has changed to meet with new demands. New cladding styles and colours have been developed and the basic timber structure has been modified to comply with changing building regulations. The Cook family are proud that Lindsay's vision of producing a quality garage at an affordable price is still upheld by Skyline today.

Recent developments

In recent years, Skyline has experienced some very exciting product and marketing developments. One of the major changes has been the introduction of a new roll formed cladding machine able to run two different profiles of cladding. This cladding, called Championboard, can be "secret nailed" and run to specific lengths. The main benefit of Championboard is that there are less joins in the cladding and no visible nail heads, making a Skyline building more aesthetically pleasing. Like its name suggests, this latest innovation is proving to be a champion of the Skyline cladding range, with over half of all Skyline buildings now constructed with this material.

With corrosion being the age-old enemy of steel clad buildings, Skyline, in conjunction with long-time supplier Pacific Coil Coaters (PCC) continually research better coatings to fight the onset of corrosion. In the mid-1990s, a new coating process for steel was introduced called Zincalume®. An innovative coating with greater anti-corrosion properties, Zincalume® was introduced to replace the galvanised variety that had been in existence.

Perhaps the biggest developmental innovation has been the Gottage. Five years ago, this name was unheard of but today, it forms a new part of the Kiwi language. The Gottage name was derived from the words garage and cottage and describes all Skyline buildings used for habitable use. Considerable effort has been put into promotion of this product, particularly through the catchy jingle "Gotta Getta Gottage".

Promotion

Early on, much of Skyline's business was generated through word-of-mouth advertising but, as the distributor network grew throughout New Zealand, other forms of media came into use.

Through much of the 1980s, New Zealand's most famous cricketer, Richard Hadlee promoted Skyline Garages on a series of television advertisements. These commercials were further reinforced through radio and print media.

Trade shows throughout the country have also been a major promotional avenue for Skyline, with Fieldays at Mystery Creek being the premier event.

The standard Skyline brochure, handed out with all customer enquiries, goes through regular design and content revamps, enabling Skyline to keep ahead of competitor advertising material.

As it did in the 1980s, Skyline continues to use television as its main form of promotion. The "Gotta Getta" campaign was launched in 1999 to resounding success, and has served to further strengthen Skyline's brand identity.

Skyline also has 20 display sites throughout New Zealand where prospective customers can see the Skyline phenomenon in full glory. Skyline firmly believes that a job well done is the best form of promotion, and nothing promotes the company better than its helpful staff on hand to provide friendly advice.

Brand values

The Skyline brand name gives customers confidence in an industry plagued with transitory companies. Part of the backbone of this stability is the comprehensive five year warranty Skyline provides.

The brand is entrenched in Lindsay Cook's vision to produce quality garages at an affordable price. Skyline's attention to detail and continual revaluations of product improvement, customer care and marketing strategies have made the brand into the powerhouse it is today.

Skyline buidlings have been built in such diverse places as England, USA, Canada, Australia, The Pacific and even the Falkland Islands.

Gotta Get a Garage
Gotta Get a Gottage
Gotta Get a Skyline

Southern Cross
Healthcare

The brand with a steady pulse

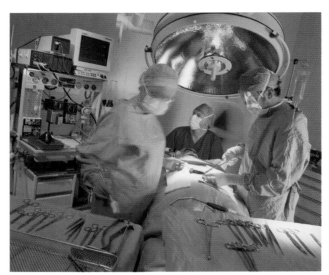

If all the exciting brands in this book are causing your pulse to race, now's probably a very good time to calm down and read about Southern Cross.

That's because a steady pulse and low blood pressure have been the hallmarks of Southern Cross Healthcare's home-grown success for more than 40 years.

Today, more than 800,000 people (about one in every five New Zealanders) have private health insurance with Southern Cross. More than 40,000 people each year undergo surgical procedures in the Southern Cross network of 11 private surgical hospitals (including two joint ventures) around the country. And when Kiwis go overseas, thousands of them take Southern Cross Travel Insurance with them.

Southern Cross's reputation has been built on its consistent delivery of value to New Zealanders through its pioneering health insurance business, the Southern Cross Medical Care Society. By the end of its 2003-2004 year, the Society had collected $5.22 billion in premiums since 1961, and paid $4.68 billion in claims. That equates to an average return to members of 90 cents in the premium dollar – a very high ratio that would seldom, if ever, be matched by other insurers.

As a not-for-profit friendly society, the health insurance organisation is owned and operated for the benefit of its members, not for the benefit of investors and shareholders.

Southern Cross Hospitals and Travel Insurance operate under the same Southern Cross brand but at arms length from the health insurer. Financial surpluses from these operations are paid into a charitable trust operated for the benefit of all New Zealanders.

Even as the costs of medical treatment have sky-rocketed over the years, all parts of the Southern Cross Healthcare Group have focused on providing New Zealanders with sustainable access to value-for-money, quality health care.

The early years

While Southern Cross first opened for business in 1961, its origins can be traced back to political ructions of the 1930's. According to Peter A Smith's history of Southern Cross – *The Private Prescription* – Labour's radical proposal of a free health service for all was viewed with great suspicion by many doctors who feared it would make them full-time public servants, and eliminate choice for patients.

After three years of argument between the government and the medical profession, the "dual system" of public and private health care sectors, and a government contribution of one guinea ($2.10) per night towards private hospital costs, were enshrined in the Social Security Act of 1938.

Twenty years later, with surgery costs burgeoning, many in the private sector felt the government contribution was falling well short of the mark. So the idea of private health insurance, which at that time was catching on in Australia and the United Kingdom, was floated.

The Private Prescription recounts that two of the earliest issues addressed by the prospective organisation's steering committee were the things that would ensure Southern Cross's success and distinctiveness in the following years: its name and its not-for-profit status.

Aware of the international recognition of the Blue Cross organisation of the United States, there was talk of a local adaptation.

Memories now differ as to why "Southern Cross" was favoured: some saw it as a link to – or localised version of - Blue Cross while others recall seeking something that had a distinctly New Zealand flavour.

As for the preferred form of constitution, from the very earliest discussions the idea that a conventional company should be formed had been ruled out; all those involved had the foresight to agree unanimously that the enterprise should be run on a not-for-profit basis.

(*The Private Prescription*, Peter A. Smith, 2000)

Supply and demand

Southern Cross's growth over the years has been driven by simple economic principles of "supply and demand". In the early 1960s it took considerable courage for the founders of Southern Cross to declare publicly what others dared not: that the Welfare State's public health system couldn't satisfy the huge demands placed upon it.

By 1970 there were 35,000 New Zealanders on waiting lists for admission to public hospitals for non-acute problems such as hernias, varicose veins, tonsils or hip joints. When patients got to the top of the list, they had limited choice over when or where the surgery would take place, or who their surgeon would be.

In subsequent years there has been little significant change. In early 2004, over 27,000 patients had been waiting more than six months just for a first specialist appointment through the public health system, let alone admission for surgery.

Little wonder that hundreds of thousands of New Zealanders have flocked to Southern Cross, many of them via thousands of group schemes set up by employers wanting better access to health care for their staff.

New health horizons

The growth and success of the health insurance market in general, and Southern Cross in particular, has had considerable impact on the rest of the private health care sector. This was particularly obvious in private hospitals in the 1970s, where capacity and quality of care came under considerable pressure as the demand for elective surgery grew.

A good example is Christchurch, where one of the city's two private surgical facilities was in real difficulty. If it closed, there would have been insufficient capacity in Canterbury to meet the elective surgery needs of Southern Cross members. So, in 1979, Southern Cross stepped in and purchased its first hospital, then known as Calvary Hospital. Very shortly afterwards Auckland's Brightside Hospital became the second. And in 1980 work began on the construction of the first all-new Southern Cross Hospital in Auckland's Gillies Ave, which *House & Garden* magazine later observed was "designed first for humans, rather than medicine."

With hundreds of thousands of members, and an expanding hospital network, Southern Cross broadened its horizons again. Its profile in the health sector meant many would-be travelers, aware of high health care costs in foreign countries, were approaching Southern Cross for advice and help. So in 1982 Southern Cross established a travel insurance operation to extend health and travel cover for members, and non-members, when they went abroad.

Your health is our business

In all of its activities over the years, Southern Cross's bread and butter has been looking after people when they're ill: providing better access to treatment backed up by efficient claims processing, setting high standards of private hospital care and helping New Zealanders in strife around the globe. But in recent times Southern Cross has been gently turning its emphasis from illness to general health and wellbeing.

This was crystalised in late 2003 with the adoption of a new by-line for the Southern Cross Healthcare brand: "Your health is our business".

For some years prior to this, Southern Cross had promoted healthy lifestyles to its membership, in particular through its member magazine *Jump!*, services like the free Health Info 0800 line, and an internet site brimming with health information. After all, a healthy diet, regular exercise and the elimination of "naughties" like smoking and excessive alcohol consumption have a proven beneficial effect on people's health.

This would be reward enough for most people. But Southern Cross research has suggested that insurance incentives could further reinforce the pursuit of a healthy lifestyle.

So, late in 2003 Southern Cross took the innovative step of introducing a "healthy lifestyle reward" for new members signing up to its new Wellbeing Plan. Applicants satisfying three out of four lifestyle criteria (built around smoking, diet, physical activity and alcohol consumption) pay lower health insurance premiums than they would otherwise pay. After about two years, the Wellbeing Plan's healthy lifestyle reward may be replaced with a low claim reward, if good living has successfully translated into low claims.

The Wellbeing Plan introduced further innovations, including preventative and natural health options such as annual check ups, weight management, acupuncture, homeopathy and naturopathy consultations to complement safety net cover for surgery, hospitalisation, diagnostic tests and specialist consultations.

Inclusion of acupuncture spawned one tongue-in-cheek advertisement proclaiming cover for "pins and needles". And many of Southern Cross's other recent advertisements have focused on health and wellbeing messages, such as the anti-stress reminder on a billboard near the Waipu holiday spot in Northland – "Relax, you're still over two hours from Auckland."

These latest health insurance innovations and advertisements demonstrate both the legacy and future directions of Southern Cross Healthcare. And they show why a steady pulse will be part of the Southern Cross brand for many years to come.

Things you might not know about Southern Cross Healthcare

• In a typical 12-month period, Southern Cross will process over 600,000 claims representing 5 million treatments. Over 128,000 of those claims will be for surgical procedures.

• Southern Cross Hospitals is the largest group of private hospitals in New Zealand. Its customers include not only people with Southern Cross health insurance, but clients of other insurers and ACC.

• Southern Cross Travel Insurace caters for all types of leisure and business travel for New Zealanders going overseas. It's also the market-leading provider of insurance for international students from around the globe studying here in New Zealand.

• Southern Cross Medical Care Society (health insurance) and Southern Cross Benefits Limited (travel insurance) both enjoy A+ (strong) financial strength ratings from international agency Standard and Poor's (as at February 2004).

• Sir Arthur Porrit, New Zealand's first home-born Governor General from 1967, was Chief Medical Adviser to Britain's leading health insurer in the late 50's. Material he provided helped get Southern Cross off the ground.

• Lawyer, MP and Minister of Health from 1951 to 1954, Jack Marshall, prepared the initial drafts of the Southern Cross constitution known as, "The Rules" in 1959. Twelve years later he became Prime Minister and was knighted in 1974.

• Southern Cross's first customer in 1961 was the then Auckland Mayor, Dove-Myer Robinson who later recalled, "I thought that as I was number one citizen, I should be number one member of Southern Cross."

• Southern Cross's current group chief executive, Dr Ian McPherson, is a former GP who worked for the International Red Cross, initially serving on the Pakistan/Afghanistan border in the early 1980s during the Russian occupation of Afghanistan.

• The chairman of the Board is Dr John Matthews, an Auckland clinical haematologist and company director. Other board members include Bruce Davidson, Dr Harley Gray, Dr Susan Macken, David May, Philip Meyer and Jeff Todd, who collectively boast a vast range and depth of experience in business leadership and governance.

Southern Cross Healthcare   Tel: **0800 800 181**   **www.southerncross.co.nz**

Never before in the history of New Zealand's beer market, has one brand permeated into the folklore of the country like Steinlager has. From its beginnings in the mid fifties, the brand has become a symbol of New Zealand achievement around the world. The story of Steinlager is about New Zealand taking on the world's best and beating them.

The Steinlager Story

Steinlager stands alone as New Zealand's most internationally acclaimed beer and has been at the forefront of our country's export drive since the early 1960s. It is now savoured around the world and comprises more than 96 per cent of this country's export beer sales.

Steinlager was first brewed in 1958 in response to a challenge by the then finance minister, Lord Nordmeyer.

New Zealand was in the financial doldrums and in the Minister's "black budget", he threatened to cut international beer imports to boost the flagging economy. This move laid down the challenge for New Zealand's leading brewers to come up with an international-style lager beer.

In response to that challenge, Steinecker was born. The name Steinecker was chosen because the brewhouse equipment used at the Auckland brewery had come from the German equipment manufacturer, Steinecker. The name also fitted the need for a European-style identity, in tune with the names of the continental beers Lord Nordmeyer had banished from New Zealand shores.

Steinecker was a huge success, but in 1962 Lion Breweries (then New Zealand breweries) was taken to court in the US to defend a "passing off" action. The accuser objected to the use of the name and image on the grounds of similarity to its own product. The opposition won, and so in 1963, Steinlager was launched instead. It was the same product, with a new name.

For the next decade, Steinlager – the beer in the brown bottle with the distinctive taste – consolidated its New Zealand position. In 1973, export sales to the American market began.

Two key changes were made which helped ensure Steinlager's success in the US – It was sold in a green bottle and in a six-pack to tap into the lucrative supermarket trade - years before New Zealand would take such a step.

Steinlager's international reputation grew quickly and by 1977, it was selling in 15 countries worldwide and winning international beer-tasting competitions.

Due to a production problem in the late 1970s, some green export bottles were sold in New Zealand and took off immediately. For the next decade, green meant "export" and brown meant "local".

Debate raged in every corner of the country about the supposed difference between the beers and which was the best. In 1980, the export variant was finally released on to the New Zealand market and was quickly established as a popular alternative.

By now, the brand was on course to becoming part of the fabric of New Zealand society, to the point where even the dedicated Steinlager sales team was mooted. The New Zealand green imagery, together with the premium feel and success of the beer on the international export scene helped to establish Steinlager as a national icon.

During the mid-1980s, the Steinlager momentum increased when the decision was made to take the brand to the people via advertising. Tony Thomas of McKay King and Saatchi & Saatchi was charged with the task reflecting the brand's international success through developing highly visible advertising campaigns for Steinlager.

By 1986, Steinlager was available in 35 countries while back at home, it led the way in the sponsorship of New Zealand rugby and yachting.

Steinlager is now firmly established as New Zealand's top-selling premium beer. It is, without a doubt, one of the best beers in the world and has the awards to prove it.

Steinlager won the Les Amis Du Vin competition four years in a row in the late 1970s – an unprecedented honour – after which the organisers politely asked if the brand could refrain from entering "to give the others a chance".

The highest accolade for Steinlager came in 1985 at the Brewing Industry's International Awards in London. Against competition from 800 of the world's leading lagers, Steinlager won both the award for its particular class, and the Championship Trophy supreme award – "truly the World's Best Bottled Lager." In 1998 it was awarded two Monde Selection gold medals in Belgium.

Steinlager's success around the world is credited to its distinctive taste and use of only pure, natural ingredients. It has a dry, tangy finish and the green bullet hops deliver a clean, crisp bitterness.

Over the years Steinlager has produced some highly memorable, iconic advertising campaigns, – many of which have become famous catchphrases for the brand. The most unforgettable of these include "The thirsty drink beer, the hungry drink Steinlager", "Stand behind the All Blacks, we are", "New Zealand's Finest" and more recently the celebrated "Know who you are" and "Unconditional". The hugely popular "They're drinking our beer. Here." campaign emphasised the success of Steinlager, both in New Zealand and abroad. Images included posh elderly people being served Steinlager on a silver tray at a garden tea party, people drinking Steinlager in France, New York and even the Arabian Desert. The commercials starred Gryff Rhys Jones and Mel Smith.

Steinlager has also been represented by a number of famous spokespeople, including Sir Peter Blake, Doug Myers, AJ Whetton and of course the All Blacks.

The most coveted among the lengthy list of sponsorships that Steinlager has been involved with are the All Blacks, Team New Zealand, and the New Zealand Golf Open.

Steinlager and the All Blacks

Steinlager's sponsorship of the All Blacks dates back to 1986 when corporate sponsorship of sporting teams was virtually non-existent. Few would have predicted its development into the big budget, highly competitive business it is today.

The reason behind the sponsorship was clear – New Zealand's finest beer was winning international awards and riding a wave of export success. Quite naturally, the brand was keen to become associated with New Zealand's premier sporting export. A year later, the All Blacks made both New Zealand and Steinlager proud in winning the 1987 Rugby World Cup.

Working together, the All Black management and Steinlager evolved the sponsorship into a partnership that has performed well for both sides for more than 15 years of good times and bad, including the development of the first All Blacks television campaign "Stand By Me".

The highs and lows are what have strengthened this famous association. From the devastating loss to South Africa in extra time during the 1995 World Cup, to the sought-after series win against the Springboks in South Africa – a victory that had eluded the All Blacks since 1928 and earned them the title of "The Incomparables".

In 1999, Steinlager's sponsorship of the All Blacks moved to a new position when Adidas took over the principal sponsorship. Steinlager has since become a major sponsor of the All Blacks and is even more committed to New Zealand's favourite team.

The 2004 "Unconditional" campaign clearly identifies the enduring relationship between Steinlager and the All Blacks. To reflect and reinforce this relationship, Steinlager has launched All Black icon Colin Mead's "Immortals", his selection of the all-time greatest past and present All Blacks.

New Zealand's highest-profile sports sponsorship is a successful, long-running partnership that will continue well into this millennium.

Steinlager and Yachting

Steinlager has been a force behind New Zealand yachting for more than 20 years.

Team New Zealand

Steinlager (and Lion Breweries) is one of the few companies to have supported every New Zealand America's Cup challenge.

Steinlager became involved in the America's Cup challenge contested in Fremantle, Perth in 1986 where $1 million was raised through the sale of Steinlager cans. New Zealand entered a 12 metre fibreglass yacht, KZ7, nicknamed Plastic Fantastic.

In 1988 Steinlager supported the next challenge for the Cup contested in San Diego, with KZ1, otherwise known as the Big Boat.

In 1992 New Zealand returned to contest the next America's Cup with NZL20 and, despite an extremely close competition, the Kiwis were unsuccessful.

In 1995 all the experience, hard work, finely tuned strategies and sheer Kiwi determination paid off when New Zealand won the America's Cup challenge of San Diego, with an outstanding 5–0 victory over Dennis Connor's Young America. Once again, Steinlager was a major sponsor of the team – one of the "Family of Five" sponsors.

With New Zealand first to see in the new millennium, the world was watching with greater interest than ever before. It was also the year that yachting's greatest prize was contested on the waters around Auckland. After an exciting challenger series, Team New Zealand repeated their 1995 performance with a stunning 5–0 victory this time over the Italian challenger, Prada. In typical Kiwi fashion, Russell Coutts handed over to Dean Barker to steer New Zealand to victory in race five. It was a successful defence of the America's Cup and the only non-American syndicate to have done so – a fantastic time for New Zealand and Steinlager!

In February 2001 Steinlager again confirmed its commitment to Team New Zealand as a member of the family of five for the 2003 challenge. Although Team NZ this time experienced a devastating loss, Steinlager remained a loyal supporter.

Whitbread Round the World Race

Steinlager proudly supported former Team New Zealand leader Sir Peter Blake throughout his career. In 1985 Blake competed in the prestigious Whitbread Round the World Race on the silver coloured Lion New Zealand. Blake again made headlines in 1988 when he built and raced around Australia, Steinlager One – the world's fastest ocean-going trimaran.

Success continued when Steinlager Two brought him victory in all six legs of the 1990 Whitbread Round the World Race.

Steinlager captures the emotions of national pride and the mood celebration in a nutshell – or in a beer bottle, as the case may be.

Due to the continual success of Steinlager's sponsorship partners, Kiwis have often found themselves celebrating New Zealand's finest victories with New Zealand's finest beer.

As New Zealand's largest premium beer, Steinlager has consistently represented success and achievement the good old Kiwi way: through grit and determination. This has been reinforced through their support for other New Zealand brands, teams and events, through their advertising and most importantly, through the beer itself.

Steinlager, New Zealand's Finest.

Ask anyone why they wear Swanndri garments and you'd think they were talking about an old friend. Affection runs deep for New Zealand's most iconic country clobber.

The market

There's a yarn or two in every Swannie. Ask any Kiwi if they've heard of Swanndri, and odds are they'll be able to describe to you a long woollen bush shirt with a lace up front.

Such is the universal awareness of Swanndri, developed over generations of service to New Zealand farming and the outdoors, that the name has become legendary in its own lifetime.

Research shows that Swanndri is still one of the nation's most recognised brands – way ahead of some of its high profile international competitors.

Swanndri is part of New Zealand's heritage and is about as Kiwi as you can get. The brand has a story that is unique and compelling; it is real, it is authentic and it performs.

Swanndri is believed to be the oldest apparel brand in New Zealand.

Grand Ole Swannie

The day grew crisp and chilly
But I didn't really care
Cause I was snug and warm now
In the best of outerwear

And when my man should finally wake
He won't mind that I've now gone
But he'll be spitting tacks and nails
Cause I'm now wearing his treasured 'swan'

- Excerpt from an entry in
"There's a yarn or two in every Swannie" competition.

History

In the 1800s, New Zealand was no place for the weak hearted. Pioneers and early settlers were at the mercy of New Zealand's tough terrain and unforgiving weather. The solution was as natural as the problem.

A man called William Broome entered the history books of New Zealand's pioneering years as he set about creating the country's first all-purpose, hardwearing, shower-proof bush shirt. With the establishment of the Bruce Woollen Mill in Milton in 1871, it became possible for woollen yarn to be woven to create such a garment.

Broome started with a basic design for a short-sleeved bush shirt. The shirt was then immersed in a drum filled with a secret water proofing formula and hung out to dry. The result was spectacular: a shirt that offered warmth in cold conditions, kept the wearer cool under the summer sun, and offered protection against the driving rain.

A legend was born

John McKendrick took the original design and added the hood, laced front and long sleeves that make the Swanndri so distinctive and practical. So in 1927 the deep olive green 103 "Swannie" became New Zealand's first choice for outdoor clothing.

A lifetime of yarns

My Swannies remind me of the good times. I got my first 103 for Scouts when I was just eight. Although it's now a little small for me, it has kept my two sons dry on many a camping trip – and it still has life in it! I bought my Swannie in the mid-1970s and those black and red checks have seen the world: rugby test matches, the Springbok tour, motorbiking through the South Island, camping trips in outback Australia and a Russian winter. I was even wearing it when my daughter was born!

- David Higgins, Publisher, New Zealand's Favourite Brands

Though the range of Swanndri garments has changed to keep pace with different fashion trends through the decades, the original 103 remains an ever popular garment. Whole generations of New Zealanders have grown up with their Swanndri bush shirt – a garment which is hardwearing enough to last a lifetime.

Swanndri today

Today Swanndri uses the finest New Zealand wools to weave a yarn more durable and hard-wearing than any competitor has been able to create. All garments are finished with a process that raises the surface to give a textured appearance and shower-proofed surface.

Beginning with the original little winner in 1913, the 103 bush shirt, the range of products on offer has continually grown in order to meet consumer demand. There are now a number of styles in the range, developed with varying weights and lengths to protect the wearer from the elements. These traditional products are made from wool from farms around New Zealand.

In 2002, a new lifestyle collection of jackets, vests and mid layer garments were introduced to the market. This range is dominated by products made from Swanndri's revolutionary Merino Flexiwool™, one of the smartest insulating fabrics on the planet. Thanks to the extra weight and finish of this incredible fabric, these classic yet fashionable styles promise all the characteristics of 100 per cent merino wool. The fabric is so soft that it can be worn next to the skin – winter or summer. Wearers have the flexibility to literally live in these versatile garments.

In winter 2004 a kids range was launched. Based on Swanndri's most popular classic adult styles, these hard-wearing little garments are tough enough to withstand the harshest battering that kids can give – the garment will be in the family for years!

The durability of Swanndri garments is mirrored in the brand itself, in its ideals and in its core company values. Such is the strength of the Swanndri brand that with the backing of private investors, two former managers of Alliance Textiles purchased the brand in June of 2004.

Julian Bowden, Gerard Kilpatrick, Chairman of the Board George Cowper and investors see the global potential for the brand, and are confident that the intrinsic value of Swanndri will be the essential elements in the company's future success.

"We want to take it to the farmers, hunters and fishermen in Australia, the United Kingdom and elsewhere," says Kilpatrick of the company vision.

There's a YARN or two in every SWANNIE.

SWANNDRI®
The New Zealand Legend.

With such high brand awareness, promotion is focused on product advertising.

Achievements

Beginning with the original 103 bush shirt developed in the pioneering days of New Zealand, the Swanndri brand has evolved into a range of clothing found on the backs of Kiwis all over the country – in fact all around the world – doing all kinds of things.

Some of these garments were chosen as the official clothing for the New Zealand team at the 2002 Winter Olympic Games in Salt Lake City.

In 2002, Swanndri was chosen as part of the Great New Zealand Red Series – a series of Westpac trust debit cards celebrating Kiwi culture.

Since 1913, Swanndri garments have been present at just about every New Zealand event that has taken place. From rugby test matches and picket lines to the land occupations and the Springbok tour, the old Swannie has been worn with pride.

For generations the products have been a trusted companion on all kinds of adventures and staff are constantly amazed by the stories people tell of their Swanndri garments. Recently, a competition was run in conjunction with *The Rural News* in which Swanndri wearers were asked to send in their best Swanndri yarn. The response to the competition reinforced just what a special place the brand has in the hearts and minds of New Zealanders.

Brand values

Swanndri has a very strong brand identity in New Zealand and the product is renowned for its quality and durability.

Swanndri New Zealand Ltd prides itself further on the fact that it has a mill based in Timaru that produces world-class fabrics. The garments are then manufactured in New Zealand and distributed to the many retailers who sell this iconic product.

Swanndri garments carry an unconditional guarantee of quality materials and workmanship. Not only does Swanndri have confidence in the physical components of the garment, but also in the heritage it is associated with.

When a customer purchases a Swanndri garment, they're buying part of New Zealand history – part of the Kiwi national character, and part of the Swanndri company pride and esteem.

Promotion

Swanndri is proud to have a strong association with New Zealand's premier agricultural event, the National Bank Young Farmer of the Year Competition. This sponsorship not only provides the opportunity to showcase the Swanndri range, but offers the chance to work with the young farmers on product development, ensuring the company is kept abreast of their needs in this ever-changing environment.

Swanndri has implemented a product programme for business and corporate solutions. Many organisations have taken advantage of the ability to supply quality garments that are all New Zealand made. Whether it is a promotional event or a corporate identity initiative, Swanndri garments will maximise the value to all its customers.

PLIMMERTON V BALTIC GREY V 100% NEW ZEALAND MERINO
FOR STOCKISTS, CALL 0800 800 446 WWW.SWANNDRI.CO.NZ

Recent evelopments

As it did in the early days, Swanndri continues to push boundaries in order to provide New Zealanders with clothing that reflects their unique lifestyles.

While the company now firmly focuses on the development of work wear styles for the rural and industrial sector, there is also a soundly established niche in the lifestyle market, focusing on products designed to meet the needs of New Zealander's looking for classic pieces of clothing from a brand they know they can trust.

The lifestyle products are developed with one simple goal in mind – to provide the ultimate in comfort and practicality for everyday wear. The range is based around timeless designs and colours for both men and women.

Developments in the work wear range include the launch of new garments featuring woollen fabric that meets daytime high visibility standards, as well as the introduction of technical linings for selected styles.

With a new company vision to take on the world, Bowden and Kilpatrick maintain that the roots of the brand will always remain proudly in New Zealand. This hard wearing, no-nonsense outdoor clothing is so deeply woven into the fabric of New Zealand culture that the nation teems with yarns of deeds done in a Swannie.

There is a legend in the weave of Swanndri, and that legend will continue to grow.

Throughout its history Telecom has been regularly assessed as one of the most trusted brands in New Zealand.

The early years

Telecom's heritage in New Zealand dates back to 1872 when the first telegraph line was installed between Wellington, Wanganui and New Plymouth. Over the succeeding 100 years a complex telecommunications network spread throughout the country, drawing together far-flung communities and enabling the rapid growth of commerce and industry.

In the mid-1980s major philosophical and technological change began to affect the industry. In 1987 Telecom was established as a State-owned enterprise. The move marked a substantial shift in the provision of telecommunications services in New Zealand away from state sector management towards a more business-focused administration.

In 1989 the industry was deregulated and telecommunications became a fully competitive market. In 1990 Telecom was sold to Bell Atlantic and Ameritech for NZ$4250 million, and a year later was listed on the New Zealand, Australian and New York stock exchanges.

It wasn't long before the new market environment made its presence felt. In the early 1990s the competitive focus was mainly on national calling services. For customers the effects were immediately rewarding as they began regularly to reap the advantages of falling prices and numerous special offers. Active competition soon spread to mobile services and across all business and residential markets as well.

Throughout this innovative period Telecom took a decisive and leading role in the development of sophisticated communications services within the country, and in the establishment of critical telecommunications connections between New Zealand and the rest of the world.

The look of the brand

The Telecom brand was launched in 1987 coinciding with the establishment of Telecom Corporation of New Zealand Limited.

The new logo featured three upward-shooting lines penetrating the centre of the Telecom "O". The lines represented the three channels of communication – copper wire, fibre optics and microwave radio. It was a logo which was to serve Telecom well for 16 years.

In September 2003 however, a new logo was introduced. It was designed to build on the heritage of the original, whilst reflecting a more modern digital characteristic. As with all famous logos which undergo revision, the change to the look of the Telecom brand was carefully managed to maintain continuity while embracing an exciting global future. The new logo was not so much revolutionary, as evolutionary.

Since the establishment of Telecom in 1987 the technological changes have been far-reaching and dramatic. The new logo is designed to be more in keeping with a brand which now provides a broadband network, wireless technology and the capacity to transmit packages of data across Telecom's Internet Protocol (IP) network.

In introducing a new logo it was important to retain the best of what had been achieved in the first one and a half decades, while at the same time moving into a more contemporary and forward-looking expression of the brand's identity.

Innovation

Of all the brands in New Zealand, Telecom is one of those most closely associated with one particular Kiwi characteristic: the ability to innovate.

As early as 1990 the company was the first to introduce phonecard technology and usher out the old era of coin payphones.

In 1993, with the launch of the Frame Relay service for high-speed data links, Telecom was once again first on the block with new broadband technology. Since its introduction 10 years ago, broadband has revolutionised the way New Zealanders communicate. With the subsequent launch of Telecom JetStream in 1999, the company took broadband communications to a totally new level altogether.

In 1995 Telecom effectively changed New Zealanders' clock-watching attitude to toll calls and put the enjoyment back into keeping in touch. With an innovative range of new services, special offers and imaginative pricing structures, average Kiwis were finally able to enjoy the freedom of talking to family and friends for as long as they liked without worrying unduly about cost. Subsequently, Telecom's campaign is credited with bringing about a significant change in New Zealanders' attitudes to the telephone.

1996 saw the launch of Xtra which grew very rapidly to become New Zealand's most popular internet service provider.

In 1999 the company launched a new nationwide payphone network using smartcard technology. In some airport locations, for instance, travellers are now able to connect their laptops to payphones to access their emails or websites.

In 2001 the introduction of Telecom's 027 mobile network expanded mobile coverage to more than 98 per cent of New Zealand's populated areas. Using the new generation GO27 mobile phones, Telecom customers are now able to check their Xtra emails as well as access other Xtra mobile services.

In 2002/2003, during the 2003 America's Cup challenge, over 400,000 people visited the Telecom Shed at Auckland's Viaduct Basin. In the shed visitors were exposed to displays showcasing the entire range of Telecom's modern telecommunications services including some of the extraordinary possibilities that communications technology holds for all of us in the future.

Famous ads we all remember

The Telecom brand has been behind several of New Zealand's most popular and memorable advertising campaigns. Commercials like "Little Boy – Are you lonesome tonight" (1985), "Life – Father and Son" (1996) and the "Animals" campaign, which started in 1988 and is still running today, have had particular impact on the nation's psyche and quickly became sentimental favourites for many New Zealanders.

Telecom campaigns have always been emotive, possessing the key elements to make New Zealanders laugh and, sometimes, cry. Key ingredients in the campaign successes have invariably been in the choice of memorable music and the unashamed use of emotion. And it's not only in New Zealand that the advertising has produced this desired result. Over the years Telecom's commercial campaigns have won numerous prestigious advertising awards from around the world.

But the campaign character that was perhaps the most famous and, in its own way, the most iconic, was "SPOT"

Keep in touch
Telecom

SPOT – the wonder dog

First arriving on screen in 1992, SPOT, a loveable Jack Russell terrier was a clever acronym for Services and Products of Telecom. SPOT's television antics for Telecom kept the nation entertained for nearly eight years.

In his career which lasted until 1998 SPOT starred in over 45 television commercials. His job was to represent Telecom's resourcefulness, reliability and efficiency. SPOT was required to speed around the city on a skateboard, get help in emergencies, leap from high buildings, balance on girders hundreds of feet in the air, ride a surfboard, parachute off cliffs and even swim among sharks while racing across the Tasman.

SPOT was a natural performer who loved every minute of working on ad shoots. In take after take he ran, jumped, swam, got sprayed with water and showered with soot, carried phones and, of course, rode his skateboard. In return the New Zealand public loved him. His ads consistently rated within the Top 5 Favourite Ads for the entire eight years they were on air.

SPOT received regular mail from children and fans all around the country and on occasion would visit local schools, IHC and the children at Starship Hospital. Sadly, SPOT died in 2000. For many New Zealanders and to those who worked closely with him over the years, he will always be remembered as SPOT, the wonder dog!

Brand positioning

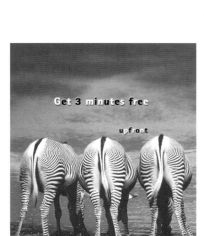

Get 3 minutes free
upfront

Telecom
NEW ZEALAND
Keep in touch.

For over 20 years one consistent expression of Telecom's brand position has been found in the words "keep in touch". "Keep in touch", which evolved from the old Post Office strapline, "Keeping in Touch", demonstrates the company's understanding of its primary role as the means by which New Zealanders stay in contact with family and friends; by which New Zealand businesses communicate with suppliers, customers, key stakeholders and each other; and by which New Zealand itself remains a contributory part of a global communications network.

While communications technology changes and evolves at a sometimes exponential rate, the core purpose expressed in these words remains the same. Despite the increasing sophistication and globalisation of telecommunications, keeping in touch is a fundamental human need which has remained central to mankind's social, intellectual and trading experience for thousands of years.

By its brand positioning, Telecom recognises this significant and important fact and its own centrally important responsibility for maintaining and improving our ability to communicate.

Through its branding and communications exercises over the years, Telecom has always tried to inspire New Zealanders to understand and think about both the human and economic importance of keeping in touch. And by regularly being the first to introduce innovative and future-focused technology, Telecom aims to retain the initiative as the communications company people will naturally choose when they want to keep in touch.

Present day

Telecom's focus today is to build preference and loyalty for its brand.

Telecom's advertising is designed to inspire people to see the almost limitless possibilities of communications technology, either for keeping in touch with friends and family, or running an efficient and successful business.

Telecom believes that helping to enrich the lives of its customers and significantly contributing to the prosperity of New Zealand are important aspects of its role as a communications provider. Telecom demonstrates this commitment through continuing development of technology, enthusiastic support of education and strong involvement in New Zealand sporting and art activities.

Telecom has grown up in New Zealand through a period of sometimes dramatic technological change. Often Telecom itself has been an integral and initiating part of that change. Today the company knows that its destiny lies in New Zealand. And as a New Zealand company, it will continue to contribute proudly to this country's future.

It's the end of one year   and the start of the next

19 c China per minute incl. GST

16 c Singapore, Hong Kong, & Taiwan per minute incl. GST

Dial 0161 first from your Telecom home phone

Time to get on the phone

Call friends and family over New Year with Telecom's 0161 service and you'll pay just 19c per minute including gst to China, and 16c per minute including gst to Singapore, Hong Kong and Taiwan. Even better, prices apply any time of day or night until midnight February 28.

Keepintouch Telecom

www.telecom.co.nz

Tip Top

At nearly 70 years old, it's a national icon, a famous corner and something we have all grown up with. Its real ice creamier Tip Top Ice Cream, and it's time to celebrate its story. So sit back, relax, and reminisce about the happy times spent devouring Tip Top ice cream, because this is the story of one of New Zealand's favourite brands.

How did it all begin?

In 1935 two gentlemen named Albert Hayman and Len Malaghan opened an ice cream parlour in Manners Street, Wellington. Little did they know, their humble store would soon catapult into a national icon.

The origin of the name Tip Top is a bit of folklore. Over a meal in a train dining car one evening, Hayman and Malaghan were discussing business when they overheard a fellow diner commenting that his meal was 'tip top'. The two men immediately decided that they would like to hear people say that about their ice cream, and so the name for their newly established ice cream business was born.

The popularity of Tip Top Ice Cream grew rapidly. In 1936 a second milk bar was opened in Wellington, and another in Dunedin. That same year, Tip Top Ice Cream was registered as a manufacturing company. By 1938, Tip Top was manufacturing its own ice cream and successfully operating stores in the lower half of the North Island, as well as in Nelson and Blenheim.

Encouraged by their success to date, Hayman and Malaghan turned their attention to Auckland, and in May 1938, Tip Top Ice Cream Company Auckland Limited was incorporated into their growing business, with capital of $15,000. Due to distribution difficulties during World War II, this was operated as a completely separate company to the Wellington Tip Top.

Tip Top Corner is born

It was November 1962 when the company sensed that New Zealand was ready for some ice cream hedonism! Their answer: the biggest and most technically advanced ice cream factory in the Southern Hemisphere, built right on Auckland's doorstep. At a cost of NZ£700,000, The Tip Top factory included staff houses, and 20 acres of farmland overlooking the Southern Motorway. The then Prime Minster Keith Holyoake was at the opening, eager to be the first to sample the creamy Tip Top Ice Cream that we still know and love today.

Like the Southern Motorway it was built aside, the Tip Top building speedily became a true New Zealand landmark and was the birthplace of the much coined namesake, "Tip Top Corner". For motorists travelling either north or south, Tip Top Corner marked the place on the motorway where work finished and the holidays began.

By 1964 the company had expanded to such an extent that its operations had spread throughout New Zealand. As well as the Mt Wellington plant, there were also manufacturing plants operating in Wellington, Nelson, Christchurch and Dunedin.

The Tip Top factory was originally a seasonal factory, operating to produce ice cream for the summer months only. Such icy treats sold for a shilling, and early innovations led to iconic brands such as Topsy, Jelly Tip, FruJu and Ice Cream Sundaes, some of which remain much-loved treats today. The overwhelming success of these products transformed the Mt Wellington site from a summer-centered seasonal factory into a 24 hour, 365 day operation. The factory's first foreman, Bertha Sutton, employed up to 80 girls to keep up with consumer demand at the height of the season. Now in 2004, Tip Top employs 380 staff, and produces over 40 million litres of ice cream per annum.

The classics are born

In retrospect, Tip Top Ice Cream cites an early culture of innovation as one of the keys to the company's longevity. Tip Top started the ball rolling with quarts (1 litre); pints (600ml) and bulk ice cream for dairies, all packed in cardboard boxes. However, it didn't take long for the first single-serve, novelty ice cream product to hit the freezers. Eskimo Pie, still a popular multi-pack flavour today, was Tip Top's first novelty product and was initially produced at Tip Top's Dunkerron Avenue factory in Epsom, Auckland in the early 1950s. Then came the "classics". First there was Topsy, a chocolate covered, vanilla ice cream creation, complete with a revolutionary idea for the time: a stick!

Tip Top soon realised they had struck a chord with consumers, and soon after, Jelly Tip, which sold for a sixpence (5c) was created. Jelly Tip was fashioned by a team of creative-minded chemists who had been briefed to develop an ice cream children could eat when out and about. Their inspiration came from a popular children's dessert of the time – jelly and ice cream.

Jelly Tip transcended time when it celebrated its 50th birthday in 2001, remaining one of the top selling ice creams in New Zealand. Not so surprising when, at the age of 99, George Hayman (former director of Tip Top Ice Cream) still walks to his local dairy to fetch a Jelly Tip. 250 Jelly Tips are produced every minute at Tip Top, and over 150 million have been sold since it launched.

Toppa, Trumpet and FruJu were added to the Tip Top portfolio during the 1950s and 60s, as was the famous 2-litre plastic bowl – a sales hit for Tip Top and a revolution in the ice cream industry. The 1970s saw the launch of R2D2, the much-loved Star Wars robot-turned-ice-block, and New Zealand's first solid chocolate-centered ice cream: Choc Bar. Still

New Zealand's number one novelty product, with 2.7 million sold every year, Choc Bar was an instant favourite for New Zealanders. Popsicle ice blocks, originally called TT2s, were also launched in the 1970s, but it was the arrival of the Popsicle Band in the 1980s that really got the Popsicle brand grooving. With a recent makeover, the Popsicle band have made guest appearances at such events as the Teddy's Bear Picnic and the Santa Parade, never failing to put a smile on their fans' faces.

In the 1980s single-serve Crofters cheesecakes changed the shape of New Zealand's dessert landscape and Rocky Road turned a classic confectionery into an ice cream novelty that would be just as popular 20 years later. New Zealanders also saw Rachel Hunter appear for the first time on television in the 1980s. At 15 years of age, she starred in her first ever TV commercial for Trumpet.

Tip Top's strategy – innovate, innovate, innovate

Tip Top Corner is home to some of the world's smartest ice cream making advances.

"Innovation has been a keynote at Tip Top from the beginning," says current managing director Ray O'Connor. The company is internationally recognised as a leader in ice cream product development and marketing, operating an in-house "think tank" in which young, creative marketers are encouraged to manage ideas through to commercial reality.

Some of Tip Top's most famous innovations are Memphis Meltdown and Moritz Extreme. In 1997, Memphis Meltdown took the ice cream world by surprise, with an award-winning layer of caramel sandwiched between two layers of chocolate. The gruff looking Southern American Sheriff launched Memphis Meltdown Gooey Caramel on New Zealand televisions when he was bribed with such a treat by a speeding motorist. Tip Top was also taken by surprise when over 2 million were sold in the first three months. Due to the unparalleled success of Memphis Meltdown Caramel, Grand ol' Gooey Chocolate followed in 1999, and Momma's Gooey Raspberry in 2001. Memphis Meltdown won the premier award at the Massy University Food Awards in 2000 and Memphis Meltdown Raspberry won the best product award at the 2002 International Ice Cream Consortium annual conference. All three Memphis Meltdown products are still star performers, and Tip Top has recently extended the brand by launching the first Memphis Meltdown in a bar.

The next major breakthrough for Tip Top, and the ice cream world, was Moritz Extreme in 2000 – the world's first ice cream on a stick containing large chunks of truffle and praline. Some of the biggest ice cream players had been trying – and failing – for years to develop the processing equipment that would enable ice cream with large inclusions to be manufactured.

The code was finally cracked when Tip Top's research and development manager at the time, John Tucker, had a sudden brainwave. Wanting to capture his idea in the manner of true Kiwi ingenuity, John developed a prototype out of an old pizza-base carton. "Project Pizza Board" was duly formed, and the Tip Top Engineers and Research & Development team spent two years developing the Pizza Board equipment.

The Pizza Board technology was patented around the world, and in 2001 Tip Top licensed the prototype machine to a US maker of food processing equipment to earn royalties on sales of the machines worldwide.

Growth through export

Tip Top has been exporting ice cream since the 1970s. The creamy ice cream manufactured from high quality fresh New Zealand ingredients is shipped to many countries including Japan, Australia, Pacific Islands, Singapore, Malaysia and Taiwan, Indonesia and Russia. Export sales currently make up 30 per cent of business and are now experiencing strong growth. Being part of the Fonterra Group, the world's largest marketer of dairy products, also opens up huge doors in the export market for Tip Top.

In early 2000, Tip Top began selling Hokey Pokey ice cream, specially reformulated for Japanese taste buds. This was the first time Hokey Pokey had been sold outside of Australasia, and became a huge hit. The Japanese not only love Hokey Pokey, but many other Kiwi favourites such as Neopolitan, Chocolate, Strawberry and Cookies and Cream also tickle their tastebuds.

All ice cream for the Japanese market is made in the Christchurch factory, which was given a major upgrade in 1990 to accommodate ice cream production for this country. From the factory, it is trucked in special frozen containers to Lyttleton Harbour and then shipped to ports throughout Japan.

New Zealand's favourite ice cream is also a favourite throughout the South Pacific. Since the early 1970s, Tip Top has been exporting its range of novelties, take-home, scoop and dessert products to the many South Pacific Nations ranging from French Polynesia to Papua New Guinea.

Tip Top factory 40th anniversary

November 2002 marked the celebration of a milestone – the Tip Top factory's 40th Birthday. Credit was certainly due considering it had pumped out 2 billion ice creams on sticks and 1 billion litres of real-ice creamier Tip Top ice cream, all of which had made their way onto dessert spoons and sticky fingers in every sunny corner of New Zealand.

Tip Top celebrated its 40th birthday by opening Licky Lane, presenting the Tip Top iceCONE award, and launching the Tip Top website, www.tiptop.co.nz. Licky Lane was the name given to the new factory tour room which, complete with wondrous ice cream trees, giant slices of chair shaped multi-flavoured ice cream and a candy striped floor, quickly became one of the most popular food technology classrooms in New Zealand.

500,000 people had already visited the Tip Top factory since it opened, but Licky Lane gave children the opportunity to not only learn all about the history of ice cream in New Zealand, how it is made and how new products are developed, but to do so in a fun filled fantasy environment. A further benefit of Licky Lane is that the $1 admission is donated to the Starship children's hospital.

Tip Top's IceCONE award revealed that people in Nelson/Marlborough are the country's biggest lickers of cone ice cream. More ice cream cones per head of population are sold in Nelson/Marlborough than anywhere else in the country. In fact, every person in the province consumes 6.46 litres of ice cream each year. No surprises there – Nelson is the undisputed sunshine capital of the world.

This just goes to show that ice cream is still a very popular offering in New Zealand. Our per capita consumption is second in the world, and we Kiwis lead in consumption of ice cream scooped in a cone.

Tip Top today

Nearly 70 years have passed since two Kiwi blokes with a passion for ice cream opened their first parlour. Today, the company is still known for its great products and delicious creamy ice cream that everyone loves.

Thanks to the company's innovation and creativity, Tip Top ice cream is synonymous with childhood; of long summer days and popping down to the dairy for an ice creamier treat. Tip Top's success is thus evident because it is deeply embedded in Kiwi culture, heritage, and of course, New Zealanders' tastebuds.

From humble beginnings in Mangatainoka to a strong national brand,
Tui is a little brewery with a big reputation.

A Proud history

Tui Brewery was established in Mangatainoka in 1889 by entrepreneur Henry Wagstaff. His dream was to supply "export quality brews to beer drinkers around the colony" and his ales quickly earned a reputation for excellence.

Legend has it that in early 1889, Henry Wagstaff stopped for a cup of tea on the banks of the Mangatainoka River and found the water made the finest cuppa he'd ever tasted. He decided on the spot it would be the ideal place to build a brewery.

He purchased the land that same year and set about excavating what was to become the cellar of the brewery (now a favourite stop for tourists). His brewing skills were such that the cry "Make mine a Wagstaff" was soon heard throughout the taverns in and around Pahiatua. The full-bodied, smooth malt taste of his beer found favour with worker and manager alike.

Henry Wagstaff may have sold his beloved brewery in 1903 but his name and the recipe he handed down still take pride of place at the Tui Brewery. Henry Cowan, the eldest son of a pioneering family from Cornwall, bought the brewery in 1903. He renamed it North Island Brewing Company Ltd and set about plans for expansion. By the following year the company had recorded the princely profit of four pounds and won its first award for Tui East India Pale Ale at the Palmerston North A & P Show.

This marked the turning point for the brewery and sales grew steadily over the next decade, reaching 2271 hogsheads by 1914. In 1923 it was renamed once again, this time as Tui Brewery. With an eye to the changing market, Tui established a bottling plant in Wellington and started building a new seven-storey brick brew tower to meet future demand. The move showed great foresight and by the mid-1930s the brewery was selling more than 100 dozen quart bottles per annum.

Tui was taken over by DB Breweries in 1969. A massive modernisation program was undertaken so that demand could be met. In 1988 Tui was launched in 375ml cans and in 1994 Tui moved into the bottle known as the stubbie.

The name – Tui, East India Pale Ale

The name East India Pale Ale originated in England last century. Beer exported to India was unpasteurised, which allowed secondary fermentation to occur in the barrel on the long boat trip to the colonies of East India.

It soon became a favourite because its natural CO_2 created a brew with an effervescent character. More than 100 years on, Tui East India Pale Ale is as popular as it was when Henry Wagstaff brewed the beer by hand and delivered it around the district by horse and cart.

The Journey

For decades Tui was a well-kept secret in the hotels throughout the Wairarapa and Hawkes Bay region. Tui established itself as their beer, accepted by generations, as they all knew that their beer came from the brewery just down the road. Any visitor to the region would soon see how popular the brand was within the local community. Ask any local what their favourite drop was and the answer will undoubtedly be "Tui of course".

Tui's expansion outside the Wairarapa and Hawkes Bay region started in the early 1990s, with many students from these areas studying at Massey University. Hotels soon learnt that the drop from Mangatainoka had a strong and passionate following from these young yet wise consumers. Tui soon became entrenched as the beer for the students at New Zealand's largest university. Other watering holes around the Manawatu and Taranaki region soon picked up on this trend and helped Tui expand into these regions.

It was during this time that Tui developed its "Yeah Right" campaign. Yeah Right was developed to reflect the provincial humour and ideals that the brand stood for – that of not taking themselves too seriously and always having a light hearted approach to any situation. The Yeah Right campaign was often seen to take the mickey from a local perspective, with messages like "Let's go to Auckland for the Holidays" and "Popping down to the pub for a few quiets". The first Tui billboards were in Manawatu and Hawkes Bay and were backed up with a very effective Yeah Right TV advert that ran in these regions.

During the 1990s much of the promotional activity focused on rewarding loyal drinkers in the home markets of Wairarapa and Hawkes Bay. To the locals the little brewery just down the road was an asset and an icon. Mangatainoka, while unknown to the wider population, was the centre of every Tui drinker's world and commonly referred to as Beer Heaven. It was not uncommon to see cars stopping outside the Tui Brewery so the occupant could pay homage to the Tui Brewery.

Throughout much of the late 1990s Tui continued to expand in the lower North Island, billboards became a regular feature within the region and a reference point for locals. In 1995, Tui brought TV time in the Wellington region that meant a Yeah Right billboard and TV campaign was now operating in all of the lower North Island.

During the 1990s, most promotional activity was based around the Tui brewery, with prizes such as Beer Heaven and the Big Bash all involving trips for you and your mates to the infamous Tui Brewery. Students also became a greater driving force for the brand, with both Massey and Victoria avid supporters of the Tui brands.

You can't keep a good thing down. (Or in the lower North Island!) In late 1998 Tui expanded into Taupo, Waikato and the Bay of Plenty. Pockets of avid Tui drinkers developed in areas north of Taupo along with expansion of Tui TV advertising and billboards. Limited activity targeted new Tui drinkers, while also supporting loyal drinkers.

Recent times

In 2000, consumer excitement about the beer from down country was so strong that Tui expanded its advertising and promotional activity into Auckland and Northland. The move into Auckland was one of relief for many Tui fans who had migrated to the big smoke. Finally their beer was here!

TV advertising and billboards were now spread from Whangarei to Wellington, New Plymouth to Gisborne, with promotions a regular occurrence in hotels, bars, bottle stores and supermarkets throughout the North Island. In 2002, TV advertising, billboards and product distribution expanded into the South Island. For the first time ever Tui was a national brand.

2002 saw a dramatic change in the way in which Tui communicated with its drinkers – Tui became involved with New Zealand's most widely supported sport – rugby. Tui became the sponsor for the Hurricanes Super 12 team and the Hawkes Bay, Taranaki, Wairarapa and Wellington NPC teams. This change was reflective of the significant position that the brand had reached in the lower North Island region.

Taking over such high-profile rugby properties gave Tui a position in the market that the brand had only once but dreamed of. Sponsorship had now become a very important component of the Tui marketing campaign.

Tui also took over the Sky TV broadcasting rights for the 2002 Super 12 and NPC. Tui now had a platform that gave the brand exposure to nearly every male in New Zealand. In 2003 Tui also gained the sponsorship of the Blues Franchise and the Auckland NPC teams. Tui now has a strong association with Super 12 teams, NPC and numerous club rugby teams throughout the North Island.

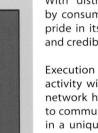

Tui's position on rugby is not so much about the serious nature of the game, but more about the occasion rugby creates, allowing guys to interact with each other (and Tui of course). It's about rugby supporters, not rugby heads.

TV advertising has played a crucial role in the brands development as a mass medium that can show the Tui drinker's world. All ATL communication is based around Tui's role in the drinker's world and stories are always told in a hard-case, intelligent and irreverent manner.

The "Yeah Right" billboard campaign is Tui's communication hero through which much of the Tui brand attitude is delivered. Now into its 8th year, the campaign remains fresh and topical because of the constantly changing messages. The hard case spin on the everyday situation allows a broad number of drinkers to gain a humorous insight into the brand, its ideals and themselves.

The drinker

Loyal drinkers are the heart of the brand; they have grown up with the brand and are avid promoters of Tui.

Mates, students and those with a zest for life have always exemplified the Tui drinker. For them life is all about the boys getting together and

spinning a few yarns. Tui is the social glue that holds the guys together, any BBQ, student party, 21st would not be the same without the boy's favourite drop – Tui.

Students have always played an important role with regard to Tui. From the initial days where Tui was involved with the students at Massey, the brand is now supportive of students at all of New Zealand's major tertiary institutions. They have become our ambassadors who spread the Tui word throughout New Zealand.

Distribution and promotions

With distribution often driven by consumer demand, Tui takes pride in its position as a worthy and credible national beer.

Execution of promotional activity with a wide distribution network has always enabled Tui to communicate its brand values in a unique and humorous way. Using clothing, gnomes or floppy hats, promotions have always involved items and activities that offer the drinker something a bit different.

Point of sale has remained consistent with the message that has been portrayed through the TV and billboards – that of hard-case, intelligent and irreverent wit.

Home market

Tui will never forget its roots (like any true New Zealander) and the brand still holds a special place for Tui drinkers in Hawkes Bay and Wairarapa. Tui continues to support these regions through relationships with the Tararua District Council, by supporting Hawkes Bay Anniversary every year, as well as sponsoring numerous local rugby clubs, the Tauherenikau Races, the Hawkes Bay Magpies and the Wairarapa Bush NPC team.

The road ahead

A successful marketing campaign over the past 10 years has seen Tui develop from a small local beer to one of the most popular New Zealand beers. Tui will continue its strong marketing campaign and the brand will continue to grow in the future.

More than just a humble loaf of bread, delicious and nutritious
Vogel's has grown to become one of New Zealand's favourites.
Kiwis won't leave home without it.

The History of Dr Vogel's

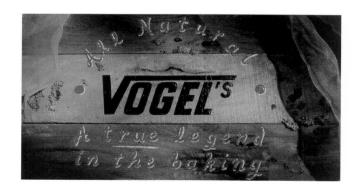

In 1902 in a small town on the outskirts of Basel, Switzerland, a unique man by the name of Alfred Vogel was born. During his childhood, his parents encouraged him to embrace natural healing and ways to live in harmony with nature to benefit both man and environment.

This early education propelled Alfred Vogel on a lifelong quest for wellbeing, and assisted him in the cultivation of a health food empire that spans almost a century.

Equipped with the unsullied optimism of youth, Dr Vogel opened his first health food store in 1920. Over the ensuing years, more people began to seek his professional dietary advice and after witnessing remarkable results, he was compelled to explore the field of herbal remedies in greater depth. His study included the work of other health authorities of the time such as Dr Ragnar Berg and Dr Bircher-Benner.

In 1952 his ideas entered popular consciousness with the publication of The Little Doctor. Following the world-wide success of this book, Dr Vogel has grown to be a respected source of knowledge on healthy living.

Vogel's was first baked by Klissers Farmhouse Bakery in the early 1960s, and originated as 'the first true alternative to white bread in New Zealand'. During the brand's formative stages, Vogel's was prominent in the Auckland region, however as demand grew so too did distribution throughout the North Island.

In 1990 the Klissers Farmhouse Bakery was sold to Goodman Fielder New Zealand Limited, the current manufacturer of Vogel's. In New Zealand today, Vogel's is the market leader in heavy health loaf bread, baking over 10 million loaves per annum.

A good brand with a great taste

A favourite brand is like a best friend – it will incite emotions and spark happy memories associated with times of enjoyment. A favourite brand will also constantly adapt to meet the changing needs of the consumer, yet remaining true to its original promise.

Vogel's original promise was to provide the first healthy alternative to white bread made from 100 per cent natural ingredients.

Already one of New Zealand's leading icon brands with Original Mixed Grain loaf, Vogel's introduced Wholemeal & Sesame and Light Grain to the range in the mid 1980s.

The best thing since sliced bread – Vogel's arrives in New Zealand

Founded on Dr Vogel's original Swiss recipe and made from carefully selected natural ingredients, Vogel's bread has become legendary throughout New Zealand for its unique taste, heavy grain texture and all-too-familiar smell.

New Zealand has Niels Stevns to thank for bringing Vogel's to their toasters, lunchboxes and pantries. In 1947, Danish-born Niels Stevns arrived in Australia together with his young bride, his brother Knud, and his parents. After a relentless illness, Knud was taken by his father to seek help from renowned Swiss naturopath Dr Alfred Vogel. It was this significant meeting that lead to Dr Vogel sharing his award winning mixed grain bread recipe with Niels Stevns.

Vogel's soon became the pioneer of mixed grain bread in Australia and based on its success, Stevns believed there was an opportunity to introduce the bread to New Zealand.

In 2002 Vogel's launched Vogel's Select, a premium range of indulgent breads that included Organic, Wheatfree and Fruit Bread. Following the success of this launch, Spelt & Rye and Muesli were introduced to the Vogel's Select range in 2004. Vogel's Select Summer Citrus Zest, a limited release summer loaf, was launched in September 2004.

As any trusted friend will do, Vogel's has continued to be true to its promise; to this day, the Original Mixed Grain loaf remains the number one bestseller in the range[1].

Pack design

Vogel's very distinctive and unique packaging design has stood the test of time, with the current packaging still featuring elements originating from the Stevns family. The stripes on the packet "ponytails" have become an icon in themselves and the original Vogel's logo and portrait of Dr Vogel himself still features prominently on current packaging. The most marked change, however, is that the general design has softened over time, transforming the perception of Vogel's from a staunch health bread to one with a more mainstream appeal.

Manufacturing milestones

The Vogel's Original Mixed Grain loaf is still baked to the same recipe as pioneered by Dr Vogel himself.

The most significant change to formulations began after Goodman Fielder bought Klissers Farmhouse Bakery. Innovation saw the introduction of new varieties such as Sunflower & Barley, Honey & Oatbran and Soy & Linseed to the Vogel's range. These were baked in an unlidded tin, with a less dense texture than the original Vogel's recipe and whilst still remaining true to Vogel's unique taste, broadened the appeal of the popular bread.

Homesick Kiwi's miss their Vogel's – award-winning advertising

And its you that I love
And it's true that I love
And its love not given lightly

    --- Chris Knox

To the soundtrack of "Not Given Lightly" by Kiwi artist Chris Knox, the Bread for New Zealander's campaign, launched in 2000, was a reminder that wherever you are in the world, there is nothing quite like Vogel's. No one can deny that the travel bug is infectious, but homesick Kiwis who are thousands of miles from home will do almost anything for a slice of Vogel's.

The memorable TV advertisements featured some very hungry Kiwis doing desperate things for a slice of their favourite bread – smuggling it out of the country, customs officials confiscating it, only to devour it themselves, and people stashing their sought after loaf while overseas. For New Zealanders the award winning campaign reaffirmed a sense of pride in an iconic and much loved brand.

Awards

Vogel's won the NZ Marketing Magazine Marketing Award for best campaign in the FMCG category in August 2003. The success of the Vogel's brand and the Vogel's Select range were key contributors to winning the award.

Vogel's also won a Silver Effie Award for Advertising Effectiveness in September 2002 for the 'Bread for New Zealander's campaign.

Vogel's munchers and crunchers

Vogel's continues to bring new and innovative loaves to the market and has a very loyal following among its consumers, who if sales are any indication, are increasingly passionate about munching their way through their bread of choice.

Vogel's bread reminds New Zealanders of what it's like to be a true Kiwi and there is simply no substitute in New Zealand or internationally.

[1] AC Nielsen Current MAT TKA data to 5 October 04

Providing New Zealanders with a century of good health.

At Sanitarium, the goal has always been to link good health with a good diet. This objective has been achieved through the example set by the Battle Creek Sanitarium in Michigan, USA. Here, doctors successfully introduced natural remedies and simple unprocessed foods into the diets of their patients. As far back as the 1890s, the Sanitarium doctors were advocating healthier eating, drinking fresh water and exercising in the fresh air to help people "learn to stay well".

In December of 1900, Edward Halsey, a Seventh-day Adventist and baker trained at the Battle Creek Sanitarium, came to New Zealand to prepare healthy food for a small health retreat. He began making batches of Granola, New Zealand's first breakfast cereal, Caramel Cereals (a coffee substitute) and wholemeal bread in a humble wooden shed in the Christchurch suburb of Papanui. These products became known as Sanitarium Health Foods. Demand began to grow outside the health retreat as patients wished to continue eating these products, even when they were fit and well.

Since Edward Halsey formed the business, the Sanitarium Health Food Company has remained at the forefront of healthy eating. The company was the initial advocator of vegetarianism as a healthy diet option long before it was trendy to do so, and was the first to introduce the concept of the health food shop to New Zealanders.

Today, Sanitarium is proudly 100 per cent New Zealand owned and has developed a reputation for manufacturing quality health and vegetarian food products – a position that has been rewarded by the strong trust consumers demonstrate toward Sanitarium products.

Of the many healthy products that Sanitarium proudly attaches to its name, there is one that has become deeply embedded in the history and culture of New Zealand. The name calls to mind those halcyon days of childhood; of breakfasts around the family table and school lunches in brown paper bags. Homesick Kiwis hunger for it; thousands of miles from home, they remember the familiar taste, smell and texture that embodies this brand, and all that is New Zealand.

That brand is Weet-Bix.

The market

Weet-Bix is a special part of the New Zealand psyche. It is one brand that can boast a history shared with generations of New Zealanders in being a proud part of many childhood breakfasts. Weet-Bix is more than just a breakfast cereal – it has become part of being a Kiwi. As the jingle goes, Kiwi kids are Weet-Bix kids.

Weet-Bix has the largest market share within the cereal category and now produces 7 million packs per year. One in four bowls of cereal at breakfast time are Weet-Bix, and the cereal also features in 60 per cent of New Zealand pantries.

History

The Sanitarium Health Food Company first manufactured Weet-Bix in the Sanitarium Papanui factory, Christchurch in 1930. At the time, there was only one other wheat biscuit in the market called Granose - also produced by Sanitarium in the early 1900s. Weet-Bix proved to be a more popular product and was described in comparison to Granose as the "sweetened wheat" biscuit. It was not long before Weet-Bix completely replaced the Granose offering, and began its journey to becoming New Zealand's most popular breakfast cereal.

Achievements

This cereal is a true success story. What you see is what you get with Weet-Bix, which is why it is ranked the number one seller in the cereal aisle. Weet-Bix was voted "first equal" in the Best Breakfast category for the Children's Food Awards in October 2003. Criteria for this category were

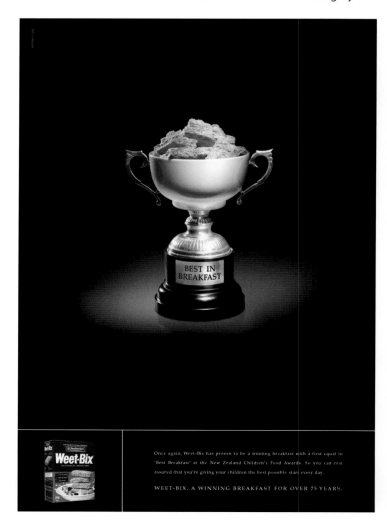

defined as "Something that makes you feel your child is leaving home with a well-filled engine", in which Weet-Bix shared the number one spot with Fleming's Porridge. The awards, a Green Party initiative were established to help counter the effects of obesity in young people. Also supporting the event is a range of groups including 5+ A Day, the Maori Women's Welfare League, Safe Food Campaign, Parent's Centre and Fight the Obesity Epidemic, with the Green Party planning to make the awards a powerful annual event.

Not only a winning cereal for kids, the annual Weet-Bix Tryathlon series is another success story worth noting. The Weet-Bix Tryathlon is one of the most popular children's multi-sports events, reaching a record of over 16,000 entrants in 2003. The Weet-Bix Tryathlon started in 1993, with a single Auckland event and has since gone from strength to strength. Entering its twelfth year in 2004, the event is now held in Auckland, Napier, Christchurch, Nelson, Dunedin, Tauranga and Wellington. The 2004 series started with a special invitation to be a part of the opening ceremony of the World Triathlon Championships in Queenstown.

The Weet-Bix Tryathlon is not about getting across the line first - it's about getting out there, having a go and achieving your personal best, which is why all participants are rewarded with a medal at the finish line. The event is open to everyone aged between eight and fifteen years and participants can enter on their own – meaning they complete the swim, bike and run, or they can participate as part of a team.

The product

Sitting amongst the many other cereal offerings, Weet-Bix is the gold star standard in nutrition. It is a simple product that is simply good for you! Sanitarium also produces many variants of Weet-Bix including Vita-Bix, Weet-Bix Hi Bran and Weet-Bix plus Oat Bran. In these, the Weet-Bix base is used as a medium to carry extra ingredients with particular nutritional advantages. The newest addition to the Weet-Bix family is Weet-Bix Crunch. Crunch has recently launched in New Zealand offering smaller wheat biscuits covered in natural honey. A honey sweetened product, the purpose of Crunch is not to offer extra nutritional benefit, but is an answer to a consumer demand – especially in the teen market - for a sweeter/tastier breakfast cereal that still delivers all the goodness and nutrition of the Weet-Bix base.

Recent developments

The original Weet-Bix recipe developed in 1926 has virtually remained unchanged. Amazingly, in today's market which is full of highly processed and "extruded energy cereals" that are often high in sugar, Weet-Bix stands tall as the most natural and unprocessed breakfast product on the shelf. Accordingly, Weet-Bix has more or less maintained the exact recipe for 75 years.

In 1961, new machinery was installed in the Pah Road Sanitarium factory, allowing Weet-Bix to be machine-made and untouched by the human hand – a very significant development for the time. Today's manufacturing of Weet-Bix of course involves modern machinery, but still Weet-Bix can claim "Nothing new, nothing added". Weet-Bix is simply a great taste that Kiwis have loved for generations.

Promotions

Weet-Bix has been a major sponsor of the All Blacks for 6 years and in 2003, the company leveraged its association with this high profile sports team to help benefit Project K - a charitable trust that designs programmes dedicated to building self-esteem and giving life-direction to at-risk teenagers.

To commemorate the centenary of All Blacks' Test Rugby (1903–2003), Weet-Bix launched a limited edition All Blacks Centenary tin. As part of the celebration of the tin launch, Weet-Bix created a special silver edition of the tin, which was signed by the entire All Blacks' squad. The tin was made available for public purchase via an on-line auction, which eventually sold for just under $5,000. The entire amount donated to Project K.

Brand values

The Weet-Bix brand is everything New Zealanders admire about being a Kiwi. It has a raw honesty that, deep down, everyone respects. It is unpretentious, trustworthy, and solid; a quiet achiever that only rises to the occasion when the time calls. The brand will keenly accept any challenge with a rugged and positive can-do attitude.

Weet-Bix never denigrates others and above all it is true to itself and the people who enjoy it.

SINCE 1896

No one goes further than Whittaker's to make the finest chocolate in New Zealand

Whittaker's was founded in 1896 by James Henry Whittaker, who had immigrated to New Zealand from Macclesfield, England.

James Henry began manufacturing confectionery on a small level from his home in Addington, Christchurch. As a small business owner, Whittaker was essentially a one-man band, splitting his time between the product manufacturing process and door-to-door sales of his chocolates.

In 1913, the business was moved to Wellington and James Henry established a partnership with his two sons, Ronald and James, to form J. H. Whittaker & Sons.

The business prospered over the ensuing years and in 1931, Woolworths Australia established shops in Auckland, Wellington, Christchurch and Dunedin. Whittaker's was selected to be their main supplier of a wide range of confectionery, which proved to be a significant boost for the company.

In July 1937, the business was turned into a limited liability company. The Whittaker's family has proudly continued to own and cultivate the business, driving it successfully into the twenty first century. Today the company is controlled by Andrew and Brian Whittaker, the third generation of Whittaker's owners.

Throughout Whittaker's history the objective of the business has always been:

"To produce high quality, premium tasting confectionary at an affordable price."

In 1969, Whittaker's moved its factory from central Wellington to the current location in Porirua. All of Whittaker's range is produced from the one factory and the products are distributed throughout New Zealand, Australia and Singapore.

Although the Whittaker's factory is in Porirua, the very first step in making Whittaker's chocolate actually begins thousands of miles away in West Africa where the cocoa beans are grown.

From bean to bar

Whittaker's is the only major chocolate manufacturer in New Zealand that controls the whole manufacturing process – from the smallest of cocoa beans to the tastiest of chocolate bars.

Whittaker's are proud of their premium quality chocolate, and Ghanaian cocoa beans are selected because they are among the highest quality beans in the world. The cocoa pods are harvested and each contain around 20 – 40 beans nestled in white pulp. The beans are allowed to ferment

for several days before a week of sun drying to remove excess moisture. The beans are then bagged and shipped to the Whittaker's factory in Porirua.

From the New Zealand factory, the beans are carefully roasted and the characteristic chocolate aroma and colour of the Whittaker's chocolate starts to develop. Roasting also loosens the outer hulls and the husk of the bean so that they can be separated easily. The beans are then cracked and the hulls blown away – a process called winnowing.

The nibs (the inside of the beans) are carefully blended to form the characteristic Whittaker's chocolate flavour. The cocoa nib is then ground and heat pressure is applied, causing the cell walls to break down, melt and produce a liquid chocolate. This occurs because the cocoa bean is approximately 50 per cent solid (cocoa liquid) and 50 per cent fat (cocoa butter) so when the nib is ground, it turns into liquid.

The next stage is refining. Cocoa butter, sugar and milk powder (for some recipes) are added to the liquid chocolate. The refining process crushes the particles to micron size, improving the texture of the chocolate. The resulting product is then ready for the last stages of production, transforming the cocoa beans into Whittaker's premium tasting chocolate.

The chocolate is tempered so that it begins to harden for its final stage of moulding. Poured into the Whittaker's mould and cooled quickly, the chocolate bar is removed and wrapped at a high speed. Automatic carton filling ensures an efficient packing operation.

Only the best for a much loved chocolate bar

Whittaker's follow strict codes of quality control throughout the entire manufacturing process, ensuring that all products are of the highest quality and have that premium Whittaker's taste.

Because of this commitment to quality control, Whittaker's has developed into a major New Zealand chocolate company. Consumers have come to recognise and appreciate the quality of Whittaker's chocolate.

Chocolate to die for

Whittaker's is most famous for the Peanut Slab chocolate bar. This

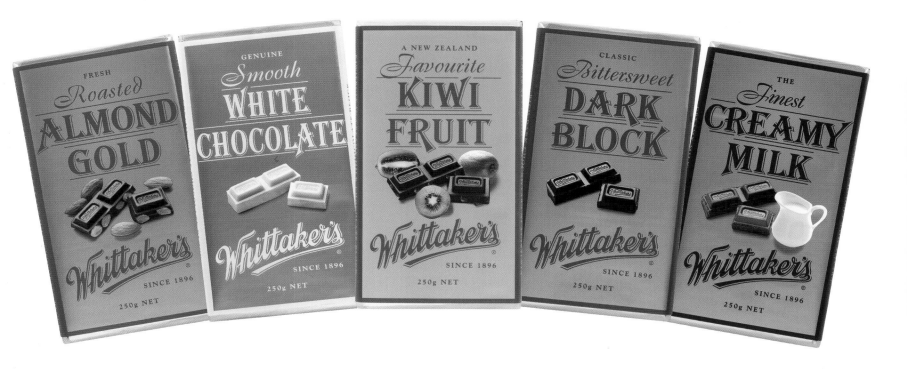

chocolatey, peanuty treat was first launched in the early 1950s in an unwrapped form and again in 1984 in its current wrapped form. The product has become one of New Zealand's most iconic brands and is still one of the best selling chocolate bars in the country today.

In recent years, the Whittaker's range of products has expanded significantly. The Slab chocolate bar range has increased from the original Whittakers Peanut Slab to include a Raisin and Peanut Slab, an Almond Gold Slab and Hazelnut Slabs. More recently the Coconut Slab variety has been added.

In a major move for Whittaker's in the mid-1990s, a 250-gram Peanut Block product was launched. This was quickly followed by the fruit and nut, hazelnut, creamy milk, almond gold and dark Block varieties. In subsequent years, further ranges have been added, including varieties of white chocolate.

There are now 18 varieties in total and the development of the Whittaker's block range has been hugely successful. Whittaker's now hold a strong position in this very competitive market.

The Whittaker's product strategy has also evolved into the premium end of the market with smaller pieces of chocolate, ideally suited for moments of relaxation with a cup of coffee or tea.

The wrapped Sante products were launched in 2002 and have proved very popular for those moments when just a small piece of chocolate is needed. Unique to Whittaker's, the Sante products have become particularly prevalent with female consumers.

Whittaker's Squares are the most recent addition to the range and again, these are new to the New Zealand market and ideally suited to complement a cup of coffee. The squares are 10.5 grams of premium quality chocolate and are each individually wrapped and presented in high quality packaging.

Packaging design

Although the Whittaker's product portfolio has developed significantly, from the Whittakers Peanut Slab chocolate bar to the Whittaker's Squares, the individual product pack designs have all retained the brand's clear identity and heritage.

The colour gold has become synonymous with Whittaker's and the brand's distinctive lettering style has allowed for Whittaker's products to have a unique identity on supermarket shelves laden with competitive products.

Always delightful

During the recent wave of product additions, changes and developments, Whittaker's have kept their commitment to producing high quality, premium tasting chocolate.

The continued success of the brand confirms that consumers appreciate the dedication that goes into the production of Whittaker's chocolate and its premium taste. Through controlling the whole process – from bean to bar – consumers are always delighted with Whittaker's chocolate.

Company Milestones

1896	Company founded by James Henry Whittaker in Christchurch.
1913	Company moves to Wellington.
1937	Whittaker's becomes a limited liability company.
1950's	Whittaker's Peanut Slab chocolate bar is launched.
1969	Company moves it premises to Porirua.
1984	The wrapped Whittaker's Peanut Slab chocolate bar is launched.
1992	Whittaker's Australia is launched.
1996	The Whittaker's 250-gram block is launched.
2002	The wrapped Whittaker's Sante chocolate bar is launched.
2004	Whittaker's Squares are launched.

J.H. Whittaker & Sons Ltd   0800 1199 68   www.whittakers.co.nz

Superior BLEND
WHISKY

The age-old adage that good things take time is certainly true of Wilson's Whisky – New Zealand's number one locally produced whisky.

Wilson's Whisky – distilling the taste of New Zealand

Wilson's Whisky has been tantalising Kiwi tastebuds for 35 years but its history stretches back nearly 150 years to when James Wilson, a school master and photographer, immigrated to Dunedin and opened the beer brewery which would begin his family's love affair with brewing and distilling.

It is little wonder that Wilson's Whisky is one of New Zealand's favourite brands since it embodies some of our most dearly prized national traits. Beginning life as a small family business in the 1800s, the Wilson's company grew up with New Zealand and proved that even though we may be a small, young country, we have the talent and entrepreneurial spirit to match our older, more experienced cousins in the Northern Hemisphere.

The Wilson's brand was built on a reputation for hard work and risk-taking; and a commitment to using the considerable talents of New Zealanders and the finest local ingredients to create a product that can hold its head up alongside leading international brands whilst retaining a distinctly Kiwi flavour.

The story for how that flavour came to be created at the Wilson's Distillery site at Willowbank in Dunedin begins in 1913, when Charles Wilson bought back the original family brewery his father James had created in the 1860s which had experienced subsequent closure during the depression of the 1890s.

While retaining the brewing side of the business, Charles decided to diversify the operation and produce a malt extract which he sold under the brand name Maltexo. The malt produced by the Wilson's Malt Extract Company found its way into a variety of products such as home brew ingredients, health food such as cod liver oil and even baby food! It also got Charles Wilson thinking about malt's most celebrated claim to fame – its part in the distillation of quality whiskies.

The march of time continued and the Wilson family gave up many of their long-standing associations with brewing, hotels, and other liquor ventures – retaining only the Wilson's Malt Extract Company. In 1964, 80 years after James Wilson opened his first brewery in Dunedin, Wilson's was granted a license to become the first legal distiller of whisky in New Zealand in almost a century.

Home sweet home – our Scotland of the South Pacific

In the same way that those emigrating from Great Britain to New Zealand in the 1800s were shaped by the new, often harsh country they found themselves in, Wilson's Whisky is a product of its birthplace.

Dunedin is the old Gaelic name for Edinburgh and it seems the city inherited its love of fine whiskies from its northern namesake. What made Dunedin and the Wilson's operation unique – compared with countless

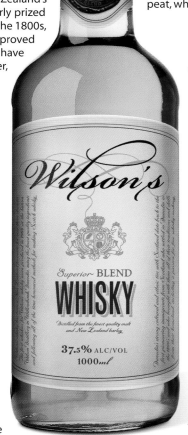

other whisky distilleries around the world attempting to follow their Scottish ancestors' footsteps – is that the region's climate and conditions allow it to produce ingredients very similar to those found in Scotland.

Often described as the Scotland of the South Pacific, the alluvial soils of the Otago region were perfect for producing the highest quality barley, while the water which tumbled down from the Lammerlaws into Deep Creek near Dunedin was very similar to the water used in Scotland's whisky production. Southland also boasted world-class peat, which is required to give whisky its distinctive characteristics.

The quest for the perfect blend

While Dunedin's similarities to the undisputed home of whisky created the perfect ingredients, seizing upon the right recipe proved to be a much more difficult challenge.

After being granted a government license to distil 50,000 gallons of whisky, Wilson's Distillers employed the talents of a young research chemist, Richard Boraman, to uncover the secret to creating the perfect tipple. At the time however, Scottish producers and distillers jealously guarded their secrets and would not give any information to outsiders – meaning Mr Boraman had to start from scratch.

Just as the distillers in Scotland had been unwilling to share their secrets with Wilson's, the company wanted their intentions to remain top-secret and Mr Boraman had to work in complete isolation, with black-out curtains drawn in case anyone caught on to the company's plans. In fact, the project was shrouded in so much mystery that it wasn't until Mr Boraman's first day on the job that he was told his job would be to develop the perfect whisky recipe for Wilson's.

Over four years Mr Boraman experimented with different ratios of varying grains and types of peat. Without "experts" to hypothesise with, Mr Boraman took advice from a number of the illegal moonshiners operating in the area at the time. This was followed by some small successes and a number of dead ends and false starts.

Finally, at the end of the decade in 1969, the first clear whisky spirit was distilled at Willowbank and was ready to be barrelled and aged. Wilson's Whisky was officially born – although it would be another five years before the ageing process was complete and the first Wilson's Whisky went on sale.

The art of distilling fine whisky

Like its lengthy origins, the process involved in creating a single bottle of Wilson's Whisky is a drawn out one that resembles more of an art than an exact science. Wilson's Whisky chooses to remain true to the traditional Scottish method of malt whisky distillation, rather than adopting the arguably easier process of producing grain whisky.

Wilson's Whisky begins with the selection of the finest barley, which is then cleaned and steeped in water for several days before being laid across the malt house floor for up to a week to allow for germination.

Once this occurs, the grain is dried in a kiln fired by a mixture of peat and coal which infuses smokey flavours into the barley. The malted barley is then taken to the distillery where it is mixed with hot water in order to convert the starch to sugars that later react with the yeast to give Wilson's Whisky its alcoholic properties. This process produces solids (a high-protein substance known as draff which is highly sought after as a stock feed) and a liquid known as wort. The wort is drained off and then pumped into large wash buckets where yeast is added to produce a crude alcohol known as "wash".

Once the wash has been produced it is time for the first distillation. The wash is heated to boiling point and the condensation collected. The liquefied condensation, known as "low wines", is then passed through a spirits safe where it undergoes a quality check before being passed into a spirit still for the second distillation. More testing is then carried out to ensure the second distillation retains Wilson's high standards. The bulk of the second distillation is then passed as spirit and the maturing process begins.

The already distinctive flavours created by using the finest local barley, peat and water are developed further when Wilson's Whisky is aged for an average of seven years (four years longer than the minimum three required to become a whisky) in white-oak barrels imported from the US. Once Wilson's are convinced that the whisky is of the finest quality, the grain and malt whiskies are blended, bottled and finally available as Wilson's Whisky.

Changing times

While tradition is the cornerstone of Wilson's Whisky, the company has been careful to make sure it has kept in step with New Zealanders increasingly sophisticated palates. A recent revision of the Wilson's blend has seen its malt to grain ratio increase to nearly a 50/50 blend – a change which allows

Wilson's
THAT WARM MELLOW GLOW, IT MUST BE WILSONS

Wilson's
THAT WARM MELLOW GLOW, IT MUST BE WILSONS

the malt to dominate the blend, resulting in an all-round better tasting drop with exceptional value for money.

From humble family beginnings, Wilson's Distillery grew into a thriving national business and in 1981, its reputation for producing a world-class scotch-inspired blended whisky was recognised when the world's largest distillers, Seagram's Company Ltd, acquired the company.

The Wilson's Distillery changed hands again in November 1999 when The Foster's Group purchased the Seagram's business in New Zealand.

Sadly, the distillery is no longer in operation. The last whisky was distilled in May 1995 and the site of the former distillery at Willowbank in Dunedin has now been converted into apartments. However, lovers of our most popular home-grown tipple need not fear as Wilson's Taieri Plains bond store still houses enough barrels of maturing Wilson's Whisky to keep Kiwi liquor cabinets stocked for several years to come.

New Zealand's favourite whisky admired worldwide

Wilson's Whisky has grown in popularity since the first bottle went on sale in the early 1970s and today it is the top selling locally produced whisky, known the length of the country and appreciated by everyone from regular enthusiasts to leading local and international Whisky experts.

Acclaimed whisky writer Jim Murray recently rated the new blend very highly during a visit to New Zealand in October 2003, saying he was hugely impressed with the quality of Wilson's Whisky. But perhaps the last word should go to David Stirk – an internationally renowned whisky expert, author of the Malt Whisky Guide and one-time tasting co-ordinator for *Whisky Magazine*. On tasting Wilson's Whisky for the first time in 2003, Mr Stirk was full of praise, proclaiming it a superior drop and saying, "Wilson's Whisky is very malty with delicious sweet esthers and a soft and extremely appealing pallet. It's a blend that needs nothing added! A drink of velvet."

With a proud 163 years of service to the agriculture sector, Wrightson is deeply embedded in the culture of rural New Zealand.

"Agriculture. It's our culture."

In all its diversity, agriculture is basic to the survival and advancement of humankind – and it is the backbone of the New Zealand economy.

Nearly half of New Zealand's land area is devoted to agricultural activities: we are the largest exporter of international traded dairy products; the world's biggest producer of lamb; we have the largest farmed deer industry; and we also export large volumes of beef and wool. From seed and genetics to farm equipment and technical expertise, New Zealand's agricultural proficiency is likewise being used around the world. It might not always be obvious, but there is likely to be a Wrightson involvement in many of these activities.

Wrightson was formed 163 years ago and is New Zealand's most diverse company, specialising in servicing the needs of the country's agricultural sector and with over 1800 staff and 70,000 clients, it is New Zealand's largest agri-business.

Although the Wrightson today is very different from the Company that was formed in 1841, over the last 163 years one aspect has remained constant – the Wrightson commitment to assisting New Zealand farmers and processors to improve their profitability.

This plays on one key strength – Wrightson's understanding of agriculture and the needs of its clients. It is not an overstatement to say that no one understands agriculture better than Wrightson. Today this commitment extends to other temperate climates, with the Company's operations in Australia and Uruguay.

History

When Nathanial Levin arrived in Wellington in a sailing ship in 1841, he could hardly have imagined that his colonial business aspirations would eventually give rise to New Zealand's largest agri-business. The history of Wrightson is the story of people of enterprise, integrity and commitment – those able to lead change - the same qualities that still distinguish Wrightson 163 years later.

The story begins in 1841 when Levin & Co opened for business, supplying merchandise to farming pioneers in the Wairarapa and from 1846, exporting wool to London on behalf of clients. It would be two decades later, in 1861, that John Wright and John Stephenson arrived in Dunedin to establish themselves as separate agents for the sale of livestock and other goods. The booming wool industry saw a partnership form between the two entrepreneurs, and in 1865, Wright Stephenson & Co was formed. Their weekly wool auctions were followed soon after by monthly sales of grain and flax.

By 1890, Wright Stephenson was already becoming well-established and very active in exporting and importing commodities and farm inputs, including the supply of high-quality seed under the Challenge brand.

Post-War 1920s saw Wright Stephenson expanding further into the North Island - buying out smaller businesses in merchandising, grain and seed, and livestock trading. The company also expanded into vehicle importing and distribution, as well as livestock and bloodstock exporting and importing.

Well on its way to becoming one of New Zealand's most iconic brands, Wright Stephenson became the country's largest stock and station firm by 1960, with a particularly strong position in wool broking, livestock marketing and seed supply. Among its diverse businesses, the company was one of the New Zealand's leading motor vehicle and home appliance retailers.

After its merger with National Mortgage & Agency to become Wrightson NMA in 1972, the company went from strength to strength. In 1981 it became a founding element of Fletcher Challenge – New Zealand's biggest conglomerate, and in 1986 Wrightson merged with Dalgety Crown. Evidence of this success was distinguished in 1993, when Wrightson joined the New Zealand Stock Exchange with more than 38,000 shareholders.

Today, Wrightson continues its commitment to agriculture by repositioning itself as an agricultural solutions business, dedicated to improving the profitability of its farmer and processor clients. This is reinforced through the development of a new brand positioning and advertising campaign.

Achievements

When New Zealanders think about agriculture, they think Wrightson. The Company has grown to become New Zealand's only national agri-business, and it offers a more diverse range of products and services than any of its competitors.

Throughout its history, the fortunes of the company have been closely tied to the cyclical nature of farming - weather, commodity prices, exchange rates, world events and international trading trends have all had an impact at some time or another. Throughout a turbulent century and a half, Wrightson's commitment to this sector has never wavered.

Many achievements stand out - from being instrumental in pioneering the first exports of wool and frozen meat to world markets, to the more recent development of grass varieties that substantially improve animal productivity, Wrightson has been integral to the development and prosperity of the agricultural sector. The support of rural communities has continually played an important part in Wrightson's vision. Sponsorships such as the Young Farmer Competition, designed to encourage young people into farming, and support for the New Zealand Symphony Orchestra to take music into rural communities and schools demonstrates Wrightson's support for those who have facilitated the company's success.

The product

The Wrightson market offering covers a diverse range of products and services.

Rural Supplies – through its 77 stores, Wrightson supplies and advises on everything from animal health and nutrition products, grain, seed and chemicals to clothing, fuel, fencing, machinery and leisure goods.

Wool – Wrightson is New Zealand's only nationwide wool broker, and the world's largest supplier of crossbred wools, providing many services to its grower clients and to international and local wool processors. Wrightson has a 35 per cent shareholding in The New Zealand Merino Company Limited, and a 50 per cent shareholding in the country's largest wool logistics company - New Zealand Wool Handlers Limited.

Livestock – Wrightson is involved in transacting the buying and selling of livestock on behalf of farmer and processor clients at auction and through forward supply contracts.

Seed and Grain – Wrightson enhances productivity and profitability with a wide range of proprietary seeds and coated seed products for temperate climates – and pioneered the Animal Friendly™ philosophy where forage seeds are bred for animal productivity as well as traditional plant characteristics.

Research – Wrightson is one of the largest private investors in agricultural research in New Zealand, focusing on plant genetics, seed enhancement and forage animal performance. An alliance with Genesis Research and Development Corporation Limited, of which Wrightson owns 15 per cent, places the company at the leading edge of forage grass genomics.

Forestry – Wrightson provides a range of services including the establishment, management, harvesting and marketing of commercial forests.

Financial Services and Insurance – Wrightson provides a comprehensive range of financial services and is a leading provider of insurance broking services.

Agricultural Consultancy – Through its nationwide team of on-farm Solutions Consultants, Wrightson works with farmers to improve their productivity and profitability. A subsidiary company, Agriculture New Zealand, is a leading provider of education and training services for agri-business and farmers around the country.

Real Estate (MREINZ) – Wrightson is New Zealand's leading specialist real estate company, providing services to local and international vendors and buyers of all forms of rural, lifestyle and coastal property throughout New Zealand.

Animal Nutrition - Agri-feeds is a Wrightson subsidiary, specialising in the importation, processing and wholesaling of animal feed supplements, molasses, and a range of products designed for animal nutrition and disease prevention.

Recent developments

In recent years, Wrightson has begun to transition from a traditional stock and station company to an agri-business solutions company and has been at the forefront of new developments in agriculture, including the

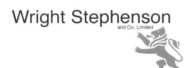

development of supply chain initiatives in the wool and meat industries. In early 2004, Wrightson re-launched its brand with an extensive advertising campaign. Designed to reinforce its position as an agricultural leader in New Zealand, the campaign was underpinned by a new positioning statement: "Agriculture. It's our culture".

The campaign tells the story of the strong relationships between Wrightson, farmers and others associated with agriculture. It shows that everything Wrightson does is ingrained in agriculture; its products, range of services and its people.

The campaign is also designed for Wrightson staff - to reinforce their pride in the company, pride in being part of the primary sector, and to clarify the responsibilities that go with being part of the Wrightson family.

What Wrightson stands for is agriculture – it is its reason for being, the essence of its spirit, soul, and culture – and the slogan "Agriculture. It's our Culture" captures the essence of this.

Promotion

Drive through any rural town, read any rural publication, attend any one of the dozens of farmer-related events in New Zealand, or look in any rural delivery mail box and you are likely see Wrightson promotional activity. Wrightson uses the broadest range of channels to communicate with its clients, potential clients and stakeholders. These activities range from in-store retail promotions geared around seasonal farm activity, to direct mail drops, and sponsorships of local rural school activities.

Brand values

The Wrightson brand signature has a proud heritage, with its roots going back to 1861 when the 'Challenge lion' first made an appearance. The current symbol of the green and blue lion and flag was developed in 1998, and was derived from the early Wright Stephenson symbol. With the lion representing strength and courage, green is a natural colour for Wrightson, working as it does, on the land.

Across rural New Zealand, and increasingly internationally, the symbol gives instant visual recognition to the company and its many businesses. It retains the values of leadership, courage and integrity inherent in the original version of the lion, but adopts a more contemporary stance, reflecting values representing strong relationships, a future-focus, breadth of knowledge, as well as a community focus.

In its simplest form, Wrightson's values reflect its passion for agriculture.

Customers know that Wrightson understands and recognises how important they are – not just as customers of Wrightson but also as the backbone of New Zealand's economy – and that Wrightson is as committed to agriculture as they are.

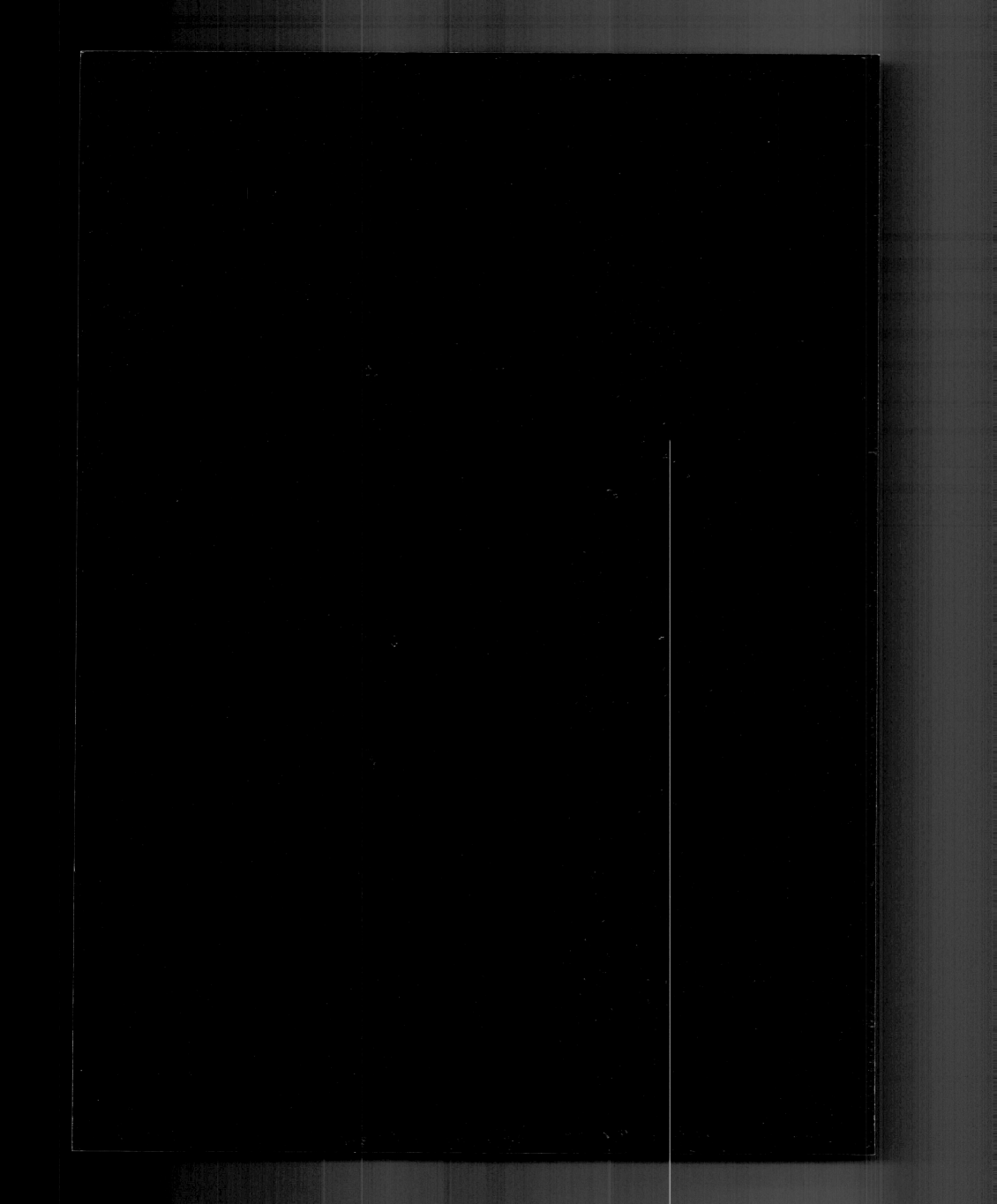